Gaeilge gan Stró!

Beginners Level

A multimedia Irish language course for adults

Éamonn Ó Dónaill

ISBN: 978-0-9563614-4-8

Grianghraif / *Photographs*: iStockphoto
Dearadh / *Design*: Gaelchultúr

Taifeadadh / *Recording*: Lime Street Sound (www.limesound.com)
Innealtóirí fuaime / *Sound engineers*: Keith Alexander & Steve McGrath

Bhí na haisteoirí seo a leanas páirteach sa taifeadadh: / *The following actors participated in the recording:*

Bernardine Nic Giolla Phádraig (láithreoir / *presenter*), Helen Hegarty, Siobhán Patten, Éamonn Ó Dónaill, Cóilín Ó Floinn, Dairíne Ní Dhonnchú, Marcus Lamb, Neasa Ní Chiaráin, Sibéal Davitt & Tristan Rosenstock

Is féidir cóipeanna breise den leabhar seo a cheannach díreach ó: / *Additional copies of this book can be bought directly from:*

Gaelchultúr
11 Sráid an Chláraigh
Baile Átha Cliath 2
Éire
D02 TD34

Gaelchultúr
11 Clare Street
Dublin 2
Ireland
D02 TD34

+353 1 484 5220
www.gaelchultur.com
www.ranganna.com

Tá an leabhar ar díol ar www.siopa.ie chomh maith. / *The book is also on sale at www.siopa.ie.*

Clár Ábhair / *Contents*

Acknowledgements / *Buíochas*

Is mian leis an údar buíochas a ghabháil leis na daoine seo a leanas: / *The author would like to thank the following people:*

Darren Ó Rodaigh, a chaith an-dua le dearadh an leabhair; a chomhghleacaithe Michelle Ryan, Helen Hegarty, Siobhán Patten agus Lisa Madden i nGaelchultúr a chabhraigh go mór leis an léamh profaí.

Tiomnaithe do Sheán Ó Tiarnaigh (1935–2008): cara, fear cúise agus fear spraoi

Introduction / *Réamhrá*

Gaeilge gan Stró! – Beginners Level is a multimedia language course for adult learners of Irish. It's aimed at those who have not previously studied Irish or who only know a few words of the language. The course is intended for learners working by themselves and seeks to give them the confidence and language skills necessary to communicate in Irish in everyday situations. The emphasis is on developing speaking and listening skills but learners are also given some opportunities to read and write the language. Grammar is taught in context, as it's required.

There is some focus initially on the three main dialects of Irish but, for the most part, an attempt is made to teach words and phrases that are common to all the dialects.

Gaeilge gan Stró! – Beginners Level consists of this book, downloadable audio files that are closely linked to the book and an online course, available on Gaelchultúr's e-learning website, www.ranganna.com. The book and audio files can be used independently of the online version of the course.

Gaeilge gan Stró! – Beginners Level aims to help the learner who undertakes the course to:

- understand and use familiar everyday expressions and basic phrases
- introduce himself/herself and others and ask and answer questions about everyday life and personal details such as where he/she lives, people he/she knows and things he/she has
- interact in a simple way in social settings with speakers of Irish
- learn core vocabulary
- gain a basic understanding of various aspects of grammar.

The book is divided into fifteen units which contain the following sections:

- *i Key sounds*
  The pronunciations which the learner should focus on in that particular unit.

- *Useful information*
  The grammar relevant to the topic covered in the unit. This grammar is presented in context and in manageable chunks, and complicated terminology is avoided.

- *Conversations*
  Four dialogues, with accompanying translations into English. The language contained in these dialogues is natural and authentic, and reflects everyday usage.

- *Vocabulary and Useful phrases*
  Core vocabulary and useful phrases relating to the theme of the unit.

- *Exercises*
  A wide range of fun-to-do activities based on the vocabulary and grammar presented in the unit. The answers to the activities are given at the back of the book.

- *Insight*
  These short passages aim to give the learner information about the history of the Irish language and a better understanding of Irish in the contemporary world.

- *Useful tips for learners*
  Handy tips on how to become a more efficient language learner.

- *Talking heads*
  This is the audio from video segments featuring a range of speakers, filmed on location in Dublin and Galway. The videos feature in the online version of this course.

The accompanying audio files contain recordings of all the vocabulary and language structures taught in the course, in addition to the sixty dialogues and a wide range of interactive exercises to help you test your knowledge of the language as you work your way through the course.

The words *Gaeilge gan Stró!* mean "Irish without stress". We hope that you find using this course a stress-free, enjoyable and rewarding experience.

Icons

The following icons appear in each unit of the book:

Indicates which CD contains the audio version of the language in a particular section and the relevant track.

Indicates a written exercise.

Indicates a spoken exercise.

How to use this course

This is the approach to study that we recommend in the case of each unit in the course:

1. *Objectives*
   Read the objectives on the first page so that you will have a better idea of what to expect in the unit.

2. *Key sounds*
   Listen to these carefully and once you're familiar with them say them with the people on the recording. Pay special attention to the letters that are highlighted in purple in the book.

3. *New language*
   Listen to the new language introduced in each section while reading these words and phrases in the book. Initially, stop the recording and repeat this new language but, once you become familiar with it, speak simultaneously with the people on the recording, without stopping it.

4. *Written exercises*
   When you have completed a written activity, have a look at the answers at the back of the book.

5. *Oral exercises*
   The first few times you attempt these exercises, look at the them in the book as you listen to the audio files. After a while, however, you should be able to do the exercises without looking at the written version. A pause is left after each question in an exercise to give you the opportunity to provide the correct answer. Initially, you might find that these pauses are too short and that you have to stop the recording.

6. *Dialogues*
   In the case of the first few units of the course, listen to the dialogues while reading the transcript in the book. Once you've learnt a reasonable amount of Irish, however, try listening to the dialogues initially without looking at the transcript. You might only manage to pick up a word here and there, but resist the temptation to consult the book until you've heard the dialogues a few times. Once you become familiar with a dialogue, say the lines simultaneously with the people on the recording, without stopping it.

7. *Vocabulary/Useful phrases*
   While reading the words and phrases contained in the *Vocabulary* and *Useful phrases* sections, you should listen to the audio files and say them out loud with the speakers on the recording. There is no need to learn all the words and phrases contained in these sections! Learn those that are most relevant to you and consult the book should you need to find a particular word or phrase.

8. *Talking heads*
   Once you've studied a few units in the book, start listening to these segments initially without consulting the book and see if you can understand any words or phrases.

9. *Review of the unit*
   Try the revision exercise at the end of the unit, *Review of the unit*, when you've covered all the material for that unit contained in the book and on the audio files. Before listening to the recording, use the book to prepare your answers. Say these out loud, and write them down if you have a chance, then use the audio file to test yourself and to verify your answers. If you have difficulty with this exercise, you will need to review some of the language in the unit.

The online version

There is an online version of *Gaeilge gan Stró! – Beginners Level* available on Gaelchultúr's e-learning website, www.ranganna.com. The explanations and exercises in the online version are the same as those contained in this book, but the exercises offer a higher level of interactivity.

All the written exercises in the online course are interactive. Once you have completed an exercise, you can click on the "Send" button and receive feedback immediately. You are told which answers were correct and which were incorrect, you are given the correct answers and a score.

Unit 1 of the online course is available free of charge at www.ranganna.com.

The Irish language: some basic information

Alphabet of the Irish Language

The Irish alphabet is made up of the following letters:

a, b, c, d, e, f, g, h, i, l, m, n, o, p, r, s, t, u

The letters **j, k, q, v, w, x, y** and **z** occur in loanwords.

Vowels can be either short or long. A mark called a *síneadh fada*, or *fada* for short, is used to indicate long vowels:

á, é, í, ó, ú

Short vowels are written without a *fada*:

a, e, i, o, u

Eclipsis (urú) *and lenition* (séimhiú)

The beginning of a word in Irish can often undergo a change in sound when it's preceded by a certain word, such as a preposition or a possessive adjective (**mo**, **do**, etc.). One change is called lenition (*séimhiú* in Irish) and the other eclipsis (*urú* in Irish).

In the old Gaelic script, a *séimhiú* was shown by placing a dot over the letter. In the new script, an **h** is written after the letter.

Urú changes the sound of a letter to that of a different letter. The new sound is written in front of the one that it replaces or "eclipses".

This table shows the changes undergone by consonants that can be lenited and eclipsed.

Consonant	Lenited form	Eclipsed form
b	**bh** Followed by **e** or **i** Pronunciation: *v* **beár** (*bar*) **sa bheár** (*in the bar*) Followed by **a**, **o** or **u** Pronunciation: *v* or *w* **buicéad** (*bucket*) **sa bhuicéad** (*in the bucket*)	**mb** Pronunciation: *m* **Baile Átha Cliath** (*Dublin*) **i mBaile Átha Cliath** (*in Dublin*)
c	**ch** Followed by **e** or **i** Pronunciation: *ch* as in German *ich* **ciseán** (*basket*) **sa chiseán** (*in the basket*) Followed by **a**, **o** or **u** Pronunciation: *ch* as in Scottish *loch* **carr** (*car*) **mo charr** (*my car*)	**gc** Followed by **e** or **i** Pronunciation: *g* as in *gift* **cearnóg** (*square*) **i gcearnóg** (*in a square*) Followed by **a**, **o** or **u** Pronunciation: *g* as in *Gordon* **curach** (*currach*) **i gcurach** (*in a currach*)
d	**dh** Followed by **e** or **i** Pronunciation: *y* as in *yell* **dinnéar** (*dinner*) **mo dhinnéar** (*my dinner*) Followed by **a**, **o** or **u** Pronunciation: This is a guttural *g* sound made in the back of the mouth. **Dáil Éireann** **geataí Dháil Éireann** (*the gates of Dáil Éireann*)	**nd** Followed by **e** or **i** Pronunciation: *n* as in *onion* **dialann** (*diary*) **i ndialann** (*in a diary*) Followed by **a**, **o** or **u** Pronunciation: *n* **Doire** (*Derry*) **i nDoire** (*in Derry*)

<table>
<tr><td>f</td><td>fh
Followed by a, e, i, o or u
Not pronounced
freagra (answer)
do fhreagra (your answer)</td><td>bhf
Followed by e or i
Pronunciation: v
filíocht (poetry)
i bhfilíocht (in poetry)

Followed by a, o or u
Pronunciation: v or w
fógra (advertisement)
i bhfógra (in an advertisement)</td></tr>
<tr><td>g</td><td>gh
Followed by e or i
Pronunciation: y as in yell
an Ghearmáin (Germany)
sa Ghearmáin (in Germany)

Followed by a, o or u
Pronunciation: This is a guttural g sound made in the back of the mouth.
an Ghaeltacht (the Gaeltacht)
sa Ghaeltacht (in the Gaeltacht)</td><td>ng
Followed by e or i
Pronunciation: ng as in king
geamaireacht (pantomime)
i ngeamaireacht (in a pantomime)

Followed by a, o or u
Pronunciation: ng as in sung
Gaeltacht Chiarraí
(the Kerry Gaeltacht)
i nGaeltacht Chiarraí
(in the Kerry Gaeltacht)</td></tr>
<tr><td>m</td><td>mh
Followed by e or i
Pronunciation: v
méar (finger)
do mhéar (your finger)

Followed by a, o or u
Pronunciation: v or w
máthair (mother)
a mháthair (his mother)</td><td>Not eclipsed</td></tr>
<tr><td>p</td><td>ph
Followed by a, e, i, o or u
Pronunciation: f
páirtí (party)
sa pháirtí (in the party)</td><td>bp
Pronunciation: b
Páirtí an Lucht Oibre
(the Labour Party)
i bPáirtí an Lucht Oibre
(in the Labour Party)</td></tr>
<tr><td>s</td><td>sh
Followed by a, e, i, o or u
Pronunciation: h
Séamas
do Shéamas (for/to Séamas)</td><td>Not eclipsed</td></tr>
<tr><td>t</td><td>th
Followed by a, e, i, o or u
Pronunciation: The t sound disappears and only h is pronounced.
talamh (land)
mo thalamh (my land)</td><td>dt
Followed by e or i
Pronunciation: j as in jeans
teideal (title)
i dteideal (in a title)

Followed by a, o or u
Pronunciation: d as in done
Tamhlacht (Tallaght)
i dTamhlacht (in Tallaght)</td></tr>
</table>

Articles
There is no equivalent in Irish to the indefinite articles *a* and *an* in English, therefore **bean** means both *woman* and *a woman*.

Word order
Irish is a VSO (verb–subject–object) language. Have a look at this example:

> **Cheannaigh Séamas carr nua.**
> *Bought Séamas a car new.*

As you can see from the above sentence, the adjective follows the noun in Irish.

Bí and is
There are two different forms in Irish that correspond to the English *to be*. One of these is the verb **bí** and the other is the copula (*an chopail*) **is**. The copula is used to describe the permanent identity or characteristics of a person or thing as opposed to temporary aspects. Here is an example of usage:

> **Bím ansin gach lá.**
> *I'm there every day.*

> **Is Sasanach í Jill.**
> *Jill is English.*

Prepositional pronouns
Prepositional pronouns, which are essentially conjugated prepositions, are used extensively in Irish. For example, **ag** means *at* and **mé** means *me*. When they're combined they become **agam**. When **agam** is used with the verb **bí** (*to be*) it indicates possession; this is the equivalent of the English *to have*. Here are two examples:

> **Tá deartháir amháin agam.**
> *I have one brother* (literally, there is one brother at me).

> **Tá deich euro aige.**
> *He has ten euro* (literally, there are ten euro at him).

This usage might seem very unfamiliar to you initially but you'll soon grow accustomed to it as you make your way through this course.

Unit 1: Meeting People

Aonad 1: Bualadh le Daoine

In this unit you will learn how to:

- greet someone and return a greeting
- ask someone if he's well and answer that question
- introduce yourself
- ask someone his name and answer that question
- say to someone that it's nice to meet him
- give your telephone number
- introduce people to each other
- say goodbye to someone.

Grammar

- the prepositional pronouns **do** and **ar**
- personal pronouns
- emphatic forms
- the numbers 0–10
- the vocative case

San aonad seo foghlaimeoidh tú conas:

- *beannú do dhuine agus beannú ar ais do dhuine*
- *ceist a chur ar dhuine an bhfuil sé go maith agus an cheist sin a fhreagairt*
- *tú féin a chur in aithne*
- *fiafraí de dhuine cén t-ainm atá air agus an cheist sin a fhreagairt*
- *a rá le duine go bhfuil sé go deas bualadh leis*
- *d'uimhir theileafóin a thabhairt*
- *daoine a chur in aithne dá chéile*
- *slán a fhágáil ag duine.*

Gramadach

- *na forainmneacha réamhfhoclacha* ***do*** *agus* ***ar***
- *forainmneacha pearsanta*
- *foirmeacha treise*
- *na huimhreacha 0–10*
- *an tuiseal gairmeach*

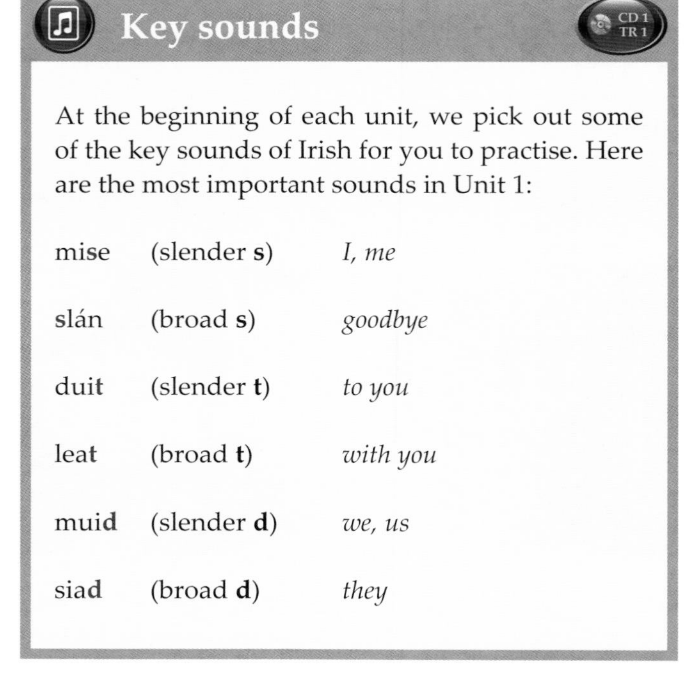

Key sounds

At the beginning of each unit, we pick out some of the key sounds of Irish for you to practise. Here are the most important sounds in Unit 1:

mise	(slender **s**)	*I, me*
slán	(broad **s**)	*goodbye*
duit	(slender **t**)	*to you*
leat	(broad **t**)	*with you*
muid	(slender **d**)	*we, us*
siad	(broad **d**)	*they*

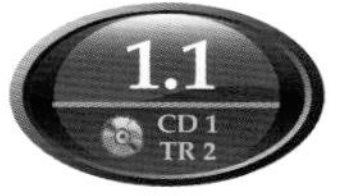

Hello

In a formal context people use the following greeting:

Dia duit (literally, *God to you*).

In reply, people say:

Dia is Muire duit (literally, *God and Mary to you*).

This is how you greet more than one person:

Dia daoibh.

How are you?

In less formal contexts, when friends are meeting, for example, people tend not to use **Dia duit**. Instead, they greet each other by asking:

Cén chaoi a bhfuil tú?
How are you?

That particular greeting is used in Connacht Irish. Note that the **n** in **Cén** is not pronounced, that the first two words run together and that the **a** before **bhfuil** is not heard either.

The greetings used in the other dialects, Ulster and Munster, are given below. As you can see, they're different from the Connacht greeting. You can choose one of those three greetings, however, and learn how to say it properly. Don't worry about being able to pronounce the other two well – you only need to understand what they mean!

Ulster dialect

Cad é mar atá tú?
How are you?

Pronunciation: Jay ma thaw thoo?

Munster dialect

Conas atá tú?
How are you?

Pronunciation: Cunis thaw thoo?

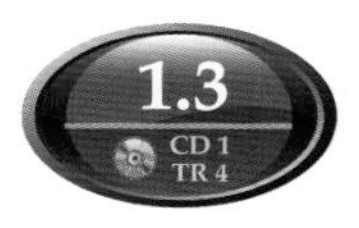

Returning a greeting

If someone greets you by asking you how you are, you can say:

Tá mé go maith.
I'm well.

or

Tá mé go breá.
I'm fine.

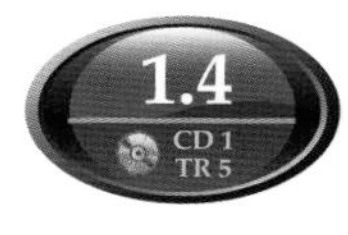

Introducing yourself

In Irish, you introduce yourself by saying **Is mise** and then your name:

Is mise Sharon.
I'm Sharon.

Is mise Dónall.
I'm Dónall.

You can leave out the **Is**, however, and just say **Mise** and your name:

Mise Siobhán.
I'm Siobhán.

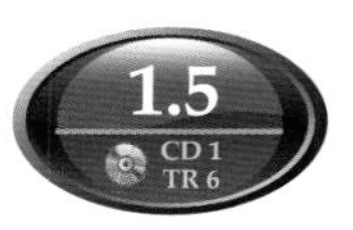

My name is Máirtín

This is how you say what your name is:

Máirtín is ainm dom.
My name is Máirtín.

A slightly different form of **dom**, **domsa**, is often used in a situation where more than one person introduces himself:

Sinéad: **Sinéad is ainm dom.**
My name is Sinéad.

Peadar: **Peadar is ainm domsa.**
***My** name is Peadar.*

Bríd: **Agus Bríd is ainm domsa.**
*And **my** name is Bríd.*

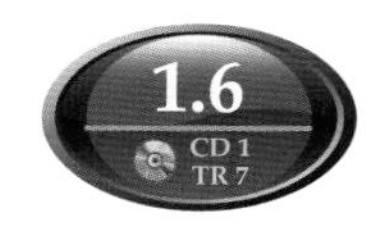

What's your name?

The way you ask someone's name varies from dialect to dialect:

Cén t-ainm atá ort? (Connacht dialect)
What's your name?

Cad is ainm duit? (Munster dialect)
What's your name?

C'ainm atá ort? (Ulster dialect)
What's your name?

Again, you only have to choose one of the above sentences and learn how to say it properly. For the rest of this unit, however, we're going to use the Connacht dialect version.

When someone introduces himself before asking someone else his/her name, the different version of **dom** referred to earlier is used. Note that **ort** changes to **ortsa** as well:

Máirtín is ainm domsa. Cén t-ainm atá ortsa?
***My** name is Máirtín. What's **your** name?*

Domsa and **ortsa** are known as emphatic forms. In English you can stress words like *my* and *your* but you can't do the same in Irish – you must use these special forms instead.

Conversation 1A

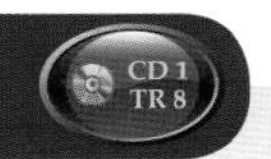

Michelle and Eoin meet for the first time, at an Irish language weekend in New York.

Michelle: Cén chaoi a bhfuil tú? Is mise Michelle – cén t-ainm atá ortsa?
*How are you? **I'm** Michelle – what's **your** name?*

Eoin: Mise Eoin.
***I'm** Eoin.*

Michelle: Tá sé go deas bualadh leat, a Eoin.
It's nice to meet you, Eoin.

Conversation 1B

At the same Irish language weekend in New York, Áine greets her teacher, Liam.

Áine: Dia duit, a Liam.
Hello, Liam.

Liam: Dia is Muire duit, a Áine. Cén chaoi a bhfuil tú na laethanta seo?
Hello, Áine. How are you these days?

Áine: Tá mé go maith, go raibh maith agat. Agus tú féin?
I'm well, thank you. And yourself?

Liam: Tá mé go breá. Tá sé go deas tú a fheiceáil arís!
I'm fine. It's nice to see you again!

1.7 The emphatic form of leat

In Conversation 1A, Michelle said:

Tá sé go deas bualadh leat, a Eoin.
It's nice to meet you, Eoin.

If Eoin wanted to say the same thing in return, he would have had to use the emphatic form of **leat**. This is what he would have said:

Tá sé go deas bualadh leatsa freisin.
*It's nice to meet **you** as well.*

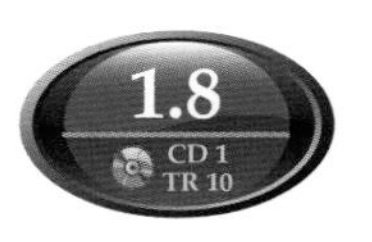

1.8 The personal pronouns

You've seen various personal pronouns used already in this unit. Here is a complete list of the pronouns now:

Singular	Plural
mé *I, me*	**muid** *us, we*
tú *you*	**sibh** *you*
sé *he, it*	**siad** *they*
sí *she, it*	

When pronouns are used in sentences, some of them sound a little different:

Tá mé go maith.
I'm well.

Tá sé go breá.
He's fine.

Don't worry too much about this, though – you'll soon get the hang of the different sounds in this unit.

Exercise 1.1: Your turn!

This is your chance to talk now. Pretend you're Michelle and that you're talking to Eoin.

Say: *How are you? **I'm** Michelle – what's **your** name?*

Eoin: Mise Eoin.

Say: *It's nice to meet you, Eoin.*

Exercise 1.2: Your turn!

This time, pretend you're Áine and that you're talking to Liam.

Say: *Hello, Liam.*

Liam: Dia is Muire duit, a Áine. Cén chaoi a bhfuil tú na laethanta seo?

Say: *I'm well, thank you. And yourself?*

Liam: Tá mé go breá. Tá sé go deas tú a fheiceáil arís!

Exercise 1.3: Fill in the gaps

Fill in the gaps in these sentences.

1. *How are you?*
   Cén ___________ a bhfuil tú?

2. *I'm well.*
   Tá mé go ___________.

3. *I'm fine.*
   Tá mé go ___________.

4. ***I**'m Alan.*
   Is __________ Alan.

5. *My name is Jennifer.*
   Jennifer is ainm ___________.

6. ***My** name is Dónall.*
   Dónall is ainm ___________.

7. *What's your name?*
   Cén t-ainm atá _________?

8. *What's **your** name?*
   Cén t-ainm atá _________?

9. *It's nice to meet you, Eoin.*
   Tá sé go deas ________________ leat, a Eoin.

10. *It's nice to see you again!*
    Tá sé go deas tú a _______________ arís!

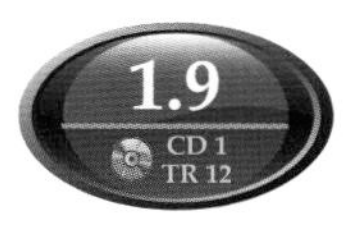

The cardinal numbers

Here are the numbers that are used when there is no noun following them:

1	**a haon** *one*
2	**a dó** *two*
3	**a trí** *three*
4	**a ceathair** *four*
5	**a cúig** *five*
6	**a sé** *six*
7	**a seacht** *seven*
8	**a hocht** *eight*
9	**a naoi** *nine*
10	**a deich** *ten*

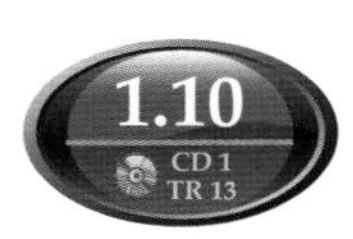

Introducing people

This is how you introduce a man:

Seo é Micheál.
This is Micheál.

This is how you introduce a woman:

Seo í Bríd.
This is Bríd.

And this is how you introduce more than one person:

Seo iad Máirtín agus Aoife.
This is Máirtín and Aoife.

Saying goodbye

The Irish for *goodbye* is **slán**. The person leaving the company uses **agat** and the person staying behind uses **leat**. In the following conversation, Éanna is staying in his office and Éilís is going out the door.

Éanna: **Slán leat, a Éilís. Feicfidh mé amárach tú.**
Goodbye, Éilís. I'll see you tomorrow.

Éilís: **Slán agat, a Éanna. Tóg go bog é!**
Goodbye, Éanna. Take it easy!

If you can't remember whether to use **leat** or **agat**, a good avoidance strategy is to use **go fóill** (*for now*) instead!

Éanna: **Slán leat, a Éilís. Feicfidh mé amárach tú.**
Goodbye, Éilís. I'll see you tomorrow.

Éilís: **Slán go fóill, a Éanna. Tóg go bog é!**
Goodbye for now, Éanna. Take it easy!

Conversation 1C

At a party, Caitlín introduces various people to her friend Nóra, who doesn't know anyone else there.

Caitlín: Seo é Barry.
This is Barry.

Barry: Tá sé go deas bualadh leat, a Nóra.
It's nice to meet you, Nóra.

Caitlín: Seo í Laura.
This is Laura.

Nóra: Cén chaoi a bhfuil tú?
How are you?

Caitlín: Agus seo iad Stiofán agus Peadar.
And this is Stiofán and Peadar.

Nóra: Cén chaoi a bhfuil sibh?
How are you?

Conversation 1D

Séamas had various friends over for dinner and now he's saying goodbye to them.

Séamas: Slán leat, a Shiobhán. Beidh mé ag caint leat amárach.
Goodbye, Siobhán. I'll be talking to you tomorrow.

Siobhán: Slán agat, a Shéamais, agus go raibh maith agat arís.
Goodbye, Séamas, and thanks again.

Séamas: Slán leat, a Mháire. Slán abhaile.
Goodbye, Máire. Safe home.

Máire: Slán agat, a Shéamais. Feicfidh mé amárach tú.
Goodbye, Séamas. I'll see you tomorrow.

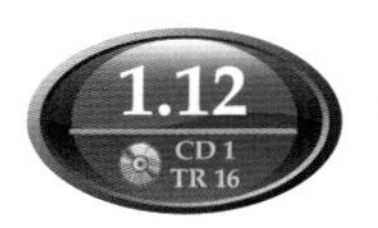

1.12 The vocative case

The vocative case is used when addressing someone directly. There were three examples in Conversation 1D:

a Shéamais
Séamas

a Shiobhán
Siobhán

a Mháire
Máire

Changes occur to the beginning of many Irish language names, both male and female, in the vocative case and also to the end of some male names.

1.13 Sibh

In Conversation 1C, Nóra said the following when she was introduced to Stiofán and Peadar:

Cén chaoi a bhfuil sibh?
How are you?

As she was speaking to more than one person, she used the personal pronoun **sibh**.

Exercise 1.4: Your turn!

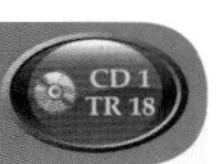

This is your chance to talk now. Pretend you're Caitlín and that you're introducing your friend Nóra to various people.

Say: *This is Barry.*

Barry: Tá sé go deas bualadh leat, a Nóra.

Say: *This is Laura.*

Nóra: Cén chaoi a bhfuil tú?

Say: *And this is Stiofán and Peadar.*

Nóra: Cén chaoi a bhfuil sibh?

Exercise 1.5: Your turn!

This time, pretend you're Séamas saying goodbye to your two friends.

Say: *Goodbye, Siobhán. I'll be talking to you tomorrow.*

Siobhán: Slán agat, a Shéamais, agus go raibh maith agat arís.

Say: *Goodbye, Máire. Safe home.*

Máire: Slán agat, a Shéamais. Feicfidh mé amárach tú.

Exercise 1.6: Numbers

Try saying the telephone numbers of various Irish language organisations below. Then, listen to the recording to see if your answers are correct.

1. Údarás na Gaeltachta: (091) 503 100
2. Gaelchultúr: (01) 484 5220
3. Oideas Gael: (074) 973 0248
4. Foras na Gaeilge: (028) 9089 0970
5. Glór na nGael: (046) 943 0974

Useful tips for learners

The three mains dialects of Irish can be found in this course.

Don't worry too much about these – remember that a majority of those who learn Irish speak a mixture of dialects.

The most important thing is that you master the sounds of the language so that people understand what you're saying.

Talking heads

In the first Talking heads in the course, you'll hear various people introducing themselves. Listen to them first without looking at the script below to see how much you'll understand. After that, listen to them with the script in front of you and, lastly, look at the English translation of their speech.

Fionnuala Croker
(filmed in Dún Laoghaire, County Dublin)
Cad é mar atá tú?
Is mise Fionnuala Croker.

Colm Mac Séalaigh
(filmed at the Civic Offices, Dublin)
Cén chaoi a bhfuil tú?
Colm is ainm domsa.

Páidí Ó Lionáird
(filmed in An Spidéal, Galway)
Conas atá tú?
Páidí Ó Lionáird is ainm domsa.

TRANSLATION

Fionnuala Croker (Ulster dialect)
How are you?
I'm Fionnuala Croker.

Colm Mac Séalaigh (Connacht dialect)
How are you?
My name is Colm.

Páidí Ó Lionáird (Munster dialect)
How are you?
My name is Páidí Ó Lionáird.

The audio versions of these excerpts are available on the sound files accompanying this book. The video segments can be seen in the online version of *Gaeilge gan Stró! – Beginners Level*, available on Gaelchultúr's e-learning website, www.ranganna.com.

Exercise 1.7: Review of Unit 1

Have a go at this activity now to see if you know the most important phrases taught in Unit 1.

How would you say the following in Irish?

1. Hello (formal).
2. How are you (Connacht dialect)?
3. I'm well.
4. **I**'m Sharon.
5. My name is Máirtín.
6. *My* name is Bríd.
7. What's your name?
8. It's nice to meet you, Eoin.
9. It's nice to meet *you* as well.
10. Goodbye (said to the person leaving).
11. Goodbye (said to the person staying).
12. Goodbye for now.
13. This is Nóra.
14. This is Seán.
15. This is Stiofán and Peadar.

Unit 2: Your Background and Where You Live
Aonad 2: Cúlra agus Áit Chónaithe

In this unit you will learn how to:
- ask someone where he's from and answer that question
- ask someone where he lives and answer that question
- say what nationality you are
- ask someone if he's of a particular nationality and answer that question
- name various countries and nationalities
- ask someone what his address is and answer that question
- name different types of places and facilities.

Grammar
- the copula **is**
- the simple prepositions **as** and **i**
- *urú* (eclipsis)
- possessive adjectives and **cónaí**
- emphatic forms of the personal pronouns **mé** and **tú**
- the numbers 11–20
- the singular and plural article
- initial changes to nouns

San aonad seo foghlaimeoidh tú conas:
- *fiafraí de dhuine cé as é agus an cheist sin a fhreagairt*
- *fiafraí de dhuine cá bhfuil sé ina chónaí agus an cheist sin a fhreagairt*
- *a rá cén náisiúntacht atá agat*
- *fiafraí de dhuine an bhfuil náisiúntacht áirithe aige agus an cheist sin a fhreagairt*
- *tíortha agus náisiúntachtaí éagsúla a ainmniú*
- *ceist a chur ar dhuine cén seoladh atá aige agus an cheist sin a fhreagairt*
- *cineálacha éagsúla áiteanna agus áiseanna a ainmniú.*

Gramadach
- *an chopail* ***is***
- *na réamhfhocail shimplí* ***as*** *agus* ***i***
- *urú*
- *aidiachtaí sealbhacha agus* ***cónaí***
- *foirmeacha treise de na forainmneacha pearsanta* ***mé*** *agus* ***tú***
- *na huimhreacha 11–20*
- *an t-alt uatha agus iolra*
- *athruithe tosaigh ar ainmfhocail*

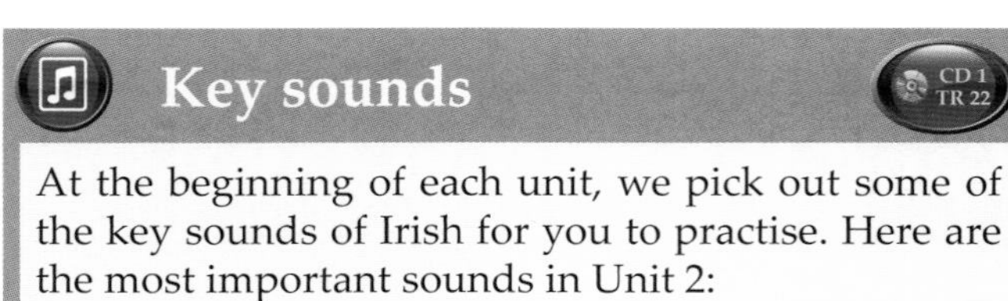

Key sounds

At the beginning of each unit, we pick out some of the key sounds of Irish for you to practise. Here are the most important sounds in Unit 2:

tír	(slender **t**)	*country*
tú	(broad **t**)	*you*
Londai**n**	(slender **n**)	*London*
Spái**nn**each	(slender **n**)	*Spanish*
An **N**ua-Shéalainn	(broad **n**)	*New Zealand*
i mo **ch**ónaí	(**c** with *séimhiú*, followed by broad vowel, **o**)	*living*
An **Bh**reatain **Bh**eag	(**b** with *séimhiú*)	*Wales*
An **t**Seapáin	(**t** before **s**)	*Japan*

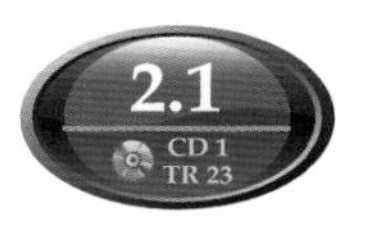

Where are you from?

There are various ways of asking where someone is from. Here is the version most commonly used in the Connacht dialect:

> **Cé as thú?**
> *Where are you from?*

The forms used in the other dialects, Ulster and Munster, are given below. You can choose one of those three versions, however, and learn how to say it properly. As we've said previously, don't worry about being able to pronounce the other two well – you only need to understand what they mean.

Ulster dialect

> **Cé as tú?**
> *Where are you from?*
>
> Pronunciation: K-hiss thoo?

Munster dialect

> **Cad as tú?**
> *Where are you from?*
>
> Pronunciation: Kad-as thoo?

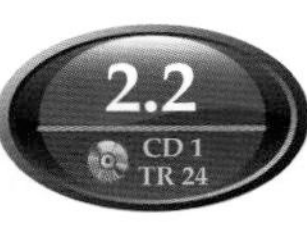

I'm from …

In reply to the question **Cé as thú?**, you say **Is as** and the name of the place, followed by **mé**:

> **Is as Londain mé.**
> *I'm from London.*

You can leave out **Is**, however, and just say **As** and the name of the place, followed by **mé**:

> **As Páras mé.**
> *I'm from Paris.*

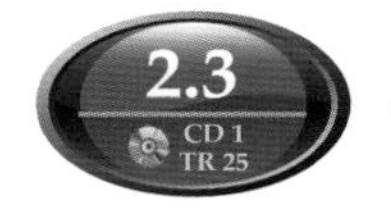

Cónaí

This is how you say where you live:

> **Tá mé i mo chónaí i Londain.**
> *I live in London*
> (literally, *I'm in my living in London).*

Be careful how you pronounce the **ch** in the word **chónaí**; it might prove difficult at first, but you'll soon get the hang of it.

This is how you find out where someone lives:

> **Cá bhfuil tú i do chónaí?**
> *Where do you live*
> (literally, *where are you in your living*)?

In reply, you can use **Tá mé i mo chónaí …** or you can use a shorter version if you wish:

> **Tá mé i mo chónaí i Londain.**
> *I live in London.*
>
> or
>
> **I Londain.**
> *In London.*

I and in

The simple preposition **i** (*in*) is used in Irish before words beginning with a consonant:

Tá mé i mo chónaí i mBaile Átha Cliath.
I live in Dublin.

Notice how **Baile** changes to **mBaile** when it's preceded by the simple preposition **i**. This is an example of *urú*.

An *urú* changes the way the word sounds – the new letter suppresses the first letter of the word and only this new letter is pronounced.

An *urú* is placed before the consonants **b**, **c**, **d**, **f**, **g**, **p** and **t** after the simple preposition **i**:

b ⇨ mb	**Béal Feirste ⇨ i mBéal Feirste**
c ⇨ gc	**Corcaigh ⇨ i gCorcaigh**
d ⇨ nd	**Doire ⇨ i nDoire**
f ⇨ bhf	**Fear Manach ⇨ i bhFear Manach**
g ⇨ ng	**Gaillimh ⇨ i nGaillimh**
p ⇨ bp	**Port Láirge ⇨ i bPort Láirge**
t ⇨ dt	**Trá Lí ⇨ i dTrá Lí**

The letters **ng** have a special sound; the new letter, **n**, does not suppress the sound of the first letter, **g**, but they combine to form a new sound. You might have difficulty with this sound initially, but you'll master it after a while!

The form **in** is used before vowels:

Aontroim
Antrim

Tá mé i mo chónaí in Aontroim.
I live in Antrim.

Inis
Ennis

Tá mé i mo chónaí in Inis.
I live in Ennis.

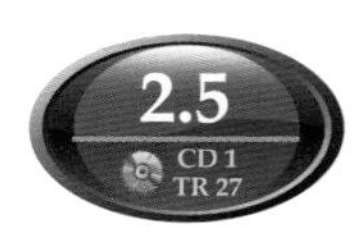

Nationality

You also use **is** when saying what your nationality is:

Is Éireannach mé.
I'm Irish.

Is Meiriceánach mé.
I'm American.

Is Astrálach mé.
I'm Australian.

This is how to find out whether or not someone is of a particular nationality:

An Francach tú?
Are you French?

An Spáinneach tú?
Are you Spanish?

This is how you answer this particular question:

An Ceanadach tú?
Are you Canadian?

Is ea.
Yes.

An Gearmánach tú?
Are you German?

Ní hea.
No.

Insight

The Irish language is recognised in the Constitution of the Republic of Ireland as the national and first official language of the country. And, since the 1st of January 2007, Irish has been an official language of the European Union.

The Irish-speaking areas, the *Gaeltachtaí* (singular: *Gaeltacht*), are mainly located on the western seaboard: in Donegal, Mayo, Galway, Cork and Kerry. There are also small *Gaeltachtaí* in County Waterford (An Rinn) and in County Meath (Ráth Chairn). There are thought to be between 70,000 and 80,000 native speakers of Irish, although many more people, particularly in Dublin and Belfast, use the language on a daily basis.

Conversation 2A

Helen and Brian are attending a one-week Irish language course in Oideas Gael in Donegal and are getting to know each other during coffee break.

Helen: Cén chaoi a bhfuil tú? Is mise Helen – cén t-ainm atá ortsa?
*How are you? **I'm** Helen – what's **your** name?*

Brian: Brian. Tá sé go deas bualadh leat, a Helen.
Brian. It's nice to meet you, Helen.

Helen: Cé as thú, a Bhriain?
Where are you from, Brian?

Brian: Is as Glaschú mé. Cé as thú féin?
I'm from Glasgow. Where are you from yourself?

Helen: As Nua-Eabhrac ach tá mé i mo chónaí i gCorcaigh anois.
From New York but I live in Cork now.

Conversation 2B

At the same Irish language course in Donegal, the learners are working in pairs in the first class. Their task is to get to know each other better.

Alan: Is mise Alan agus is Astrálach mé. Cén t-ainm atá ortsa?
***I'm** Alan and I'm Australian. What's **your** name?*

Francesca: Francesca. Francesca Saltini.
Francesca. Francesca Saltini.

Alan: An Iodálach tú, a Francesca?
Are you Italian, Francesca?

Francesca: Is ea. Is as an Róimh mé ach tá mé i mo chónaí i mBaile Átha Cliath anois.
Yes. I'm from Rome but I live in Dublin now.

Alan: Tá an Róimh go hálainn. Bhí mé ansin anuraidh.
Rome is lovely. I was there last year.

Francesca: Cá bhfuil tusa i do chónaí, a Alan?
*Where do **you** live, Alan?*

Alan: As Sydney mé ach tá mé i mo chónaí i Londain anois.
I'm from Sydney but I live in London now.

2.6 The vocative case

In Unit 1, we saw that the vocative case is used when addressing someone directly. This is an example from Conversation 2A:

Helen: **Cé as thú, a Bhriain?**
Where are you from, Brian?

As we mentioned in Unit 1, changes occur to the beginning of many Irish language names, both male and female, in the vocative case and also to the end of some male names.

2.7 Emphatic forms

In Conversation 2B, Francesca asked:

Cá bhfuil tusa i do chónaí, a Alan?
*Where do **you** live, Alan?*

Tusa is the emphatic form of the pronoun **tú**. In English you can stress pronouns such as *you* and *she* but you can't do the same in Irish – instead, you must use a special form, known as an emphatic form.

The emphatic form of the pronoun **mé** is **mise**:

Peadar: **Tá mé i mo chónaí i gCorcaigh anois.**
I live in Cork now.

Róisín: **Tá mise i mo chónaí ansin freisin!**
***I** live there as well!*

Exercise 2.1: Your turn!

This is your chance to talk now. Pretend you're Helen and that you're talking to Brian.

Say:	*How are you? **I'm** Helen – what's **your** name?*
Brian:	Brian. Tá sé go deas bualadh leat, a Helen.
Say:	*Where are you from, Brian?*
Brian:	Is as Glaschú mé. Cé as thú féin?
Say:	*From New York but I live in Cork now.*

Exercise 2.2: Your turn!

This time, pretend you're Alan and that you're talking to Francesca.

Say:	***I'm** Alan and I'm Australian. What's **your** name?*
Francesca:	Francesca. Francesca Saltini.
Say:	*Are you Italian, Francesca?*
Francesca:	Is ea. Is as an Róimh mé ach tá mé i mo chónaí i mBaile Átha Cliath anois.
Say:	*Rome is lovely. I was there last year.*
Francesca:	Cá bhfuil tusa i do chónaí, a Alan?
Say:	*I'm from Sydney but I live in London now.*

Exercise 2.3: Fill in the gaps

Fill in the gaps in these sentences.

1. *Where are you from?*
   Cé as ______?

2. *Where are you from yourself?*
   Cé as ______ _______?

3. *I'm from Derry.*
   Is as Doire ________.

4. ***I'm** from Madrid.*
   Is as Maidrid ________.

5. *Where do you live?*
   Cá bhfuil ______ i do chónaí?

6. *Where do **you** live?*
   Cá bhfuil ______ i do chónaí?

7. *I live in Paris.*
   Tá mé i ____ chónaí i bPáras.

8. *Are you American? No.*
   _____ Meiriceánach tú? Ní ________.

9. *I'm German.*
   _____ Gearmánach mé.

10. *It's nice to meet you, Brian.*
    Tá sé go deas bualadh leat, a ____________.

Vocabulary 1: Countries

- Éire — *Ireland*
- Sasana — *England*
- Albain — *Scotland*
- An Bhreatain Bheag — *Wales*
- An Fhrainc — *France*
- An Ghearmáin — *Germany*
- An Ísiltír — *The Netherlands*
- An Spáinn — *Spain*
- An Iodáil — *Italy*
- An Ghréig — *Greece*
- An Pholainn — *Poland*
- An Rúis — *Russia*
- An tSualainn — *Sweden*
- Meiriceá — *America*
- Na Stáit Aontaithe — *The United States*
- Ceanada — *Canada*
- An Astráil — *Australia*
- An Nua-Shéalainn — *New Zealand*
- An tSín — *China*
- An tSeapáin — *Japan*

If you wish to find the Irish version of other country names, go to the website www.focal.ie.

Vocabulary 2: Nationalities

- Éireannach — *(an) Irish person*
- Sasanach — *(an) English person*
- Albanach — *(a) Scottish person*
- Breatnach — *(a) Welsh person*
- Francach — *(a) French person*
- Gearmánach — *(a) German person*
- Ísiltíreach — *(a) Dutch person*
- Spáinneach — *(a) Spanish person*
- Iodálach — *(an) Italian person*
- Gréagach — *(a) Greek person*
- Polannach — *(a) Polish person*
- Rúiseach — *(a) Russian person*
- Sualannach — *(a) Swedish person*
- Meiriceánach — *(an) American person*
- Ceanadach — *(a) Canadian person*
- Astrálach — *(an) Australian person*
- Nua-Shéalannach — *(a) New Zealander*
- Síneach — *(a) Chinese person*
- Seapánach — *(a) Japanese person*

Exercise 2.4: Answer the questions

Answer each of these questions as indicated.

1. Cé as thú?
   Say: I'm from Paris.
2. Cé as thú?
   Say: I'm from Spain.
3. Cé as thú?
   Say: I'm from America.
4. Cá bhfuil tú i do chónaí?
   Say: In Dublin.
5. Cá bhfuil tú i do chónaí?
   Say: In Belfast.
6. Cá bhfuil tú i do chónaí?
   Say: In Derry.
7. An Sasanach tú?
   Say: Yes. I'm from Birmingham.
8. An Francach tú?
   Say: No. I'm Spanish.

The numbers 11–20

In Unit 1, we looked at the numbers up to ten. Here now are the numbers from 11 to 20:

11 **a haon déag**
eleven

12 **a dó dhéag**
twelve

13 **a trí déag**
thirteen

14 **a ceathair déag**
fourteen

15 **a cúig déag**
fifteen

16 **a sé déag**
sixteen

17 **a seacht déag**
seventeen

18 **a hocht déag**
eighteen

19 **a naoi déag**
nineteen

20 **fiche**
twenty

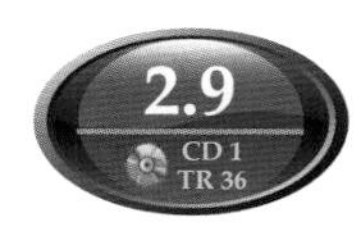

Addresses

This is how you ask for someone's address:

Cén seoladh atá agat?
What's your address?

Here are some nouns commonly used in addresses:

bóthar
road

sráid
street

ascaill
avenue

páirc
park

Exercise 2.5: Addresses

Listen to people giving their addresses and fill in the missing numbers in those addresses.

1. ______ Páirc na Coille (*Wood Park*)
2. ______ Ascaill na Mainistreach (*Abbey Avenue*)
3. ______ Bóthar an tSléibhe (*Mountain Road*)
4. ______ Sráid na Siopaí (*Shop Street*)
5. ______ Páirc Bhríde (*Bridget's Park*)
6. ______ Ascaill an Lagáin (*Lagan Avenue*)
7. ______ Bóthar na Trá (*Strand Road*)
8. ______ Sráid na hEaglaise (*Church Street*)

Vocabulary 3: Types of places and facilities

• sráidbhaile / an sráidbhaile / sráidbhailte	*(a) village / the village / villages*
• baile / an baile / bailte	*(a) town / the town / towns*
• cathair / an chathair / cathracha	*(a) city / the city / cities*
• bruachbhaile / an bruachbhaile / bruachbhailte	*(a) suburb / the suburb / suburbs*
• contae / an contae / contaetha	*(a) county / the county / counties*
• siopa / an siopa / siopaí	*(a) shop / the shop / shops*
• banc / an banc / bainc	*(a) bank / the bank / banks*
• ollmhargadh / an t-ollmhargadh / ollmhargaí	*(a) supermarket / the supermarket / supermarkets*
• ionad siopadóireachta / an t-ionad siopadóireachta / ionaid siopadóireachta	*(a) shopping centre / the shopping centre / shopping centres*
• scoil / an scoil / scoileanna	*(a) school / the school / schools*
• oifig an phoist	*(a) post office / the post office*
• teach tábhairne / an teach tábhairne / tithe tábhairne	*(a) pub / the pub / pubs*
• óstán / an t-óstán / óstáin	*(an) hotel / the hotel / hotels*
• linn snámha	*(a) swimming pool*
• pictiúrlann / an phictiúrlann / pictiúrlanna	*(a) cinema / the cinema / cinemas*
• siopa nuachtán / an siopa nuachtán / siopaí nuachtán	*(a) newsagent / the newsagent / newsagents*
• gruagaire / an gruagaire / gruagairí	*(a) hairdresser / the hairdresser / hairdressers*
• páirc / an pháirc / páirceanna	*(a) park / the park / parks*

Useful phrases

• Tá mé i mo chónaí …	*I live …*
• i gContae Mhaigh Eo.	*in County Mayo.*
• i sráidbhaile.	*in a village.*
• i mbaile beag.	*in a small town.*
• i gcathair mhór.	*in a big city.*
• i mbruachbhaile darb ainm Kingston.	*in a suburb called Kingston.*
• Tá mé i mo chónaí …	*I live …*
• faoin tuath.	*in the country.*
• cois farraige.	*beside the sea.*
• in aice le San Francisco.	*beside San Francisco.*
• gar do Luimneach.	*near Limerick.*
• cúpla míle ó Ghaillimh.	*a few miles from Galway.*

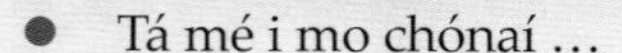

Conversation 2C

Stuart and Caitríona haven't met in a while. They bump into each other at a party and he tells her about where he now lives.

Caitríona: Cá bhfuil tú i do chónaí anois, a Stuart?
Where are you living now, Stuart?

Stuart: Tá mé i mo chónaí i mbaile beag i gContae Chill Dara na laethanta seo.
I'm living in a small town in County Kildare these days.

Caitríona: An maith leat an baile?
Do you like the town?

Stuart: Is breá liom é. Tá áiseanna maithe ann: ionad siopadóireachta, cúpla teach tábhairne, bialann álainn, óstán agus linn snámha.
I love it. There are good facilities there: a shopping centre, a few pubs, a lovely restaurant, an hotel and a swimming pool.

Caitríona: Tá áiseanna maithe ann, mar sin.
There are good facilities there, then.

Stuart: Tá. Tá mé an-sásta ansin.
Yes. I'm very happy there.

Conversation 2D

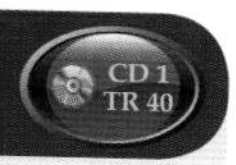

Caitríona now tells Stuart about the place where she lives.

Stuart: Cá bhfuil tusa i do chónaí anois, a Chaitríona?
*Where are **you** living now, Caitríona?*

Caitríona: Tá mé i mo chónaí in Órán Mór i gContae na Gaillimhe.
I'm living in Oranmore in County Galway.

Stuart: Tá an baile sin in aice le cathair na Gaillimhe, nach bhfuil?
That town is beside Galway city, isn't it?

Caitríona: Tá. Níl sé ach cúpla míle ó Ghaillimh.
Yes. It's only a few miles from Galway.

The article in Irish

There is no equivalent in Irish to the indefinite articles *a* and *an* in English, therefore **siopa** means both *shop* and *a shop*.

The definite article **an** is used in the singular in Irish:

an teach tábhairne
the pub

The plural form of the article is **na**:

na tithe tábhairne
the pubs

Initial changes to nouns

The initial consonant or vowel of a noun often changes when it's preceded by the article **an**. You might have noticed these changes to some of the nouns contained in the last vocabulary section:

cathair *(a) city*	**an chathair** *the city*
óstán *(an) hotel*	**an t-óstán** *the hotel*

A *séimhiú* is added to **cathair** because it's a feminine noun and **t-** is placed before **óstán** because it's a masculine noun. Don't worry about these rules at the moment – we'll be returning to them later in the book.

Exercise 2.6: Your turn!

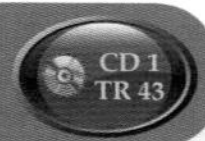

This is your chance to talk now. Pretend you're Caitríona and that you're talking to Stuart.

Say: *Where are you living now, Stuart?*

Stuart: Tá mé i mo chónaí i mbaile beag i gContae Chill Dara na laethanta seo.

Say: *Do you like the town?*

Stuart: Is breá liom é. Tá áiseanna maithe ann: ionad siopadóireachta, cúpla teach tábhairne, bialann álainn, óstán agus linn snámha.

Say: *There are good facilities there, then.*

Stuart: Tá. Tá mé an-sásta ansin.

Exercise 2.7: Your turn!

This time, pretend you're Stuart and that you're talking to Caitríona.

Say: *Where are **you** living now, Caitríona?*

Caitríona: Tá mé i mo chónaí in Órán Mór i gContae na Gaillimhe.

Say: *That town is beside Galway city, isn't it?*

Caitríona: Tá. Níl sé ach cúpla míle ó Ghaillimh.

Useful tips for learners

Irish language spelling and pronunciation can be quite a challenge initially, but you'll soon begin to recognise the patterns. You'll notice, for example, that when a *séimhiú* is added to **f**, neither **f** nor the *séimhiú* is pronounced. And when a *séimhiú* is added to **s** and **t**, only the *séimhiú* is pronounced.

Talking heads

You'll hear various people saying where they're from and where they live now. Listen to them first without looking at the script below to see how much you'll understand. After that, listen to them with the script in front of you and, lastly, look at the English translation of their speech.

Dairíne Ní Dhonnchú
(filmed in Temple Bar, Dublin)
Is mise Dairíne Ní Dhonnchú agus is as Baile Átha Luain mé, ach tá mé i mo chónaí i Raghnallach i mBaile Átha Cliath anois. Is breá liom an ceantar agus tá áiseanna maithe ann – siopaí, bialanna, scoileanna, banc agus oifig an phoist.

Cóilín Ó Floinn
(filmed in Temple Bar, Dublin)
Is mise Cóilín Ó Floinn agus is Meiriceánach mé. As Nua-Eabhrac sna Stáit Aontaithe ó dhúchas mé ach tá mé i mo chónaí i mBaile Átha Cliath anois. Tá mé i mo chónaí sa chathair agus is breá liom an ceantar – tá áiseanna maithe ann agus tá mé gar don obair.

Meadhbh Ní Eadhra
(filmed in An Spidéal, Galway)
Is mise Meadhbh Ní Eadhra. Rugadh i mBaile Átha Cliath mé agus is as Béal Feirste do mo mháthair agus m'athair. Tá mé i mo chónaí sa Spidéal anois, in aice le cathair na Gaillimhe. Is breá liom bheith i mo chónaí anseo – tá sé cois farraige ach gar don chathair freisin.

TRANSLATION

Dairíne Ní Dhonnchú
I'm Dairíne Ní Dhonnchú and I'm from Athlone, but I live in Ranelagh in Dublin now. I love the area and it has good facilities – shops, restaurants, schools, a bank and a post office.

Cóilín Ó Floinn
I'm Cóilín Ó Floinn and I'm American. I'm originally from New York in the United States but I live in Dublin now. I live in the city and I love the area – there are good facilities and I'm close to work.

Meadhbh Ní Eadhra
I'm Meadhbh Ní Eadhra. I was born in Dublin and my mother and father are from Belfast. I live in An Spidéal now, beside Galway city. I love living here – it's beside the sea but close to the city as well.

The audio versions of these excerpts are available on the sound files accompanying this book. The video segments can be seen in the online version of *Gaeilge gan Stró! – Beginners Level*, available on Gaelchultúr's e-learning website, www.ranganna.com.

Exercise 2.8: Review of Unit 2

Have a go at this activity now to see if you know the most important phrases taught in Unit 2.

How would you say the following in Irish?

1. Where are you from?
2. Where are *you* from?
3. I'm from London.
4. Where do you live?
5. Where do *you* live?
6. I live in Dublin.
7. I'm American.
8. I'm Australian.
9. Are you Canadian? Yes.
10. Are you German? No.
11. What's your address?
12. I live in a small town.
13. I live beside the sea.
14. I live in the country.
15. Do you like the town? I love it.

Unit 3: The Family

Aonad 3: An Teaghlach

In this unit you will learn how to:

- say what your marital status is
- ask someone if he's married
- name members of the family
- ask someone if he has children and answer that question
- ask someone how many children he has and answer that question
- ask what ages children are and answer that question
- ask someone how many brothers and sisters he has and answer that question
- introduce various members of the family.

Grammar

- questions with yes and no answers
- initial changes to nouns
- the first and second person singular and plural of the prepositional pronoun **ag**
- the emphatic form of the prepositional pronoun **ag** in the second person singular and plural
- personal numerals
- the noun **bliain** after the numbers 1–20
- the possessive adjectives **mo** and **do**

San aonad seo foghlaimeoidh tú conas:

- *a rá cad é do stádas pósta*
- *fiafraí de dhuine an bhfuil sé pósta*
- *baill den teaghlach a ainmniú*
- *fiafraí de dhuine an bhfuil páistí aige agus an cheist sin a fhreagairt*
- *fiafraí de dhuine cé mhéad páiste atá aige agus an cheist sin a fhreagairt*
- *fiafraí cén aois atá páistí agus an cheist sin a fhreagairt*
- *fiafraí de dhuine cé mhéad deartháir agus deirfiúr atá aige agus an cheist sin a fhreagairt*
- *baill éagsúla den teaghlach a chur in aithne.*

Gramadach

- *ceisteanna a bhfuil* yes/no *mar fhreagra orthu*
- *athruithe tosaigh ar ainmfhocail*
- *an chéad agus an dara pearsa uimhir uatha agus iolra den fhorainm réamhfhoclach* ***ag***
- *an fhoirm threise den fhorainm réamhfhoclach* ***ag*** *sa dara pearsa uimhir uatha agus iolra*
- *uimhreacha pearsanta*
- *an t-ainmfhocal* ***bliain*** *tar éis na n-uimhreacha 1–20*
- *na haidiachtaí sealbhacha* ***mo*** *agus* ***do***

Key sounds

At the beginning of each unit, we pick out some of the key sounds of Irish for you to practise. Here are the most important sounds in Unit 3:

beirt	(slender **b**)	*two people*
baintreach	(broad **b**)	*widow*
deirfiúr	(slender **d**)	*sister*
sia**d**	(broad **d**)	*they*
mo **dh**eirfiúr	(**d** with *séimhiú*, followed by slender vowel, **e**)	*my sister*
cai**l**ín	(slender **l**)	*girl*
c**l**ann	(broad **l**)	*children*
scar**th**a	(**t** with *séimhiú*)	*separated*
a**th**air	(**t** with *séimhiú*)	*father*

3.1 Marital status

This is how you describe your marital status:

Tá mé pósta.
I'm married.

Níl mé pósta.
I'm not married.

Tá mé singil.
I'm single.

Tá mé scartha.
I'm separated.

Tá mé colscartha.
I'm divorced.

Is baintreach mé.
I'm a widow/widower.

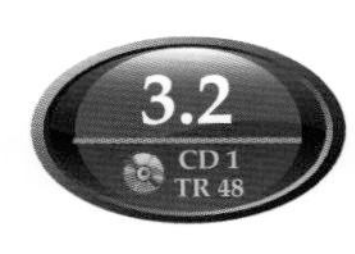

3.2 Are you married?

This is how you find out whether or not someone is married:

An bhfuil tú pósta?
Are you married?

Tá./Níl.
Yes./No.

As we mentioned before, personal pronouns cannot be stressed in Irish – you must use an emphatic form or the word **féin**:

An bhfuil tusa pósta?
*Are **you** married?*

An bhfuil tú féin pósta?
Are you married yourself?

3.3 Answering questions

There is no equivalent in Irish to *yes* and *no* in English. When you're asked a question, you must use the same verb in your answer that was used in the question:

An dtéann tú ansin go minic?
Do you go there often?

Téim./Ní théim.
Yes./No.

The verb **bí** (*be*) is very irregular:

An bhfuil tú pósta?
Are you married?

Tá./Níl.
Yes./No.

We'll be returning to questions and answers later in this course.

Vocabulary: Family members

- tuismitheoir / an tuismitheoir / tuismitheoirí — *(a) parent / the parent / parents*
- athair / an t-athair / aithreacha — *(a) father / the father / fathers*
- máthair / an mháthair / máithreacha — *(a) mother / the mother / mothers*
- teaghlach / an teaghlach / teaghlaigh — *(a) family / the family / families*
- clann / an chlann — *children / the children*
- páiste / an páiste / páistí — *(a) child / the child / children*
- leanbh / an leanbh / leanaí — *(a) baby / the baby / babies*
- mac / an mac / mic — *(a) son / the son / sons*
- iníon / an iníon / iníonacha — *(a) daughter / the daughter / daughters*
- buachaill / an buachaill / buachaillí — *(a) boy / the boy / boys*
- cailín / an cailín / cailíní — *(a) girl / the girl / girls*
- deartháir / an deartháir / deartháireacha — *(a) brother / the brother / brothers*
- deirfiúr / an deirfiúr / deirfiúracha — *(a) sister / the sister / sisters*
- fear céile / an fear céile / fir chéile — *(a) husband / the husband / husbands*
- bean chéile / an bhean chéile / mná céile — *(a) wife / the wife / wives*
- uncail / an t-uncail / uncailí — *(an) uncle / the uncle / uncles*
- aintín / an aintín / aintíní — *(an) aunt / the aunt / aunts*
- nia / an nia / nianna — *(a) nephew / the nephew / nephews*
- neacht / an neacht / neachtanna — *(a) niece / the niece / nieces*
- seanathair / an seanathair / seanaithreacha — *(a) grandfather / the grandfather / grandfathers*
- seanmháthair / an tseanmháthair / seanmháithreacha — *(a) grandmother / the grandmother / grandmothers*
- garmhac / an garmhac / garmhic — *(a) grandson / the grandson / grandsons*
- gariníon / an ghariníon / gariníonacha — *(a) granddaughter / the granddaughter / granddaughters*

3.4 Initial changes to nouns

The beginning of a noun in Irish can change when it's preceded by the article **an**, depending on the gender of the noun. The table on the right shows the changes which occur to both feminine and masculine nouns that are preceded by the article in the nominative and accusative cases singular.

There's no need to worry too much about these rules at the moment – just look out for them in the "Vocabulary" section of each unit.

We'll return to the rules in the next unit and in other units to give you the chance to familiarise yourself with them.

	Masculine	Feminine
(a) Nouns beginning with a vowel	**an t-athair** *the father*	**an iníon** *the daughter*
(b) Nouns beginning with a consonant	**an fear céile** *the husband*	**an bhean chéile** *the wife*
(c) Nouns beginning with **s**	**an seanathair** *the grandfather*	**an tseanmháthair** *the grandmother*
(d) Nouns beginning with **d** or **t**	**an deartháir** *the brother* **an tuismitheoir** *the parent*	**an deirfiúr** *the sister* A *séimhiú* is not added to feminine nouns beginning with **d** or **t** in the nominative and accusative cases

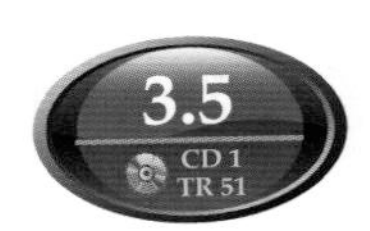

Do you have children?

There are two ways of asking someone if he has children:

An bhfuil páistí agat?
or
An bhfuil clann agat?
Do you have children (literally, *are there children at you*)*?*

Tá./Níl.
Yes./No.

The emphatic form of **agat** is **agatsa**:

An bhfuil páistí agatsa?
Do ***you*** *have children?*

If you're asking more than one person if they have children, you must use **agaibh**:

An bhfuil páistí agaibh?
Do you have children?

The emphatic form of **agaibh** is **agaibhse**:

An bhfuil páistí agaibhse?
Do ***you*** *have children?*

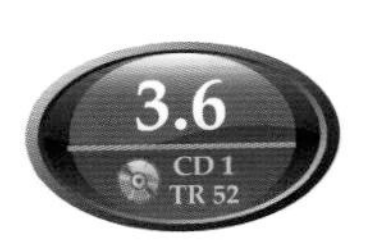

I have no children

This is how you say that you have no children:

Níl páistí ar bith agam.
or
Níl clann ar bith agam.
I have no children.

In the first person plural, you use **againn**:

Níl páistí ar bith againn.
or
Níl clann ar bith againn.
We have no children.

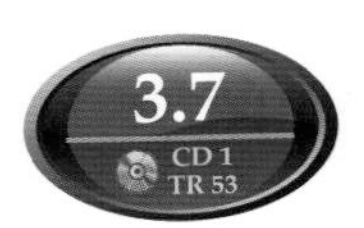

Counting people

This is how you ask someone how many children he has:

Cé mhéad páiste atá agat?
How many children do you have?

Note that **cé mhéad** is always followed by the singular of the noun.

This is how you count people in Irish:

duine amháin
one (person)

beirt
two (people)

triúr
three (people)

ceathrar
four (people)

cúigear
five (people)

seisear
six (people)

seachtar
seven (people)

ochtar
eight (people)

naonúr
nine (people)

deichniúr
ten (people)

Insight

Irish was the predominant language of the Irish people but went into decline from the 16th century onwards due mainly to British rule, famine and emigration.

The Irish brought their language with them to Scotland and the Isle of Man, where it gave rise to Scottish Gaelic and Manx.

Irish, Scottish Gaelic and Manx are referred to as Goidelic languages and are part of the Q-Celtic division of the Celtic languages. Speakers of the three languages can understand each other reasonably well but cannot understand speakers of the so-called P-Celtic languages: Welsh, Cornish and Breton.

Conversation 3A

Siobhán and Bernie have only been working together for a week and are still getting to know each other.

Siobhán: Níl tú féin pósta?
You're not married yourself?

Bernie: Níl. Bhí mé pósta ach tá mé colscartha anois.
No. I was married but I'm divorced now.

Siobhán: Tá brón orm é sin a chloisteáil.
I'm sorry to hear that.

Bernie: Tá tú féin geallta.
You're engaged yourself.

Siobhán: Tá, tá mé geallta le Caoimhín. Táimid an-sona le chéile.
Yes, I'm engaged to Caoimhín. We're very happy together.

Bernie: Tá sé sin go hiontach!
That's great!

Conversation 3B

Siobhán and Bernie then talk about children.

Siobhán: An bhfuil páistí agat?
Do you have children?

Bernie: Tá, tá beirt agam – mac agus iníon.
Yes, I have two – a son and a daughter.

Siobhán: Agus cén aois atá siad?
And what ages are they?

Bernie: Tá Eimear seacht mbliana agus tá Dara deich mbliana. An bhfuil páistí agat féin?
Eimear is seven years (old) and Dara is ten years (old). Do you have children yourself?

Siobhán: Tá mac amháin agam, Stiofán – tá sé cúig bliana d'aois.
I have one son, Stiofán – he's five years old.

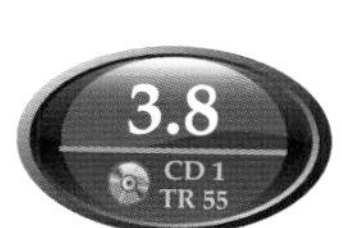

3.8 What age is he?

This is how you ask about age:

Cén aois atá sé?
What age is he?

Cén aois atá sí?
What age is she?

Cén aois atá siad?
What ages are they?

Bliain

There is a different system in Irish for counting people and counting things. We'll return to counting things in a later unit, but let's have a look in the meantime at how you count years.

1–10 years

1	2	3–6	7–10
bliain amháin *one year*	**dhá bhliain** *two years*	**trí bliana** *three years* **ceithre bliana** *four years* **cúig bliana** *five years* **sé bliana** *six years*	**seacht mbliana** *seven years* **ocht mbliana** *eight years* **naoi mbliana** *nine years* **deich mbliana** *ten years*

11–20 years

The system for counting 11–20 years is easy enough – the only difficult one is *eleven years*: **aon bhliain déag**. In the case of 12–19, you simply add **déag** to the forms in columns two, three and four above:

dhá bhliain déag
twelve years

ceithre bliana déag
fourteen years

The Irish for *twenty years* is **fiche bliain**.

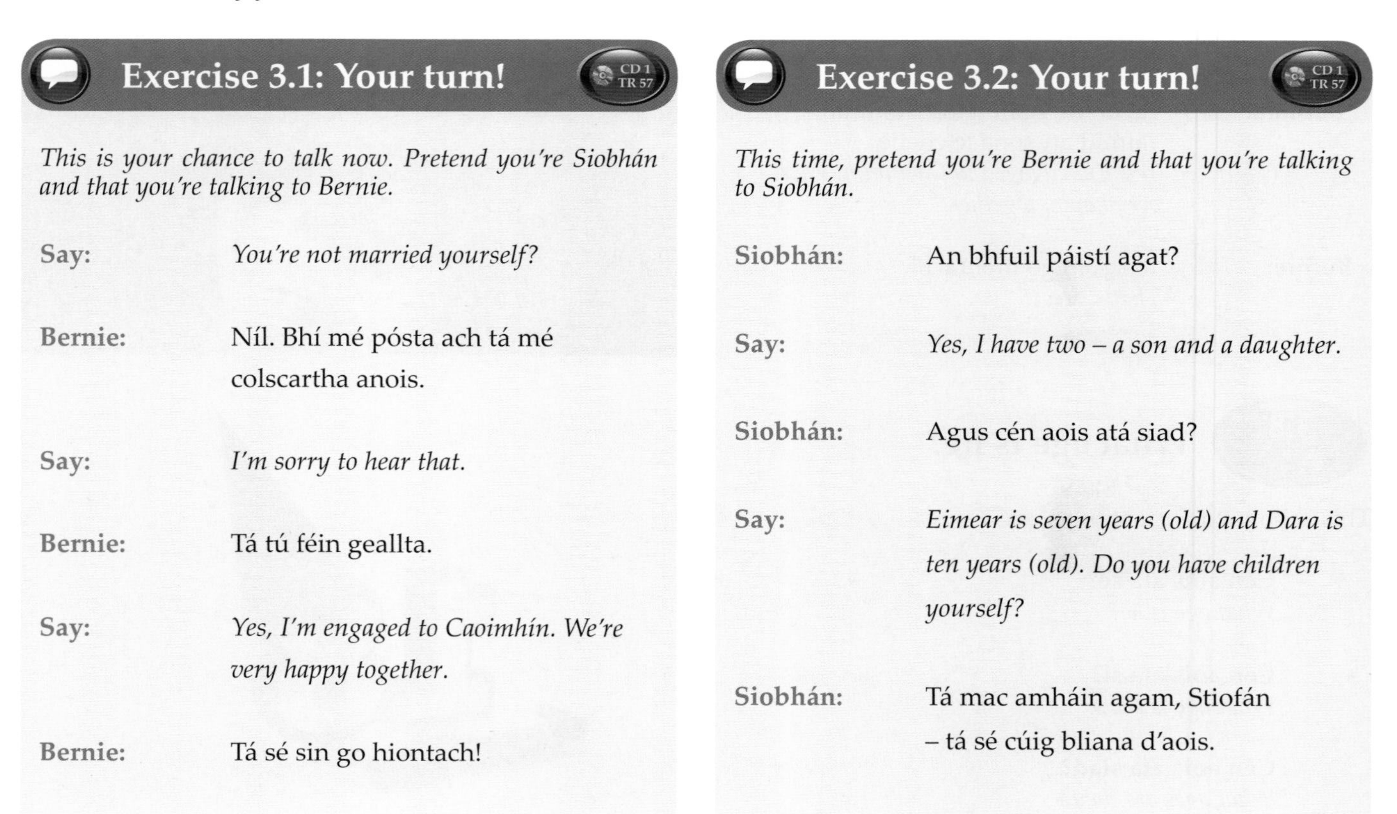

Exercise 3.1: Your turn!

CD 1 TR 57

This is your chance to talk now. Pretend you're Siobhán and that you're talking to Bernie.

Say: *You're not married yourself?*

Bernie: Níl. Bhí mé pósta ach tá mé colscartha anois.

Say: *I'm sorry to hear that.*

Bernie: Tá tú féin geallta.

Say: *Yes, I'm engaged to Caoimhín. We're very happy together.*

Bernie: Tá sé sin go hiontach!

Exercise 3.2: Your turn!

CD 1 TR 57

This time, pretend you're Bernie and that you're talking to Siobhán.

Siobhán: An bhfuil páistí agat?

Say: *Yes, I have two – a son and a daughter.*

Siobhán: Agus cén aois atá siad?

Say: *Eimear is seven years (old) and Dara is ten years (old). Do you have children yourself?*

Siobhán: Tá mac amháin agam, Stiofán – tá sé cúig bliana d'aois.

Exercise 3.3: Fill in the gaps

Fill in the gaps in these sentences.

1. *Are you married?*
   An bhfuil _______ pósta?
2. *Are **you** married?*
   An bhfuil _______ pósta?
3. *Are you married yourself?*
   An bhfuil tú _______ pósta?
4. *I'm divorced.*
   Tá mé ________________.
5. *I'm a widow.*
   Is __________________ mé.
6. *Do you have children (addressing one person)?*
   An bhfuil páistí ___________?
7. *Do you have children (addressing more than one person)?*
   An bhfuil páistí ___________?
8. *How many children do you have?*
   Cé mhéad __________ atá agat?

9. *I have no children.*
   Níl páistí ____ _______ agam.
10. *Two – a son and a daughter.*
   ________ – mac agus ____________.

Exercise 3.4: Answer the questions

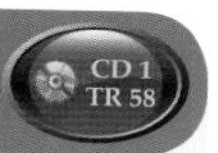

Answer each of these questions as indicated.

1. An bhfuil tú pósta?
   Say: No.
2. An bhfuil tú pósta?
   Say: Yes. Are you married yourself?

3. An bhfuil páistí agat?
   Say: Yes, two.
4. An bhfuil páistí agat?
   *Say: No. Do **you** have children (speaking to one person)?*
5. An bhfuil páistí agaibh?
   *Say: No. Do **you** have children (speaking to more than one person)?*
6. An bhfuil páistí agat?
   Say: I have no children.
7. An bhfuil páistí agaibh?
   Say: We have no children.
8. Cé mhéad páiste atá agat?
   Say: Four.
9. Cé mhéad páiste atá agat?
   Say: Three.
10. Cén aois atá siad?
   Say: Three years (old) and seven years (old).

How many brothers do you have?

This is how to find out how many brothers and sisters someone has:

Cé mhéad deartháir atá agat?
How many brothers do you have?

Triúr.
Three.

Cé mhéad deirfiúr atá agat?
How many sisters do you have?

Beirt.
Two.

My brother

The Irish for *my* is **mo** and the Irish for *your* is **do**. A *séimhiú* is added to nouns beginning with a consonant which follow them:

deartháir *brother*	**mo dheartháir** *my brother*
deirfiúr *sister*	**do dheirfiúr** *your sister*
máthair *mother*	**mo mháthair** *my mother*

Mo and **do** are shortened when they precede a noun beginning with a vowel:

athair *father*	**m'athair** *my father*
aintín *aunt*	**d'aintín** *your aunt*

Introducing members of the family

In Unit 1, we looked at how you introduce people. Let's do a recap of the rules now.

This is how you introduce a man:

Seo é mo dheartháir.
This is my brother.

This is how you introduce a woman:

Seo í mo dheirfiúr.
This is my sister.

And this is how you introduce more than one person:

Seo iad mo thuismitheoirí.
These are my parents.

Exercise 3.5: Fill in the gaps

Fill in the gaps in the sentences below.

1. *This is my Aunt Síle.*
   Seo ____ ____________ Síle.
2. *This is my uncle Seosamh.*
   Seo ____ ____________ Seosamh.
3. *These are my sisters Michelle and Bríd.*
   Seo ______ mo ______________ Michelle agus Bríd.
4. *These are my brothers Liam and Aodán.*
   Seo ______ mo ______________ Liam agus Aodán.
5. *These are my parents Cóilín and Sorcha.*
   Seo _____ mo ______________ Cóilín agus Sorcha.
6. *This is my brother Tomás.*
   Seo ___ mo ____________ Tomás.
7. *This my father Ciarán.*
   Seo ___ __________ Ciarán.
8. *This is my sister Órla.*
   Seo ___ mo ____________ Órla.

Conversation 3C

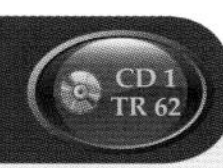

Deirdre brings her boyfriend Cathal home to meet the family for the first time.

Deirdre: Seo iad mo thuismitheoirí Séamas agus Regina.
These are my parents Séamas and Regina.

Cathal: Dia daoibh.
Hello.

Deirdre: Agus seo í mo dheirfiúr Laoise.
And this is my sister Laoise.

Laoise: Tá sé go deas bualadh leat.
It's nice to meet you.

Deirdre: Agus seo iad mo dheartháireacha Cormac agus Eoin.
And these are my brothers Cormac and Eoin.

Cathal: Cén chaoi a bhfuil sibh?
How are you?

Regina: An mbeidh cupán tae agat, a Chathail?
Will you have a cup of tea, Cathal?

Conversation 3D

Cáit and Gearóid are on their second date and are finding out more about each other's families.

Cáit: Cé mhéad deartháir atá agat?
How many brothers do you have?

Gearóid: Beirt – Máirtín agus Ruairí.
Two – Máirtín and Ruairí.

Cáit: Agus cé mhéad deirfiúr atá agat?
And how many sisters do you have?

Gearóid: Deirfiúr amháin – Sinéad. Cé mhéad deartháir agus deirfiúr atá agatsa?
*One sister – Sinéad. How many brothers and sisters do **you** have?*

Cáit: Níl deartháir ná deirfiúr ar bith agam – is páiste aonair mé.
I have no brothers or sisters – I'm an only child.

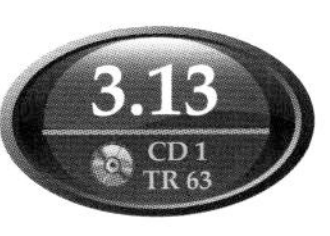

3.13 Plural forms

CD 1 TR 63

In Conversation 3C, Cathal addressed more than one person on two occasions and therefore used plural forms:

Cathal: **Dia daoibh.**
Hello.

Cathal: **Cén chaoi a bhfuil sibh?**
How are you?

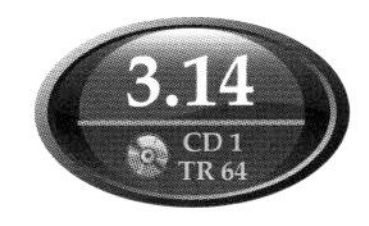

3.14 The vocative case

CD 1 TR 64

As Regina was addressing Cathal at the end of Conversation 3C, she used the vocative case form of his name:

Regina: **An mbeidh cupán tae agat, a Chathail?**
Will you have a cup of tea, Cathal?

Exercise 3.6: Your turn!

This is your chance to talk now. Pretend you're Deirdre and that you're talking to Cathal.

Say: *These are my parents Séamas and Regina.*

Cathal: Dia daoibh.

Say: *And this is my sister Laoise.*

Laoise: Tá sé go deas bualadh leat.

Say: *And these are my brothers Cormac and Eoin.*

Cathal: Cén chaoi a bhfuil sibh?

Regina: An mbeidh cupán tae agat, a Chathail?

Exercise 3.7: Your turn!

This time, pretend you're Cáit and that you're talking to Gearóid.

Say: *How many brothers do you have?*

Gearóid: Beirt – Máirtín agus Ruairí.

Say: *And how many sisters do you have?*

Gearóid: Deirfiúr amháin – Sinéad. Cé mhéad deartháir agus deirfiúr atá agatsa?

Say: *I have no brothers or sisters – I'm an only child.*

Useful tips for learners

Try a technique called shadow reading, using the dialogues contained in this unit or in any other unit in the book.

Listen to the dialogues at first without looking at the script, then listen to them with the script in front of you. After a while, when you've become familiar with them, listen, read and speak at the same time as the speakers on the audio file. Don't stop the recording as you do this.

This exercise will help you learn the sounds and the rhythm of Irish.

Talking heads

You'll hear various people talking about their family. Listen to them first without looking at the script below to see how much you'll understand. After that, listen to them with the script in front of you and, lastly, look at the English translation of their speech.

Tadhg Mac Dhonnagáin
(filmed in An Spidéal, Galway)
Tá mé pósta le Cristín agus tá ceathrar páistí againn – beirt mhac agus beirt iníon. Tá Marcus naoi mbliana déag d'aois, tá Éabha cúig bliana déag d'aois, tá Tadhg Óg dhá bhliain déag agus tá Róise deich mbliana d'aois.

Tá ceathrar deartháir agus beirt deirfiúr agam féin agus is mise an tríú duine is sine.

Colm Mac Séalaigh
(filmed at the Civic Offices, Dublin)
Tá mé pósta le Nóirín. Tá triúr páistí againn – beirt mhac, Colmán agus Cathal, agus iníon amháin, Neasa.

Tá beirt deirfiúracha agam agus deartháir amháin.

Fionnuala Croker
(filmed in Dún Laoghaire, County Dublin)
Níl mé pósta ach tá mé ag siúl amach le duine éigin le trí bliana anois. Níl páistí ar bith againn.

Tá deirfiúr amháin agus beirt deartháireacha agam. Is mise an duine is sine sa teaghlach.

Notes
The personal numerals, used for counting people, can be followed by the singular or plural of the noun in Irish. Most of the speakers in these excerpts use the plural form of the noun after the personal numerals.

TRANSLATION

Tadhg Mac Dhonnagáin
I'm married to Cristín and we have four children – two sons and two daughters. Marcus is nineteen years old, Éabha is fifteen years old, Tadhg Óg is twelve years (old) and Róise is ten years old.

I have four brothers and two sisters myself and **I**'m the third eldest.

Colm Mac Séalaigh
I'm married to Nóirín. We have three children – two sons, Colmán and Cathal, and one daughter, Neasa.

I have two sisters and one brother.

Fionnuala Croker
I'm not married but I've been going out with someone for three years now. We have no children.

I have one sister and two brothers. **I**'m the eldest in the family.

The audio versions of these excerpts are available on the sound files accompanying this book. The video segments can be seen in the online version of *Gaeilge gan Stró! – Beginners Level*, available on Gaelchultúr's e-learning website, www.ranganna.com.

Exercise 3.8: Review of Unit 3

Have a go at this activity now to see if you know the most important phrases taught in Unit 3.

How would you say the following in Irish?

1. I'm married.
2. I'm separated.
3. Are you married?
4. Are *you* married?
5. Do you have children (speaking to one person)?
6. Do *you* have children (speaking to one person)?
7. I have no children.
8. We have no children.
9. How many children do you have?
10. What age is she?
11. What ages are they?
12. How many brothers and sisters do you have?
13. This is my sister.
14. This is my brother.
15. These are my parents.

Unit 4: The House and Accommodation
Aonad 4: An Teach agus Lóistín

In this unit you will learn how to:
- ask someone what type of accommodation he has and answer that question
- name different types of houses and accommodation
- ask where a house or apartment is located and answer that question
- name the main rooms in the house
- name various things inside the house
- ask how many bedrooms there are and answer that question
- seek and give information about rent
- ask someone if he likes his accommodation and answer that question.

Grammar
- the simple preposition **i(n)**
- initial changes to nouns
- counting things
- **ceann**

San aonad seo foghlaimeoidh tú conas:
- *fiafraí de dhuine cén cineál lóistín atá aige agus an cheist sin a fhreagairt*
- *cineálacha éagsúla tithe agus lóistín a ainmniú*
- *fiafraí cá bhfuil teach nó árasán suite agus an cheist sin a fhreagairt*
- *na príomhsheomraí sa teach a ainmniú*
- *nithe éagsúla taobh istigh den teach a ainmniú*
- *ceist a chur cé mhéad seomra codlata atá ann agus an cheist sin a fhreagairt*
- *eolas a lorg agus a thabhairt faoi chíos*
- *fiafraí de dhuine an maith leis a lóistín agus an cheist sin a fhreagairt.*

Gramadach
- *an réamhfhocal simplí* ***i(n)***
- *athruithe tosaigh ar ainmfhocail*
- *rudaí a chomhaireamh*
- ***ceann***

Key sounds

CD 1 TR 68

cistin	(slender **c**)	*(a) kitchen*
cara	(broad **c**)	*(a) friend*
íoslach	(**c** with *séimhiú*, preceded by broad vowel, **a**)	*(a) basement*
an fhuinneog	(**f** with *séimhiú*)	*the window*
leaba	(slender **l**)	*(a) bed*
tolg	(broad **l**)	*(a) couch*
árasáin	(slender **n**)	*apartments*
árasán	(broad **n**)	*(an) apartment*
cuisneoir	(slender **r**)	*(a) fridge*
sorn	(broad **r**)	*(a) cooker*
i dteach	(**t** with *urú*)	*in a house*

4.1 What kind of accommodation do you have?

CD 1 TR 69

This is how you find out what type of accommodation someone has or where he lives:

Cén cineál lóistín atá agat?
What kind of accommodation do you have?

Cá bhfuil tú i do chónaí faoi láthair?
Where are you living at the moment?

Here are some possible answers:

Tá mé i mo chónaí i dteach scoite.
I live in a detached house.

Tá mé i mo chónaí i dteach leathscoite.
I live in a semi-detached house.

Tá mé i mo chónaí i m'aonar.
I'm living alone.

Tá mé ag roinnt árasáin le beirt eile.
I'm sharing an apartment with two others.

Tá mé ag roinnt tí le cara liom.
I'm sharing a house with a friend of mine.

4.2 I and in

CD 1 TR 70

As we saw in Unit 2, the simple preposition **i** (*in*) is used in Irish before words beginning with a consonant and the form **in** is used before vowels:

i dteach scoite
in a detached house

in árasán
in an apartment

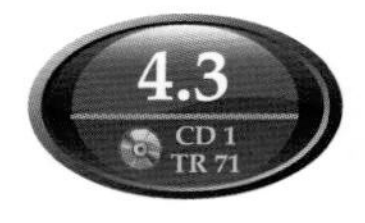

4.3 It's on the edge of the city

CD 1 TR 71

This is how you ask where a house or an apartment is situated:

Cá bhfuil an t-árasán suite?
Where is the apartment situated?

Cá bhfuil an teach suite?
Where is the house situated?

Here are some possible answers:

Tá sé ar imeall na cathrach.
It's on the edge of the city.

Tá sé ar imeall an bhaile.
It's on the edge of town.

Tá sé i lár na cathrach.
It's in the city centre.

Tá sé i lár an bhaile.
It's in the centre of town.

Tá sé san eastát nua sin.
It's in that new estate.

Tá sé faoin tuath.
It's in the country.

Words which are used to describe location, such as **ar imeall** and **i lár**, are often followed by the genitive case. **Cathair** and **baile** above are in the genitive case, which is why both words look different.

We'll come across other examples of the genitive case in later units, but at this level, there's no need to learn the rules governing the genitive.

Vocabulary 1: Houses and rooms

- teach scoite / an teach scoite / tithe scoite — *(a) detached house / the detached house / detached houses*
- teach leathscoite / an teach leathscoite / tithe leathscoite — *(a) semi-detached house / the semi-detached house / semi-detached houses*
- teach sraithe / an teach sraithe / tithe sraithe — *(a) terraced house / the terraced house / terraced houses*
- teach dhá stór / an teach dhá stór / tithe dhá stór — *(a) two-storey house / the two-storey house / two-storey houses*
- eastát tithíochta / an t-eastát tithíochta — *(a) housing estate / the housing estate*
- árasán / an t-árasán / árasáin — *(an) apartment / the apartment / apartments*
- seomra suí / an seomra suí — *(a) sitting room / the sitting room*
- seomra codlata / an seomra codlata / seomraí codlata — *(a) bedroom / the bedroom / bedrooms*
- halla / an halla — *(a) hall / the hall*
- cistin / an chistin — *(a) kitchen / the kitchen*
- seomra folctha / an seomra folctha — *(a) bathroom / the bathroom*
- leithreas / an leithreas / leithris — *(a) toilet / the toilet / toilets*
- áiléar / an t-áiléar — *(an) attic / the attic*
- íoslach / an t-íoslach — *(a) basement / the basement*

Vocabulary 2: Inside the house

- bord / an bord / boird — *(a) table / the table / tables*
- cathaoir / an chathaoir / cathaoireacha — *(a) chair / the chair / chairs*
- cathaoir uilleach / an chathaoir uilleach — *(an) armchair / the armchair*
- tolg / an tolg — *(a) couch / the couch*
- leaba / an leaba / leapacha — *(a) bed / the bed / beds*
- cófra / an cófra / cófraí — *(a) press / the press / presses*
- cuisneoir / an cuisneoir — *(a) fridge / the fridge*
- reoiteoir / an reoiteoir — *(a) freezer / the freezer*
- sorn / an sorn — *(a) cooker / the cooker*
- doras / an doras / doirse — *(a) door / the door / doors*
- an doras tosaigh — *the front door*
- an doras cúil — *the back door*
- fuinneog / an fhuinneog / fuinneoga — *(a) window / the window / windows*
- staighre / an staighre — *(a) stairs / the stairs*
- thuas staighre — *upstairs*
- thíos staighre — *downstairs*
- teas lárnach / an teas lárnach — *central heating / the central heating*

Exercise 4.1: Answer the questions

Answer each of these questions as indicated.

1. Cén cineál lóistín atá agat?
   Say: I'm living alone.
2. Cén cineál lóistín atá agat?
   Say: I'm sharing an apartment with three others.
3. Cén cineál lóistín atá agat?
   Say: I'm sharing a house with two others.
4. Cá bhfuil tú i do chónaí faoi láthair?
   Say: I live in a detached house.
5. Cá bhfuil tú i do chónaí faoi láthair?
   Say: I live in a semi-detached house.
6. Cá bhfuil an t-árasán suite?
   Say: It's on the edge of town.
7. Cá bhfuil an t-árasán suite?
   Say: It's in the city centre.
8. Cá bhfuil an teach suite?
   Say: It's in that new estate.

Exercise 4.2: Fill in the gaps

Write the correct version of each noun in the gap after the article and change the noun if necessary. Use the table in 4.4 as a guide.

1. eastát (masculine) (*estate*)
   an ________________
2. íoslach (masculine) (*basement*)
   an ________________
3. cathaoir (feminine) (*chair*)
   an ________________
4. cuisneoir (masculine) (*fridge*)
   an ________________
5. bord (masculine) (*table*)
   an ________________
6. sorn (masculine) (*cooker*)
   an ________________
7. cathair (feminine) (*city*)
   an ________________
8. fuinneog (feminine) (*window*)
   an ________________

Initial changes to nouns

In Unit 3, we saw that the beginning of a noun in Irish can change when it's preceded by the article **an**, depending on the gender of the noun. Let's have another look at the changes which occur to both feminine and masculine nouns that are preceded by the article in the nominative and accusative cases.

	Masculine	Feminine
(a) Nouns beginning with a vowel	**an t-árasán** *the apartment*	**an éarlais** *the deposit*
(b) Nouns beginning with a consonant	**an baile** *the town*	**an chistin** *the kitchen*
(c) Nouns beginning with **s**	**an seomra suí** *the sitting room*	**an tsíleáil** *the ceiling*
(d) Nouns beginning with **d** or **t**	**an doras** *the door* **an teach** *the house*	**an tine** *the fire* A *séimhiú* is not added to feminine nouns beginning with **d** or **t** in the nominative and accusative cases

Insight

Although English is the most widely spoken language in Ireland, many Irish language words are used in everyday life. Here are some of the most prominent:

an lár (*the centre* – it appears on buses in Dublin)
Dáil Éireann (the Irish parliament)
Teachta Dála (member of parliament)
Ceann Comhairle (speaker of Dáil Éireann)
An Taoiseach (the Irish prime minister)
An Tánaiste (the deputy prime minister)
Seanad Éireann (the Senate)
Fianna Fáil (*soldiers of Ireland* – political party)
Fine Gael (*Gaelic kindred* – political party)
An Garda Síochána (the police service)
Bus Éireann (public bus service)
feis cheoil (*festival of music* – annual Irish cultural festival of music and dance)

Conversation 4A

Jim is describing his new apartment to his friend Simon.

Simon: An bhfuil an t-árasán mór?
Is the apartment big?

Jim: Tá. Tá dhá sheomra codlata ann, cistin an-deas agus seomra suí an-mhór.
Yes. There are two bedrooms, a very nice kitchen and a very big sitting room.

Simon: An bhfuil tú i do chónaí i d'aonar?
Are you living alone?

Jim: Níl. Tá mé ag roinnt an árasáin le cara liom, Judy. Tá sí an-deas.
No. I'm sharing the apartment with a friend of mine, Judy. She's very nice.

Conversation 4B

Simon now tells Jim about his accommodation.

Jim: Cá bhfuil tú féin i do chónaí faoi láthair?
Where are you living yourself at the moment?

Simon: Tá mé i mo chónaí i m'aonar i lár na cathrach.
I'm living alone in the city centre.

Jim: In árasán nó i dteach?
In an apartment or in a house?

Simon: I dteach sraithe. Tá sé an-deas.
In a terraced house. It's very nice.

Jim: Cá bhfuil an teach suite?
Where's the house located?

Simon: Tá sé gar don abhainn.
It's near the river.

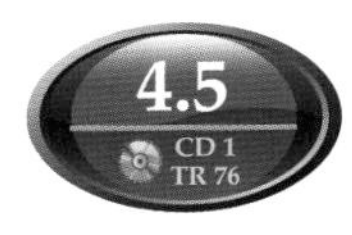

Nouns with the cardinal numbers 1

These are the numbers used when counting things in Irish:

1	**aon chathaoir amháin** *one chair*	11	**aon chathaoir déag**
2	**dhá chathaoir**	12	**dhá chathaoir déag**
3	**trí chathaoir**	13	**trí chathaoir déag**
4	**ceithre chathaoir**	14	**ceithre chathaoir déag**
5	**cúig chathaoir**	15	**cúig chathaoir déag**
6	**sé chathaoir**	16	**sé chathaoir déag**
7	**seacht gcathaoir**	17	**seacht gcathaoir déag**
8	**ocht gcathaoir**	18	**ocht gcathaoir déag**
9	**naoi gcathaoir**	19	**naoi gcathaoir déag**
10	**deich gcathaoir**	20	**fiche cathaoir**

Nouns with the cardinal numbers 2

The singular form of the noun is usually used after cardinal numbers:

trí bhord
three tables

cúig chathaoir
five chairs

There is a *séimhiú* on words beginning with a consonant which follow the numbers **2–6** and an *urú* on words beginning with a consonant or a vowel after the numbers **7–10**. Have a look at the pattern on the right.

	Consonants	Vowels
1 *séimhiú* on consonants except **d**, **t**, **s**	**aon chathaoir amháin** *one chair*	**aon óstán amháin** *one hotel*
2–6 *séimhiú* on consonants	**dhá sheomra** *two rooms*	**trí óstán** *three hotels*
	cúig sheomra *five rooms*	**sé óstán** *six hotels*
7–10 *urú* on consonants and on vowels	**seacht gcathaoir** *seven chairs*	**seacht n-oíche** *seven nights*
	ocht gcathaoir *eight chairs*	**ocht n-óstán** *eight hotels*
	deich gcathaoir *ten chairs*	**deich n-oíche** *ten nights*

Exercise 4.3: Your turn!

This is your chance to talk now. Pretend you're Jim and that you're talking to Simon.

Simon: An bhfuil an t-árasán mór?

Say: *Yes. There are two bedrooms, a very nice kitchen and a very big sitting room.*

Simon: An bhfuil tú i do chónaí i d'aonar?

Say: *No. I'm sharing the apartment with a friend of mine, Judy. She's very nice.*

Exercise 4.4: Your turn!

This time, pretend you're Simon and that you're talking to Jim.

Jim: Cá bhfuil tú féin i do chónaí faoi láthair?

Say: *I'm living alone in the city centre.*

Jim: In árasán nó i dteach?

Say: *In a terraced house. It's very nice.*

Jim: Cá bhfuil an teach suite?

Say: *It's near the river.*

Exercise 4.5: Fill in the gaps

Fill in the gaps in these sentences.

1. *What kind of accommodation do you have?*
   Cén cineál __________ atá agat?
2. *I live in a detached house.*
   Tá mé i mo chónaí i __________ __________.
3. *I'm living alone.*
   Tá mé i mo chónaí i __________.
4. *I live in an apartment.*
   Tá mé i mo chónaí _____ __________.
5. *Where is the apartment situated?*
   Cá bhfuil an __________ suite?
6. *It's on the edge of the city.*
   Tá sé ar __________ na cathrach.
7. *It's in the centre of town.*
   Tá sé i ________ an bhaile.
8. *It's in the country.*
   Tá sé ________ __________.
9. *Are you living alone?*
   An bhfuil tú i do chónaí i __________?
10. *Where's the house located?*
    Cá bhfuil an teach __________?

Ceann

When you're counting objects in Irish, the cardinal numbers we saw earlier cannot be used on their own – you must use the word **ceann** (*one*, of things, animals) with them:

Cé mhéad seomra atá sa teach?
How many rooms are there in the house?

Trí cinn.
Three.

It would be incorrect to use **trí** on its own in the above example.

Ceann is similar to the noun **bliain** (*year*) that we looked at in Unit 3 as it has special forms that are used after the cardinal numbers. There are only a few nouns in Irish that don't follow the normal rules for counting and it's worth learning how to use them properly as they occur very frequently.

Here are the various forms of **ceann** used after the cardinal numbers:

1	2	3–6	7–10
ceann amháin *one of something*	**dhá cheann** *two of something*	**trí cinn** *three of something* **ceithre cinn** *four of something* **cúig cinn** *five of something* **sé cinn** *six of something*	**seacht gcinn** *seven of something* **ocht gcinn** *eight of something* **naoi gcinn** *nine of something* **deich gcinn** *ten of something*

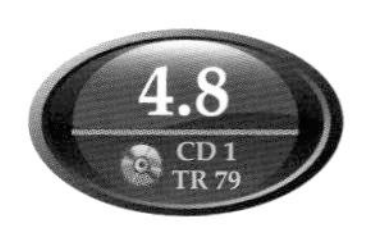

Is the rent expensive?

To find out whether someone's rent is expensive or not you can ask:

An bhfuil an cíos daor?
Is the rent expensive?

Here are some possible answers:

Tá sé ceart go leor.
It's okay.

Tá sé an-saor.
It's very cheap.

Tá sé daor go leor.
It's quite expensive.

Tá sé an-daor.
It's very expensive.

Another useful question is:

Cé mhéad a íocann tú sa mhí?
How much do you pay per month?

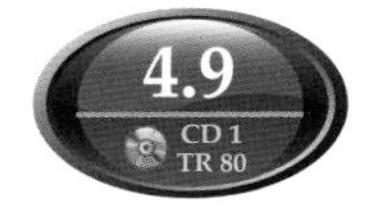

Three hundred euro

Here are some numbers which might prove useful for saying how much rent you pay:

Céad euro an duine sa tseachtain.
One hundred euro per person per week.

Dhá chéad euro an duine sa tseachtain.
Two hundred euro per person per week.

Trí chéad euro sa mhí.
Three hundred euro per month.

Ceithre chéad euro sa mhí.
Four hundred euro per month.

Cúig chéad euro sa mhí.
Five hundred euro per month.

The Irish for *fifty* is **caoga**. This is how you use it:

Ceithre chéad caoga euro sa mhí.
Four hundred and fifty euro per month.

Exercise 4.6: Give the Irish version

Give the Irish version of each of the following:

1. two rooms
2. three hotels
3. eight nights
4. seven hotels
5. ten chairs
6. two of something
7. three of something
8. seven of something
9. three hundred euro per week
10. five hundred and fifty euro per month

Conversation 4C

Seosamh describes his new accommodation to his friend Jill.

Jill: Cá bhfuil an teach suite?
Where is the house located?

Seosamh: Tá sé san eastát nua sin ar imeall an bhaile: Cois Abhann.
It's in that new estate on the edge of town: Riverside.

Jill: Go deas. Cé mhéad seomra codlata atá ann?
Very nice. How many bedrooms are there?

Seosamh: Trí cinn. Tá dhá cheann acu an-mhór ach tá an ceann eile an-bheag.
Three. Two of them are very big but the other one is very small.

Jill: An bhfuil an cíos daor?
Is the rent expensive?

Seosamh: Tá sé ceart go leor: trí chéad euro an duine sa mhí.
It's okay: three hundred euro each per month.

Conversation 4D

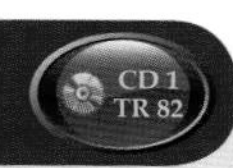

Jill now tells Seosamh about her accommodation.

Seosamh: An bhfuil tusa fós ag roinnt árasáin le Laura?
*Are **you** still sharing an apartment with Laura?*

Jill: Tá. Táimid ansin le dhá bhliain anois.
Yes. We've been there for two years now.

Seosamh: Cá bhfuil an t-árasán?
Where is the apartment?

Jill: Tá sé gar do lár an bhaile, in aice leis an ionad siopadóireachta.
It's near the centre of town, beside the shopping centre.

Seosamh: Agus an maith leat é?
And do you like it?

Jill: Is maith. Tá sé breá ciúin.
Yes. It's nice and quiet.

4.10 Do you like it?

CD 1 TR 83

This is how you say you like or don't like something:

Is maith liom an teach.
I like the house.

Ní maith liom an t-árasán.
I don't like the apartment.

To find out if someone likes something you can ask:

An maith leat é?
Do you like it?

In reply you can say:

Is maith.
Yes.
or
Ní maith.
No.

Exercise 4.7: Your turn!

CD 1 TR 84

This is your chance to talk now. Pretend you're Seosamh and that you're talking to Jill.

Jill:	Cá bhfuil an teach suite?
Say:	*It's in that new estate on the edge of town: Riverside.*
Jill:	Go deas. Cé mhéad seomra codlata atá ann?
Say:	*Three. Two of them are very big but the other one is very small.*

Jill:	An bhfuil an cíos daor?
Say:	*It's okay: three hundred euro each per month.*

Exercise 4.8: Your turn!

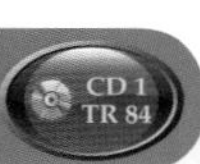

CD 1 TR 84

This time, pretend you're Jill and that you're talking to Seosamh.

Seosamh:	An bhfuil tusa fós ag roinnt árasáin le Laura?
Say:	*Yes. We've been there for two years now.*
Seosamh:	Cá bhfuil an t-árasán?
Say:	*It's near the centre of town, beside the shopping centre.*
Seosamh:	Agus an maith leat é?
Say:	*Yes. It's nice and quiet.*

Useful tips for learners

Try studying Irish on a regular basis. It's better to do twenty minutes or half an hour of work on this course a few times a week, rather than trying to cover all the material in a unit in one sitting.

You should spend an average of about six hours studying each unit in the book.

Talking heads

Cóilín Ó Floinn (filmed in Temple Bar, Dublin)
Tá mé ag roinnt árasáin le mo chailín. Is maith liom an t-árasán; níl sé ródhaor agus tá sé ciúin agus compordach. Tá cistin, seomra suí, seomra folctha, seomra codlata amháin agus oifig ann.

Siobhán Patten (filmed in Temple Bar, Dublin)
Tá mé i mo chónaí i dteach beag, gar do lár na cathrach i mBaile Átha Cliath. Tá an teach suite i gcearnóg bheag thart ar dhá chiliméadar ó lár na cathrach.

Seanteach sraithe atá ann agus níl ach trí sheomra ann: seomra leapa, seomra folctha agus tá an chistin agus seomra suite mar sheomra amháin.

Níl gairdín ar bith agam, faraor, ach tá páirc mhór, Páirc an Fhionnuisce, an-ghar do mo theach. Is breá liom dul ansin agus luí faoin ngrian nuair a bhíonn an aimsir go maith.

Páidí Ó Lionáird (filmed in An Spidéal, Galway)
Tá mé i mo chónaí i dteach scoite in Indreabhán i gConamara le mo bhean agus mo chlann. Tá cúig sheomra leapa sa teach agus tá an chistin agus an seomra suite go breá mór.

Táimid inár gcónaí sa teach anois le sé bliana agus táimid an-sásta leis.

Táimid dhá mhíle siar ón Spidéal agus dhá mhíle dhéag siar ó chathair na Gaillimhe.

Notes
There are two versions in Irish of *sitting room*: **seomra suí** and **seomra suite**.

There are also two versions of *bedroom*: **seomra codlata** and **seomra leapa**.

Translation

Cóilín Ó Floinn
I'm sharing an apartment with my girlfriend. I like the apartment; it's not too expensive and it's quiet and comfortable. There's a kitchen, sitting room, bathroom, one bedroom and an office.

Siobhán Patten
I live in a small house, close to the city centre in Dublin. The house is located in a small square, about two kilometres from the city centre.

It's an old terraced house and there are only three rooms: a bedroom, bathroom and the kitchen and sitting room are one room.

I have no garden, alas, but there's a big park, The Phoenix Park, very close to my house. I love to go there and lie under the sun when the weather is good.

Páidí Ó Lionáird
I live in a detached house in Indreabhán in Conamara with my wife and my children. There are five bedrooms in the house and the kitchen and the sitting room are nice and big.

We've been living in the house now for six years and we're very happy with it.

We're two miles west of An Spidéal and twelve miles west of Galway city.

The audio versions of these excerpts are available on the sound files accompanying this book. The video segments can be seen in the online version of *Gaeilge gan Stró! – Beginners Level*, available on Gaelchultúr's e-learning website, www.ranganna.com.

Exercise 4.9: Review of Unit 4

Have a go at this activity now to see if you know the most important phrases taught in Unit 4.

How would you say the following in Irish?

1. What kind of accommodation do you have?
2. Where are you living at the moment?
3. I'm living alone.
4. I'm sharing a house with a friend of mine.
5. I'm sharing an apartment with two others.
6. Where is the house situated?
7. It's on the edge of town.
8. It's in the city centre.
9. It's in that new estate.
10. Is the rent expensive?
11. It's okay.
12. It's very expensive.
13. I like the house.
14. I don't like the apartment.
15. Do you like it? Yes.

Unit 5: Pastimes
Aonad 5: Caitheamh Aimsire

In this unit you will learn how to:

- ask someone what he does when he's free and answer that question
- ask someone if he does a particular pastime and answer that question
- ask someone if he likes a particular pastime and answer that question
- express opinions about a pastime
- say that you have the ability to do a certain thing
- name different pastimes
- say how often you do certain things.

San aonad seo foghlaimeoidh tú conas:

- *fiafraí de dhuine cad é a dhéanann sé nuair a bhíonn sé saor agus an cheist sin a fhreagairt*
- *fiafraí de dhuine an ndéanann sé caitheamh aimsire áirithe agus an cheist sin a fhreagairt*
- *fiafraí de dhuine an maith leis caitheamh aimsire áirithe agus an cheist sin a fhreagairt*
- *tuairimí a chur in iúl faoi chaitheamh aimsire*
- *a rá go bhfuil sé ar do chumas rud áirithe a dhéanamh*
- *cineálacha difriúla caitheamh aimsire a ainmniú*
- *a rá cé chomh minic is a dhéanann tú rudaí áirithe.*

Grammar

- questions and answers in the present tense
- the copula **is**
- **chuig** and **go dtí**
- adverbs of freqency

Gramadach

- *ceisteanna agus freagraí san aimsir láithreach*
- *an chopail* ***is***
- ***chuig*** *agus* ***go dtí***
- *dobhriathra minicíochta*

Key sounds

CD 1 TR 87

céard	(slender **c**)	*what*
a**c**laí	(broad **c**)	*fit*
cad a **dh**éanann tú	(**d** with *séimhiú* followed by slender vowel, **e**)	*what do you do*
chui**g**	(slender **g**)	*to, toward*
gach	(broad **g**)	*every*
an fhidi**l**	(slender **l**)	*the fiddle*
ceo**l**	(broad **l**)	*music*
an **ph**ictiúrlann	(**p** with *séimhiú*)	*the cinema*
teach **t**ábhairne	(slender **t** and broad **t**)	*(a) pub*
an **bhf**éachann tú	(**f** with *urú*)	*do you watch*

What do you do when you have free time?

This is how you find out what someone does in their free time:

Céard a dhéanann tú nuair a bhíonn am saor agat?
What do you do when you have free time?

Here are some possible answers:

Téim ag snámh.
I go swimming.

Téim ag rith.
I go running.

Imrím leadóg.
I play tennis.

Imrím peil.
I play football.

Féachaim ar an teilifís.
I watch television.

Éistim le ceol.
I listen to music.

Éistim leis an raidió.
I listen to the radio.

Téim go dtí an phictiúrlann.
I go to the cinema.

Téim go dtí an teach tábhairne.
I go to the pub.

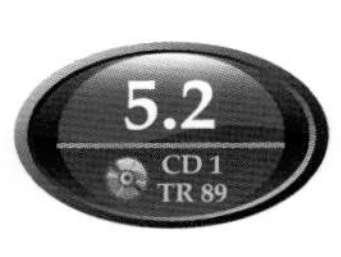

Do you play tennis?

This is how you find out if someone does a particular pastime:

An imríonn tú leadóg?
Do you play tennis?

Imrím./Ní imrím.
Yes./No.

An dtéann tú go dtí an phictiúrlann?
Do you go to the cinema?

Téim./Ní théim.
Yes./No.

To form a question in the present tense, **an** is placed before the verb. After **an**, an *urú* is added to verbs beginning with **b**, **c**, **d**, **f**, **g** or **p**. Verbs beginning with a vowel remain unchanged:

An dtéann tú ag snámh?
Do you go swimming?

An imríonn tú sacar?
Do you play soccer?

In the negative, **ní** is placed before the verb. A *séimhiú* is added to consonants which follow **ní**:

Ní théim ag snámh.
I don't go swimming.

Ní fhéachaim ar an teilifís.
I don't watch television.

Answering questions

As we mentioned in Unit 3, there is no equivalent in Irish to *yes* and *no* in English. When you're asked a question, you must use the same verb in your answer that was used in the question:

An bhféachann tú ar an teilifís?
Do you watch television?

Féachaim./Ní fhéachaim.
Yes./No.

An éisteann tú le ceol?
Do you listen to music?

Éistim./Ní éistim.
Yes./No.

An dtéann tú go dtí an teach tábhairne?
Do you go to the pub?

Téim./Ní théim.
Yes./No.

Note the following:

- The beginning of **bhféachann** is pronounced like *v* in English.
- When a *séimhiú* is added to **f** it becomes silent, e.g. **ní fhéachaim**.
- The **t** in **dtéann** is silent.

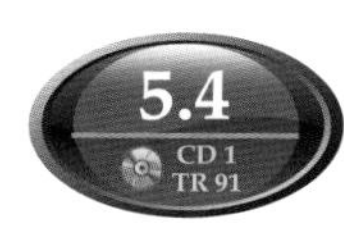

Do you like ...?

In Unit 4, you learnt how to say you like or dislike something:

Is maith liom an teach.
I like the house.

Ní maith liom an t-árasán.
I don't like the apartment.

You also learnt how to ask someone if he likes something:

An maith leat an teach?
Do you like the house?

Is maith./Ní maith.
Yes./No.

Let's have a look at three other possible answers to a question containing the words **An maith leat ...?**:

An maith leat ceol traidisiúnta?
Do you like traditional music?

Tá sé ceart go leor.
It's okay.

Is breá liom é.
I love it.

Is fuath liom é.
I hate it.

Exercise 5.1: Answer the questions

Answer each of these questions as indicated.

1. Céard a dhéanann tú nuair a bhíonn am saor agat?
   Say: I go to the pub.

2. Céard a dhéanann tú nuair a bhíonn am saor agat?
   Say: I watch television.

3. An imríonn tú leadóg?
   Say: Yes.

4. An dtéann tú go dtí an phictiúrlann?
   Say: No.

5. An bhféachann tú ar an teilifís?
   Say: No.

6. An éisteann tú le ceol?
   Say: Yes.

7. An maith leat ceol traidisiúnta?
   Say: No.

8. An maith leat ceol traidisiúnta?
   Say: No. I hate it.

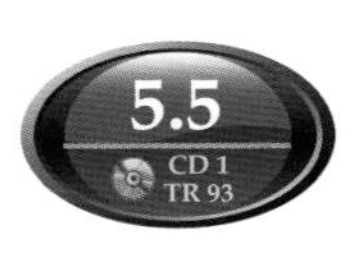

I like to read

You often use **bheith** in Irish when you're saying you like to or don't like to engage in certain pastimes:

Is maith liom bheith ag snámh.
I like to swim.

Is maith liom bheith ag léamh.
I like to read.

Is maith liom bheith ag canadh.
I like to sing.

Is breá liom bheith ag seinm ceoil.
I love to play music.

Is breá liom bheith ag scimeáil ar an Idirlíon.
I love to surf the Internet.

The **g** in **ag** is not usually pronounced when it precedes a consonant. It is pronounced, however, when it precedes a vowel.

Insight

The dialect of English spoken in Ireland, Hiberno-English, is heavily influenced by the Irish language. The following phrases would seem unfamiliar to speakers from outside the country:

I do be there often. (I'm often there.)
I'm after doing it. (I've just done it.)
I have the work done. (I've done the work.)
He gave out to her. (He told her off.)

As we mentioned earlier, Irish lacks words that directly translate as *yes* or *no*, and instead repeats the verb in a question to answer that question. Speakers of Hiberno-English tend to do the same and consequently use *yes* and *no* less frequently than speakers of other dialects. Here are two examples:

"Are you coming back tomorrow?"
– "I am."
"Is it a good film?" – "It's not."

Conversation 5A

Susan and David meet at a speed-dating event for people who want to fall in love through Irish!

Susan: Céard a dhéanann tú nuair a bhíonn am saor agat?
What do you do when you have free time?

David: Tá mé an-aclaí. Téim ag rith agus ag snámh gach lá.
I'm very fit. I go running and swimming every day.

Susan: Gach lá! Maith thú!
Every day! Fair play to you!

David: Céard a dhéanann tú féin nuair a bhíonn am saor agat?
What do you do yourself when you have free time?

Susan: Is maith liom bheith ag léamh agus is breá liom bheith ag seinm ceoil.
I like to read and I love playing music.

Conversation 5B

Caroline and Breandán are attending the same speed-dating event.

Breandán: An éisteann tú le ceol?
Do you listen to music?

Caroline: Éistim. Is breá liom ceol traidisiúnta.
Yes. I love traditional music.

Breandán: An bhfuil ceol agat féin?
Are you musical yourself?

Caroline: Tá. Seinnim an fhidil. An bhfuil ceol agatsa?
*Yes. I play the fiddle. Are **you** musical?*

Breandán: Níl. Níl ceol ar bith agam – faraor!
No. I'm not musical at all – alas!

Caroline: An imríonn tú spórt?
Do you play sport?

Breandán: Imrím. Imrím peil agus leadóg.
Yes. I play football and tennis.

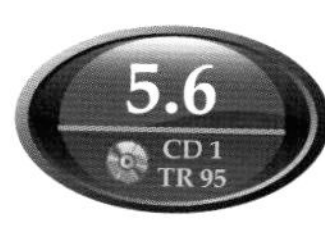

I'm musical

When you talk about ability in Irish, you often use **agam**:

Tá ceol agam.
I'm musical (literally, *there is music at me*).

Tá snámh agam.
I can swim (literally, *there is swimming at me*).

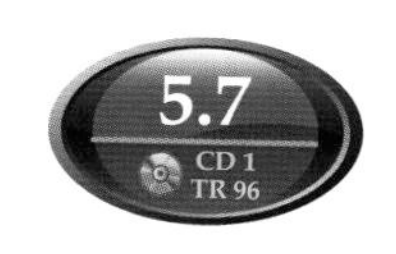

I play the fiddle

In Conversation 5B, when Caroline was asked if she was musical, she replied:

Tá. Seinnim an fhidil.
Yes. I play the fiddle.

Don't forget what we mentioned earlier: when a *séimhiú* is added to **f** it becomes silent, e.g. **ní fhéachaim**, **an fhidil**.

Exercise 5.2: Your turn!

This is your chance to talk now. Pretend you're David and that you're talking to Susan.

Susan:	Céard a dhéanann tú nuair a bhíonn am saor agat?
Say:	*I'm very fit. I go running and swimming every day.*
Susan:	Gach lá! Maith thú!
Say:	*What do you do yourself when you have free time?*
Susan:	Is maith liom bheith ag léamh agus is breá liom bheith ag seinm ceoil.

Exercise 5.3: Your turn!

This time, pretend you're Caroline and that you're talking to Breandán.

Breandán:	An éisteann tú le ceol?
Say:	*Yes. I love traditional music.*
Breandán:	An bhfuil ceol agat féin?
Say:	*Yes. I play the fiddle. Are **you** musical?*
Breandán:	Níl. Níl ceol ar bith agam – faraor!
Say:	*Do you play sport?*
Breandán:	Imrím. Imrím peil agus leadóg.

Exercise 5.4: Fill in the gaps

Fill in the gaps in these sentences.

1. *What do you do when you have free time?*
   Céard a ________________ tú nuair a bhíonn am saor agat?
2. *I go running.*
   Téim ag _______.
3. *I watch television.*
   _______________ ar an teilifís.
4. *I listen to music.*
   _______________ le ceol.

5. *I go to the cinema.*
   ___________ go dtí an phictiúrlann.
6. *Do you play tennis?*
   An _______________ tú leadóg?
7. *Do you go to the pub?*
   An _______________ tú go dtí an teach tábhairne?
8. *Do you like traditional music?*
   An _________ leat ceol traidisiúnta?
9. *It's okay.*
   Tá sé __________ go leor.
10. *I like to read.*
    Is maith liom __________ ag léamh.

Vocabulary: Pastimes

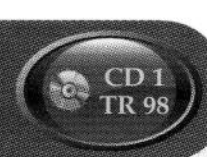

spórt	*sport*
peil Ghaelach	*Gaelic football*
iománaíocht	*hurling*
sacar	*soccer*
rugbaí	*rugby*
leadóg	*tennis*
galf	*golf*
cispheil	*basketball*
amharclann / an amharclann	*(a) theatre / the theatre*
dráma / an dráma / drámaí	*(a) play / the play / plays*
pictiúrlann / an phictiúrlann	*(a) cinema / the cinema*
scannán / an scannán / scannáin	*(a) film / the film / films*
teach tábhairne / an teach tábhairne / tithe tábhairne	*(a) pub / the pub / pubs*
seisiún ceoil / an seisiún ceoil / seisiúin cheoil	*(a) music session / the music session / music sessions*
ceolchoirm / an cheolchoirm / ceolchoirmeacha	*(a) concert / the concert / concerts*
ceol	*music*
amhrán / an t-amhrán / amhráin	*(a) song / the song / songs*
ceol traidisiúnta	*traditional music*
ceol tíre	*folk music*
popcheol	*pop music*
rac-cheol	*rock music*
snagcheol	*jazz*
ceol clasaiceach	*classical music*
ceol tuaithe	*country music*

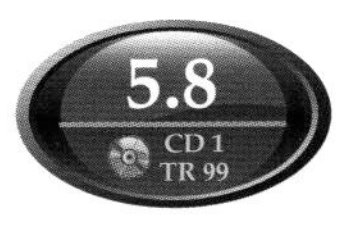

Chuig and go dtí

The preposition **chuig** is usually used when talking about going to an event or an appointment:

Téim chuig ceolchoirmeacha go minic.
I often go to concerts.

Téim chuig drámaí.
I go to plays.

Go dtí is usually used when talking about going to a particular place:

Téim go dtí an phictiúrlann.
I go to the cinema.

Téim go dtí an teach tábhairne.
I go to the pub.

Useful phrases

CD 1 TR 99

Is maith liom cispheil a imirt.	*I like to play basketball.*
Is breá liom rugbaí a imirt.	*I love to play rugby.*
Is maith dul go dtí an phictiúrlann.	*I like to go to the cinema.*
Is maith liom dul chuig scannáin.	*I like to go to films.*
Is breá liom dul go dtí an teach tábhairne.	*I love going to the pub.*
Is breá liom dul chuig seisiúin cheoil.	*I love going to music sessions.*

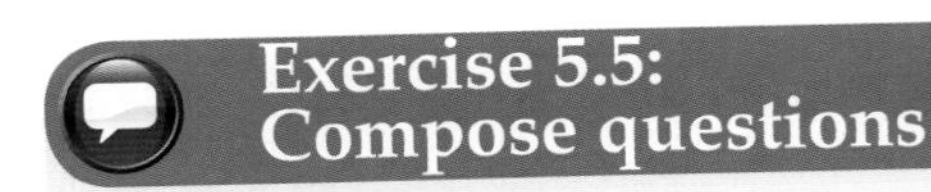

Exercise 5.5: Compose questions

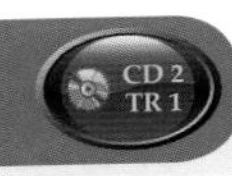

Change each statement into a question in the second person singular.

1. Téim ag rith.
2. Imrím peil.
3. Éistim leis an raidió.
4. Féachaim ar an teilifís.
5. Téim chuig ceolchoirmeacha.
6. Éistim le ceol.
7. Is maith liom ceol clasaiceach.
8. Tá ceol agam.

5.9 I haven't the slightest interest in it

CD 2 TR 2

You've already learnt how to express opinions on pastimes. Here's another useful sentence that can be used in this context:

Níl suim dá laghad agam i rugbaí.
I haven't the slightest interest in rugby.

This is how you say *in it* in Irish:

Níl suim dá laghad agam ann.
I haven't the slightest interest in it.

To find out if someone has an interest in a particular pastime you can ask:

An bhfuil suim agat i rugbaí?
Are you interested in rugby?

Tá suim mhór agam ann.
I have a big interest in it.

Níl suim ar bith agam ann.
I have no interest in it.

Conversation 5C

Áine recently moved from the country to the city and is telling her friend Lucy about her social life.

Áine: Téim go dtí an teach tábhairne beagnach gach oíche!
I go to the pub nearly every night!

Lucy: Tá sé sin an-dána! An dtéann tú chuig ceolchoirmeacha?
That's very bold! Do you go to concerts?

Áine: Téim, oíche Dé hAoine nó oíche Dé Sathairn de ghnáth.
Yes, usually on Friday night or on Saturday night.

Lucy: Go hiontach.
Great.

Áine: Agus téim chuig dráma nó chuig scannán go minic freisin.
And I often go to a play or a film as well.

Lucy: Tá saol iontach agat!
You have a great life!

Conversation 5D

Mark is attending an interview for a job as a critic with an arts magazine but isn't making much of an effort to impress!

Interviewer: Céard a dhéanann tú nuair a bhíonn am saor agat?
What do you do when you have free time?

Mark: Féachaim ar an teilifís.
I watch television.

Interviewer: An imríonn tú spórt?
Do you play sport?

Mark: Ní imrím. Níl suim dá laghad agam ann.
No. I haven't the slightest interest in it.

Interviewer: Em. Cé chomh minic is a théann tú chuig drámaí?
Em. How often do you go to plays?

Mark: Go fíorannamh.
Very seldom.

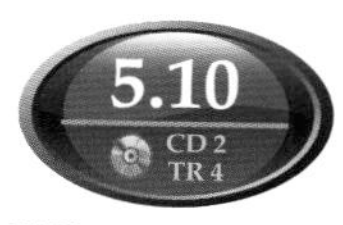

5.10 Adverbs of frequency

When Mark was asked how often he went to plays, he said:

Go fíorannamh.
Very seldom.

Here are other ways of referring to frequency:

Imrím peil go minic.
I often play football.

Éistim leis an raidió anois is arís.
I listen to the radio now and again.

Féachaim ar an teilifís an t-am ar fad.
I watch television all the time.

Téim chuig scannán uair sa tseachtain.
I go to a film once a week.

Exercise 5.6: Your turn!

This is your chance to talk now. Pretend you're Áine and that you're talking to Lucy.

Say:	*I go to the pub nearly every night!*
Lucy:	Tá sé sin an-dána! An dtéann tú chuig ceolchoirmeacha?
Say:	*Yes, usually on Friday night or on Saturday night.*
Lucy:	Go hiontach.
Say:	*And I often go to a play or a film as well.*
Lucy:	Tá saol iontach agat!

Exercise 5.7: Your turn!

This time, pretend you're Mark and that you're talking to the interviewer.

Interviewer:	Céard a dhéanann tú nuair a bhíonn am saor agat?
Say:	*I watch television.*
Interviewer:	An imríonn tú spórt?
Say:	*No. I haven't the slightest interest in it.*
Interviewer:	Em. Cé chomh minic is a théann tú chuig drámaí?
Say:	*Very seldom.*

Useful tips for learners

Since Irish lacks words that directly translate as *yes* or *no*, and instead repeats the verb in a question to answer that question, it's important to learn how to ask and answer questions in the various tenses. If you master that particular aspect of grammar, it'll be a lot easier to engage in conversation through Irish with others!

In this course, we focus on the most frequently used verbs in the present and past tenses.

Talking heads

Meadhbh Ní Eadhra
(filmed in An Spidéal, Galway)
Is maith liom bheith ag imirt camógaíochta. Téim go dtí an phictiúrlann go minic chun scannán a fheiceáil agus is aoibhinn liom dul chuig an amharclann freisin. Téim ar shiúlóidí fada de ghnáth ag an deireadh seachtaine; is breá liom bheith amuigh faoin aer.

Tadhg Mac Dhonnagáin
(filmed in An Spidéal, Galway)
Is maith liom bheith ag garraíodóireacht. Is breá liom dul chuig an bpictiúrlann le scannán a fheiceáil agus téim chuig ceolchoirmeacha freisin. Imrím leadóg sa samhradh.

Is ceoltóir mé agus seinnim an giotár go minic sa bhaile. Is breá liom an t-amhránaí Albanach Julie Fowlis.

Dairíne Ní Dhonnchú
(filmed in Temple Bar, Dublin)
Is maith liom bheith ag léamh, ag scríobh agus ag péinteáil. Téim go dtí an amharclann go minic chun drámaí a fheiceáil agus is breá liom dul chuig scannáin chomh maith. Téim ar shiúlóidí fada ag an deireadh seachtaine de ghnáth. Is breá liom bheith amuigh faoin aer.

Translation

Meadhbh Ní Eadhra
I like to play camogie. I often go to the cinema to see a film and I love going to the theatre as well. I usually go for long walks at the weekend; I love being out in the open air.

Tadhg Mac Dhonnagáin
I like to garden. I love going to the cinema to see a film and I go to concerts as well. I play tennis in the summer.

I'm a musician and I often play guitar at home. I love the Scottish singer Julie Fowlis.

Dairíne Ní Dhonnchú
I like to read, write and paint. I often go to the theatre to see plays and I also love to go to films. I usually go for long walks at the weekend. I love being out in the open air.

The audio versions of these excerpts are available on the sound files accompanying this book. The video segments can be seen in the online version of *Gaeilge gan Stró! – Beginners Level*, available on Gaelchultúr's e-learning website, www.ranganna.com.

Exercise 5.8: Review of Unit 5

Have a go at this activity now to see if you know the most important phrases taught in Unit 5.

How would you say the following in Irish?

1. I go swimming.
2. I play tennis.
3. I listen to the radio.
4. I go to the cinema.
5. Do you play tennis? No.
6. Do you go to the pub? Yes.
7. Do you watch television? No.
8. Do you like classical music? Yes.
9. Do you like rugby? I love it.
10. I like to read.
11. I love to sing.
12. I often go to concerts.
13. I like to play soccer.
14. I haven't the slightest interest in tennis.
15. I go to a play once a week.

Unit 6: Daily Life
Aonad 6: An Saol Laethúil

In this unit you will learn how to:

- ask someone what time it is and answer that question
- ask someone what time he does a particular thing
- say what time you do various things
- name various parts of the day
- talk about the things you do every day
- ask someone if he does a particular thing
- name the days of the week.

Grammar

- numbers and time
- **ar** + *séimhiú*
- *séimhiú* on verbs following **cén t-am**
- the present tense of the verb
- the present habitual tense
- **abhaile** vs. **sa bhaile**

San aonad seo foghlaimeoidh tú conas:

- *ceist a chur ar dhuine cén t-am atá sé agus an cheist sin a fhreagairt*
- *ceist a chur ar dhuine cén t-am a dhéanann sé rud ar leith*
- *a rá cén t-am a dhéanann tú rudaí éagsúla*
- *codanna éagsúla den lá a ainmniú*
- *labhairt faoi na rudaí a dhéanann tú gach lá*
- *ceist a chur ar dhuine an ndéanann sé rud ar leith*
- *laethanta na seachtaine a ainmniú.*

Gramadach

- *uimhreacha agus am*
- ***ar*** + *séimhiú*
- *séimhiú ar bhriathra tar éis* ***cén t-am***
- *an aimsir láithreach den bhriathar*
- *an aimsir ghnáthláithreach*
- ***abhaile*** *vs.* ***sa bhaile***

Key sounds

CD 2 TR 8

a seacht a **ch**log	(**c** with *séimhiú* followed by broad vowel, **o**)	*seven o'clock*
ar **ch**eathrú tar éis	(**c** with *séimhiú* followed by slender vowel, **e**)	*at a quarter past*
an-**gh**nóthach	(**g** with *séimhiú*)	*very busy*
mise	(slender **m**)	*I, me*
maidin	(broad **m**)	*morning*
an-**mh**aith	(**m** with *séimhiú* followed by broad vowel, **a**)	*very good*
i**nn**iu	(slender **n**)	*today*
nua	(broad **n**)	*new*
obai**r**	(slender **r**)	*work*
seachtain	(slender **s**)	*(a) week*
sos	(broad **s**)	*(a) break*
le do **th**oil	(**t** with *séimhiú*)	*please*

What time is it?

To find out what time it is, you ask:

Cén t-am atá sé?
What time is it?

You can start your reply with **Tá sé ...** (*It's ...*) or simply say the time:

a haon a chlog
one o'clock

a dó a chlog
two o'clock

a trí a chlog
three o'clock

a ceathair a chlog
four o'clock

a cúig a chlog
five o'clock

a sé a chlog
six o'clock

a seacht a chlog
seven o'clock

a hocht a chlog
eight o'clock

a naoi a chlog
nine o'clock

a deich a chlog
ten o'clock

a haon déag a chlog
eleven o'clock

a dó dhéag a chlog
twelve o'clock

ceathrú tar éis
a quarter past

leathuair tar éis
half past

ceathrú chun
a quarter to

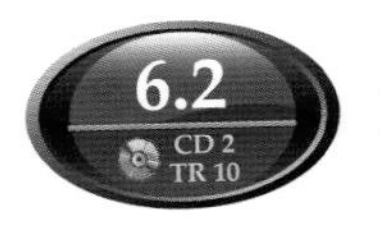

Being polite

If you want to be polite, you can say:

Gabh mo leithscéal. Cén t-am atá sé?
Excuse me. What time is it?

or

Cén t-am atá sé, le do thoil?
What time is it, please?

Exercise 6.1: It's three o'clock

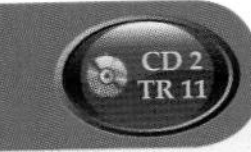

Listen to six people saying what time it is and indicate in the spaces provided which clock each one of them is referring to.

Person	Clock
1	
2	
3	
4	
5	
6	

When you've finished the exercise, try saying the times indicated on the clocks.

Ag or ar

When you're referring to the time in Irish, you can use either **ag** or **ar** to translate *at*:

ag a cúig a chlog
or
ar a cúig a chlog
at five o'clock

Ag is the easier of the two prepositions to use as consonants which directly follow it remain unchanged. A *séimhiú* is added to consonants which follow **ar**:

ag ceathrú tar éis a dó
but
ar cheathrú tar éis a dó
at a quarter past two

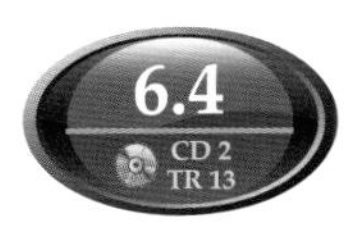

What time do you get up?

Here are sentences you can use if you want to find out about someone's daily routine:

Cén t-am a éiríonn tú ar maidin?
What time do you get up in the morning?

or

Cén t-am a éiríonn tú de ghnáth?
What time do you usually get up?

Cén t-am a théann tú ag obair?
What time do you go to work?

If one of the above questions is being asked for the second time in a conversation, you must, of course, use an emphatic form:

Cén t-am a théann tusa ag obair?
*What time do **you** go to work?*

Notice how a *séimhiú* is added to verbs beginning with a consonant which follow **cén t-am**.

I start working at nine

These are some activities people do on a daily basis:

Tosaím ag obair ag a naoi a chlog.
I start working at nine o'clock.

Bíonn sos agam timpeall a haon déag.
I have a break around eleven.

Bíonn mo lón agam idir a haon agus a dó.
I have my lunch between one and two.

Fágaim an obair timpeall a cúig.
I leave work around five.

Faighim an bus abhaile.
I get the bus home.

Bím sa bhaile timpeall a sé a chlog.
I'm home around six o'clock.

Ithim mo dhinnéar idir a seacht agus a hocht.
I eat my dinner between seven and eight.

Téim amach uaireanta.
I sometimes go out.

Téim a chodladh ag a haon déag ar a dhéanaí.
I go to bed/to sleep at eleven at the latest.

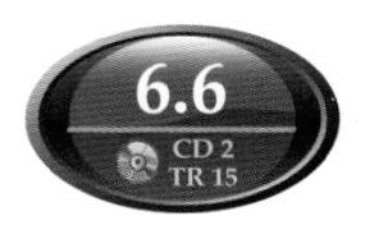

6.6 What time do you start working?

This is how you would change the statements in the last section into questions:

Cén t-am a thosaíonn tú ag obair?
What time do you start working?

Cén t-am a bhíonn sos agat?
What time do you have a break?

Cén t-am a bhíonn do lón agat?
What time do you have your lunch?

Cén t-am a fhágann tú an obair?
What time do you leave work?

An bhfaigheann tú an bus abhaile?
Do you get the bus home?

Cén t-am a bhíonn tú sa bhaile?
What time are you home?

Cén t-am a itheann tú do dhinnéar?
What time do you eat your dinner?

An dtéann tú amach uaireanta?
Do you go out sometimes?

Cén t-am a théann tú a chodladh?
What time do you go to bed/to sleep?

Exercise 6.2: Answer the questions

Answer each of these questions as indicated.

1. Cén t-am a éiríonn tú ar maidin?
   Say: Around seven o'clock.
2. Cén t-am a éiríonn tú ar maidin?
   Say: At half past seven.
3. Cén t-am a théann tú ag obair?
   Say: At a quarter past eight.
4. Cén t-am a théann tú ag obair de ghnáth?
   Say: At five o'clock.
5. Cén t-am a bhíonn do lón agat?
   Say: Between one and two.
6. Cén t-am a bhíonn do lón agat?
   Say: Around two o'clock.
7. Cén t-am a bhíonn tú sa bhaile?
   Say: At six o'clock.
8. Cén t-am a bhíonn tú sa bhaile?
   Say: At a quarter to eight.
9. Cén t-am a itheann tú do dhinnéar?
   Say: At half past eight.
10. Cén t-am a théann tú a chodladh?
    Say: Between ten and eleven.

Exercise 6.3: Translate the sentences

Translate each of the following:

1. Excuse me. What time is it?
2. Half past three.
3. A quarter to eleven.
4. What time do you get up in the morning?
5. What time do you usually go to work?
6. What time do *you* go to work?
7. I start working at eight o'clock.
8. I'm home around seven o'clock.
9. I eat my dinner between seven and eight.
10. I go to bed at eleven.

Conversation 6A

Pádraig recently moved to a new town. His friend Jenny wants to find out about his life there.

Jenny: Cén t-am a éiríonn tú de ghnáth?
What time do you usually get up?

Pádraig: Éirím timpeall a hocht agus bíonn bricfeasta agam sa bhaile.
I get up around eight and I have breakfast at home.

Jenny: Níl sé sin róluath.
That's not too early.

Pádraig: Níl, níl sé ró-olc. Bím san obair timpeall a naoi.
No, it's not too bad. I'm at work around nine.

Jenny: Agus cén t-am a fhágann tú an obair?
And what time do you leave work?

Pádraig: Idir a cúig agus leathuair tar éis a cúig.
Between five and half past five.

Conversation 6B

Jenny now wants to find out what Pádraig does after work.

Jenny: An mbíonn dinnéar agat sa bhaile?
Do you have dinner at home?

Pádraig: Bíonn, de ghnáth. Uaireanta bíonn dinnéar agam i mbialann le mo chairde.
Yes, usually. Sometimes I have dinner in a restaurant with my friends.

Jenny: An dtéann tú amach mórán san oíche?
Do you go out much at night?

Pádraig: Bím an-tuirseach tar éis na hoibre ach téim amach oíche nó dhó.
I'm very tired after work but I go out one or two nights.

Jenny: Céard a dhéanann tú?
What do you do?

Pádraig: Téim chuig ceolchoirm nó chuig seisiún ceoil de ghnáth.
I usually go to a concert or a music session.

Insight

The English language contains quite a few words of Irish origin, including the following:

galore (from **go leor**, plenty)
glen (from **gleann**, a valley)
lough (from **loch**, a lake)
poteen (from **poitín**, a home-distilled illicit alcoholic drink)
shamrock (from **seamróg**, a clover)
shebeen (from **síbín**, an illicit drinking place)
slew (from **slua**, a large number or quantity)
smashing (from **is maith sin**, that's good)
whiskey (from **uisce beatha**, water of life)

6.7 Present habitual tense

CD 2 TR 19

The verb **bí** (*be*) differs from other verbs because it has two distinct forms in the present tense and in the present habitual tense.

The present habitual tense is used to express actions that recur, whether frequently or infrequently. Compare the sentences in the table.

Present tense	Present habitual tense
Tá mé san obair faoi láthair. *I'm in work at the moment.*	**Bím san obair gach maidin timpeall a naoi.** *I'm in work every morning around nine.*
Tá an lón seo go deas. *This lunch is nice.*	**Bíonn an lón go deas anseo i gcónaí.** *Lunch is always nice here.*
Tá mé an-tuirseach. *I'm very tired.*	**Bím an-tuirseach gach tráthnóna.** *I'm very tired every evening.*
An bhfuil tú tuirseach inniu? Tá.* *Are you tired today? Yes.*	**An mbíonn tú tuirseach gach tráthnóna? Bím.** *Are you tired every evening? Yes.*

*Notice that the pronoun **mé** is not used in the answer.

Here are the present tense and present habitual tense forms of **bí**:

Present tense		Present habitual tense	
tá mé *I am*	**táimid** *we are*	**bím** *I am*	**bímid** *we are*
tá tú *you are*	**tá sibh** *you are*	**bíonn tú** *you are*	**bíonn sibh** *you are*
tá sé *he is*	**tá siad** *they are*	**bíonn sé** *he is*	**bíonn siad** *they are*
tá sí *she is*		**bíonn sí** *she is*	

Have a look again at Conversations 6A and 6B and pick out the present habitual tense forms of **bí**.

Vocabulary: Daily life

CD 2 TR 20

- ar maidin — *in the morning*
- tráthnóna — *in the evening*
- san oíche — *at night*
- meán lae / ag meán lae — *midday / at midday*
- meán oíche / ag meán oíche — *midnight / at midnight*
- bricfeasta — *breakfast*
- lón — *lunch*
- dinnéar — *dinner*
- sos tae — *(a) tea break*

- sos caife — *(a) coffee break*
- rothar — *(a) bicycle*
- bus — *(a) bus*
- traein — *(a) train*
- obair / an obair — *work / the work*
- oifig / an oifig — *(an) office / the office*
- de ghnáth — *usually*
- anois is arís — *now and again*
- uaireanta — *sometimes*
- go minic — *often*
- i gcónaí — *always*

Useful phrases

- Bíonn mo bhricfeasta agam sa bhaile. — *I have my breakfast at home.*
- Bíonn bricfeasta agam i gcaifé. — *I have breakfast in a café.*
- Bíonn ceapaire liom go dtí an obair. — *I bring a sandwich to work.*
- Bíonn lón agam san oifig. — *I have lunch in the office.*
- Téim go dtí an obair … — *I go to work …*
- ar mo rothar. — *on my bike.*
- ar an mbus. — *by bus.*
- ar an traein. — *by train.*
- Siúlaim go dtí an obair. — *I walk to work.*
- Cén chaoi a dtéann tú go dtí an obair? — *How do you go to work?*
- Ar an traein. — *By train.*

Exercise 6.4: Your turn!

This is your chance to talk now. Pretend you're Pádraig and that you're talking to Jenny.

Jenny: Cén t-am a éiríonn tú de ghnáth?

Say: *I get up around eight and I have breakfast at home.*

Jenny: Níl sé sin róluath.

Say: *No, it's not too bad. I'm at work around nine.*

Jenny: Agus cén t-am a fhágann tú an obair?

Say: *Between five and half past five.*

Exercise 6.5: Your turn!

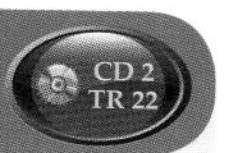

Again, pretend you're Pádraig and that you're talking to Jenny.

Jenny: An mbíonn dinnéar agat sa bhaile?

Say: *Yes, usually. Sometimes I have dinner in a restaurant with my friends.*

Jenny: An dtéann tú amach mórán san oíche?

Say: *I'm very tired after work but I go out one or two nights.*

Jenny: Céard a dhéanann tú?

Say: *I usually go to a concert or a music session.*

Exercise 6.6: Fill in the gaps

Fill in the gaps in these sentences.

1. *What time is it, please?*
   Cén t-am atá sé, le ____ ___________?

2. *It's half past ten.*
   Tá sé _______________ tar éis a deich.

3. *What time do you go to work?*
   Cén t-am a ___________ tú ag obair?

4. *I start working at nine o'clock.*
   _____________ ag obair ag a naoi a chlog.

5. *I leave work around five.*
   _____________ an obair timpeall a cúig.

6. *I go to bed at eleven at the latest.*
   Téim a chodladh ag a haon déag ar ___ __________.

7. *What time do you have a break?*
   Cén t-am a ___________ sos agat?

8. *Do you go out sometimes?*
   An __________ tú amach uaireanta?

9. *I'm very tired after work.*
   ________ an-tuirseach tar éis na hoibre.

10. *I'm very tired today.*
    ____ mé an-tuirseach inniu.

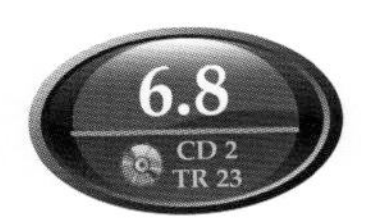

Questions and answers

In Conversation 6B, Jenny asked Pádraig if he did certain things:

An mbíonn dinnéar agat sa bhaile?
Do you have dinner at home?

An dtéann tú amach mórán san oíche?
Do you go out much at night?

Here are other questions you can ask to find out if someone does certain things:

An éiríonn tú go luath?
Do you get up early?
Éirím./Ní éirím.
Yes./No.

An mbíonn bricfeasta agat sa bhaile?
Do you have breakfast at home?
Bíonn./Ní bhíonn.
Yes./No.

An bhfágann tú an obair ag a cúig de ghnáth?
Do you usually leave work at five?
Fágaim./Ní fhágaim.
Yes./No.

An bhfaigheann tú bus abhaile?
Do you get a bus home?
Faighim./Ní fhaighim.
Yes./No.

An itheann tú do dhinnéar ag a seacht?
Do you eat your dinner at seven?
Ithim./Ní ithim.
Yes./No.

An dtéann tú amach uaireanta?
Do you go out sometimes?
Téim./Ní théim.
Yes./No.

An mbíonn tú tuirseach gach tráthnóna?
Are you tired every evening?
Bím./Ní bhím.
Yes./No.

An bhfuil tú tuirseach anois?
Are you tired now?
Tá./Níl.
Yes./No.

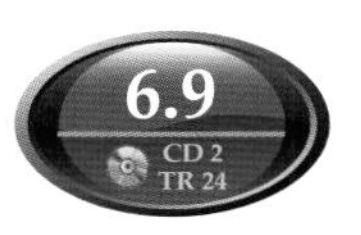

Abhaile vs. sa bhaile

Learners often confuse **abhaile** (*homewards*) and **sa bhaile** (*at home*).

Abhaile is used when movement is being referred to:

> **Tá mé ag dul abhaile tráthnóna.**
> *I'm going home this evening.*

Sa bhaile is used when location is being referred to:

> **Tá mé sa bhaile faoi láthair.**
> *I'm at home at the moment.*

Exercise 6.7: Answer the questions

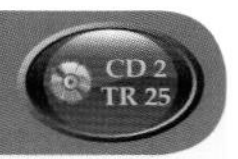

Answer each of these questions in the affirmative (yes) and negative (no).

1. An mbíonn dinnéar agat sa bhaile?
2. An éiríonn tú go luath?
3. An itheann tú do dhinnéar sa bhaile?
4. An dtéann tú chuig drámaí?
5. An bhfaigheann tú traein abhaile?
6. An bhfágann tú an obair ag a sé a chlog?
7. An bhfuil tú tuirseach inniu?
8. An mbíonn tú tuirseach gach tráthnóna?

Conversation 6C

Cathy has recently moved abroad. Her friend Peter rings her to find out how she's getting on in her new bar job.

Peter: An maith leat an post nua?
Do you like the new job?

Cathy: Is breá liom é. Tá sé an-suimiúil.
I love it. It's very interesting.

Peter: An mbíonn tú ag obair gach deireadh seachtaine?
Do you work every weekend?

Cathy: Bím. Bíonn an beár an-ghnóthach Dé hAoine agus Dé Sathairn.
Yes. The bar is very busy on Friday and Saturday.

Peter: An mbíonn tú ag obair déanach?
Do you work late?

Cathy: Bím. Faighim tacsaí abhaile timpeall a trí a chlog de ghnáth.
Yes. I usually get a taxi home around three o'clock.

Conversation 6D

Peter now asks Cathy about her social life.

Peter: An mbíonn tú i gcónaí an-tuirseach tar éis an deireadh seachtaine?
Are you always very tired after the weekend?

Cathy: Bím. Bím traochta.
Yes. I'm exhausted.

Cathy yawns.

Peter: Tá tú an-tuirseach faoi láthair, nach bhfuil?
You're very tired at the moment, aren't you?

Cathy: Tá brón orm – tá mé an-tuirseach. Bhí an deireadh seachtaine dian.
Sorry – I'm very tired. The weekend was tough.

Peter: An bhfuil tú ag obair gan stop?
Are you working non-stop?

Cathy: Níl. Tá saol sóisialta an-mhaith agam freisin.
No. I have a very good social life as well.

The days of the week 1

This is how the days of the week are named in Irish:

An Luan *Monday*	or	**Dé Luain**
An Mháirt *Tuesday*	or	**Dé Máirt**
an Chéadaoin *Wednesday*	or	**Dé Céadaoin**
an Déardaoin *Thursday*	or	**Déardaoin**
an Aoine *Friday*	or	**Dé hAoine**
an Satharn *Saturday*	or	**Dé Sathairn**
an Domhnach *Sunday*	or	**Dé Domhnaigh**

The forms in the left-hand column are usually used when speaking in a general way about the days of the week or when stating what day it is:

Is breá liom an Satharn.
I love Saturdays.

Is é an Satharn an lá is fearr liom.
Saturday is my favourite day.

Inniu an Mháirt.
Today is Tuesday.

The forms in the right-hand column above are used when referring to a particular day just gone or about to come:

Tháinig sé abhaile Dé hAoine.
He came home (last) Friday.

Feicfidh mé tú Déardaoin.
I'll see you on Thursday.

Notice that **Dé** is already incorporated into **Déardaoin**. Learners often say or write ***Dé Déardaoin**, but this is an incorrect form.

The days of the week 2

In Conversation 6C Cathy said:

Bíonn an beár an-ghnóthach Dé hAoine agus Dé Sathairn.
The bar is very busy on Friday and Saturday.

There's no need to use the simple preposition **ar** (*on*) in this case – it would be incorrect, in fact, to say or to write ***ar Dé hAoine agus Dé Sathairn**. Here are two more examples of the same rule:

Beidh sí ar ais oíche Dé Máirt.
She'll be back on Tuesday night.

Ní bhím saor oíche Dé Luain.
I'm not free on Monday nights.

Exercise 6.8: Your turn!

This is your chance to talk now. Pretend you're Cathy and that you're talking to Peter.

Peter: An maith leat an post nua?

Say: *I love it. It's very interesting.*

Peter: An mbíonn tú ag obair gach deireadh seachtaine?

Say: *Yes. The bar is very busy on Friday and Saturday.*

Peter: An mbíonn tú ag obair déanach?

Say: *Yes. I usually get a taxi home around three o'clock.*

Exercise 6.9: Your turn!

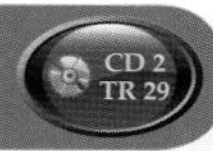

Again, pretend you're Cathy and that you're talking to Peter.

Peter:	An mbíonn tú i gcónaí an-tuirseach tar éis an deireadh seachtaine?
Say:	*Yes. I'm exhausted.*
Peter:	Tá tú an-tuirseach faoi láthair, nach bhfuil?
Say:	*Sorry – I'm very tired. The weekend was tough.*
Peter:	An bhfuil tú ag obair gan stop?
Say:	*No. I have a very good social life as well.*

Useful tips for learners

Buy index cards and use them to practise your Irish. Write an Irish word or sentence on one side of the card and the English translation on the other side. It would be worth using the cards to practise questions and answers in the various tenses, for example, and the sentences contained in the review exercise at the end of each unit. Try to get through the cards as quickly as possible and shuffle them frequently.

Talking heads

Cóilín Ó Floinn (filmed in Temple Bar, Dublin)
Éirim ar a hocht a chlog agus ithim mo bhricfeasta. Tosaím ag obair ar a naoi. Críochnaíonn an obair ar leathuair tar éis a cúig. Ithim mo dhinnéar timpeall a hocht a chlog.

Déanaim rudaí éagsúla san oíche – léim leabhar nó féachaim ar an teilifís nó buailim le cairde.

Caoimhe Ní Chonchoille (filmed in An Spidéal, Galway)
Nuair a bhíonn lá saor ón obair agam, éirím ar leath i ndiaidh a hocht de ghnáth. Déanaim iarracht bualadh le mo chuid cairde fosta agus freastal ar ranganna aclaíochta i nGaillimh.

Téim abhaile go Dún na nGall go rialta nuair a bhíonn cúpla lá saor agam.

Páidí Ó Lionáird (filmed in An Spidéal, Galway)
Nuair a bhím ag obair in TG4, fágaim an teach thart ar a naoi a chlog. Ní thógann an turas ach deich nóiméad sa charr. Tosaím ag obair ag a deich agus tógaim sos thart ar a haon a chlog. Críochnaím ag obair ag TG4 ag leathuair tar éis a hocht agus bím sa bhaile ag ceathrú chun a naoi.

Ag an deireadh seachtaine, tógaim rudaí go deas bog agus éasca. Éirím thart ar a hocht a chlog agus déanaim roinnt léitheoireachta nó staidéir. Má bhíonn an aimsir go breá, téim ag rothaíocht.

Notes
The second speaker is from Donegal and uses the form **leath i ndiaidh** (*half past*) instead of **leathuair tar éis**.

When referring to a particular time, two of the speakers use **ar** and the other **ag**.

Translation

Cóilín Ó Floinn
I get up at eight o'clock and I eat my breakfast. I start working at nine. Work finishes at half past five. I eat my dinner around eight o'clock.

I do various things at night – I read a book or I watch television or I meet friends.

Caoimhe Ní Chonchoille
When I have a free day from work, I usually get up at half past eight. I make an effort to meet my friends as well and to attend fitness classes in Galway.

I regularly go home to Donegal when I have a few free days.

Páidí Ó Lionáird
When I work in TG4, I leave the house around nine o'clock. The journey only takes ten minutes in the car. I start work at ten and I take a break around one o'clock. I finish working at TG4 at half past eight and I'm home at a quarter to nine.

At the weekend, I take things nice and easy. I get up at around eight o'clock and I do some reading or studying. If the weather is fine, I go cycling.

Exercise 6.10: Review of Unit 6

Have a go at this activity now to see if you know the most important phrases taught in Unit 6.

How would you say the following in Irish?

1. What time is it, please?
2. It's a quarter to twelve.
3. It's half past six.
4. What time do you have a break?
5. At a quarter past ten.
6. What time are you home?
7. Do you get the train home?
8. Do you have dinner at home? Yes.
9. Do you eat your dinner around seven?
10. What time do you go to bed/to sleep?
11. At midnight at the latest.
12. I get a taxi home around three o'clock.
13. Are you tired every Saturday?
14. You're very tired at the moment, aren't you?
15. The weekend was tough.

Unit 7: Talents and Skills
Aonad 7: Buanna agus Scileanna

In this unit you will learn how to:

- ask someone if he can do something and answer that question
- ask someone how good he is at something and answer that question
- say how easy or difficult something is
- ask someone how long he's been doing something and answer that question
- ask someone how he's getting on with something and answer that question
- seek and give information about languages
- say how well you know a language
- deal with communication problems.

Grammar

- questions and answers in the present tense
- the prepositional pronoun **ag**
- the prefixes **an-** and **ró-**

San aonad seo foghlaimeoidh tú conas:

- *ceist a chur ar dhuine an bhfuil sé ábalta rud éigin a dhéanamh agus an cheist sin a fhreagairt*
- *fiafraí de dhuine cé chomh maith is atá sé ag rud éigin agus an cheist sin a fhreagairt*
- *a rá cé chomh furasta nó deacair is atá rud éigin*
- *fiafraí de dhuine cén fhad atá sé ag déanamh rud éigin agus an cheist sin a fhreagairt*
- *ceist a chur ar dhuine conas atá ag éirí leis le rud éigin agus an cheist sin a fhreagairt*
- *eolas a lorg agus a thabhairt faoi theangacha*
- *a rá cé chomh maith is atá teanga agat*
- *déileáil le fadhbanna cumarsáide.*

Gramadach

- *ceisteanna agus freagraí san aimsir láithreach*
- *an forainm réamhfhoclach* ***ag***
- *na réimíreanna* ***an-*** *agus* ***ró-***

Key sounds

CD 2 TR 32

fi**d**il	(slender **d**)	*(a) fiddle*
fea**d**óg	(broad **d**)	*(a) whistle*
an **Ghe**armáinis	(**g** with *séimhiú* followed by slender vowel, **e**)	*German*
fo**gha**laim	(**g** with *séimhiú* followed by broad vowel, **a**)	*learning*
ag foghlai**m**	(slender **m**)	*learning*
maith	(broad **m**)	*good*
suim **mhó**r	(**m** with *séimhiú* followed by broad vowel, **o**)	*a lot of interest*
Spáinni**s**	(broad and slender **s**)	*Spanish*
ró**sh**ean	(**s** with *séimhiú*)	*too old*
an **tS**eapáinis	(**t** before **s**)	*Japanese*

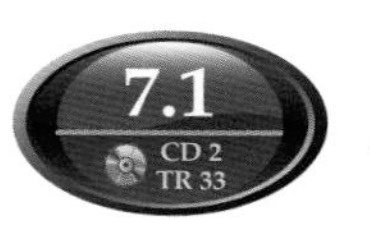

Are you musical?

In Unit 5, we saw how **agam** is often used when ability is being referred to:

Tá ceol agam.
I'm musical (literally, *there is music at me*).

Tá snámh agam.
I can swim (literally, *there is swimming at me*).

To find out if someone can do something, you can ask:

An bhfuil ceol agat?
Are you musical?

Here are two other examples:

An bhfuil clóscríobh agat?
Can you type?

An bhfuil Fraincis agat?
Can you speak French?

Here is another structure you can use in this context:

An bhfuil tú ábalta carr a thiomáint?
Can you drive a car?

An bhfuil tú ábalta ríomhaire a úsáid?
Can you use a computer?

To reply in the affirmative or in the negative to the above questions, you say:

Tá.
Yes.
or
Níl.
No.

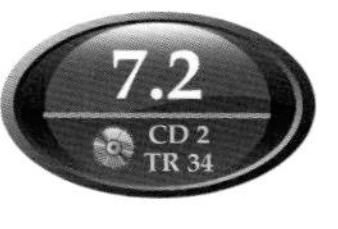

How good are you?

To find out how good someone is at something, you can ask:

Cé chomh maith is atá tú?
How good are you?

Here are some possible answers:

Tá mé réasúnta maith.
I'm reasonably good.

Tá mé maith go leor.
I'm okay.

Tá mé an-mhaith.
I'm very good.

Níl mé rómhaith.
I'm not too good.

Tá mé ag foghlaim.
I'm learning.

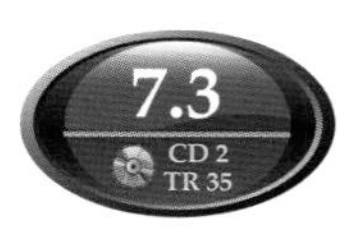

It's easy

This is how you say that something is easy:

Tá sé furasta.
or
Tá sé éasca.
It's easy.

To find out if something is easy, you can ask:

An bhfuil sé furasta?
or
An bhfuil sé éasca?
Is it easy?

Here are some possible answers:

Níl sé rófhurasta.
It's not too easy.

Tá sé furasta go leor.
It's easy enough.

Tá sé an-fhurasta.
It's very easy.

Tá sé rófhurasta.
It's too easy.

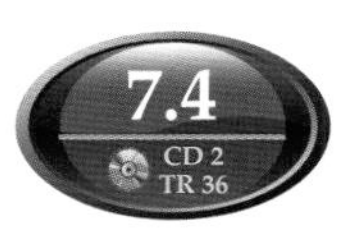

It's difficult

This is how you say that something is difficult:

Tá sé deacair.
It's difficult.

To find out if something is difficult, you can ask:

An bhfuil sé deacair?
Is it difficult?

Here are some possible answers:

Níl sé ródheacair.
It's not too difficult.

Tá sé deacair go leor.
It's difficult enough.

Tá sé an-deacair.
It's very difficult.

Tá sé ródheacair.
It's too difficult.

The prefix an-

As you've probably noticed, the Irish for *very* is **an-**. There is a *séimhiú* on consonants (other than **d**, **t**, **s**) that follow **an-**; vowels that follow it remain unchanged.

The consonants (other than d, t, s) *Séimhiú*	The consonants d, t, s No *séimhiú*	The vowels (a, e, i, o, u) They don't change
an-mhaith *very good*	**an-deacair** *very difficult*	**an-óg** *very young*
an-chairdiúil *very friendly*	**an-sean** *very old*	**an-íseal** *very low*
an-fhurasta *very easy*	**an-te** *very hot*	**an-éasca** *very easy*

The prefix **an-** always contains a hyphen.

The prefix ró-

The Irish for *too* is **ró-**. There is a *séimhiú* on consonants that follow **ró-**; again, vowels that follow it remain unchanged.

mór *big*	**rómhór** *too big*
deacair *difficult*	**ródheacair** *too difficult*
sean *old*	**róshean** *too old*
óg *young*	**ró-óg** *too young*
éasca *easy*	**ró-éasca** *too easy*
amaideach *foolish*	**ró-amaideach** *too foolish*

Note that there's always a hyphen between **ró-** and a vowel; there isn't usually a hyphen between **ró-** and a consonant.

Exercise 7.1: Answer the questions

Answer each of these questions as indicated.

1. An bhfuil Fraincis agat?
   Say: Yes.

2. Cé chomh maith is atá tú?
   Say: I'm okay.

3. Cé chomh maith is atá tú?
   Say: I'm not too good.

4. Cé chomh maith is atá tú?
   Say: I'm very good.

5. An bhfuil sé furasta?
   Say: It's easy enough.

6. An bhfuil sé furasta?
   Say: It's very easy.

7. An bhfuil sé deacair?
   Say: It's very difficult.

8. An bhfuil sé deacair?
   Say: It's not too difficult.

Exercise 7.2: Give the Irish version

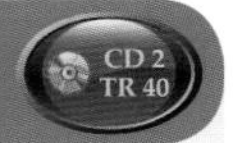

Give the Irish version of each of the following:

1. very good

2. very hot

3. too difficult

4. very difficult

5. too easy (use **éasca**)

6. very easy (use **éasca**)

7. too old

8. very easy (use **furasta**)

Insight

In Ireland, the Irish language is usually referred to by English speakers as *Irish*. Outside the country, the language is often called *Gaelic* or *Irish Gaelic*. Irish people tend to avoid calling the language *Gaelic* and use that word to refer to Scottish Gaelic.

The official standard name of the language in Irish is *Gaeilge*. Before the introduction of *An Caighdeán Oifigiúil* (The Official Standard) in 1948, this was spelled *Gaedhilge*.

Conversation 7A

Sinéad is being interviewed for a summer job in a cultural centre.

Interviewer: Cé chomh maith is atá tú ag clóscríobh?
How good are you at typing?

Sinéad: Tá mé réasúnta maith – tá mé ábalta caoga focal sa nóiméad a chlóscríobh.
I'm reasonably good – I can type fifty words per minute.

Interviewer: Go breá. Tá Fraincis agat, feicim. Cé chomh maith is atá tú?
Fine. You speak French, I see. How good are you?

Sinéad: Tá mé an-mhaith. Rinne mé Fraincis san ollscoil. Agus tá mé ag foghlaim Spáinnise.
I'm very good. I did French in university. And I'm learning Spanish.

Interviewer: An bhfuil an Spáinnis deacair?
Is Spanish difficult?

Sinéad: Tá sí deacair go leor.
It's difficult enough.

Conversation 7B

The interviewer now asks Sinéad about her free time.

Interviewer: Céard a dhéanann tú nuair a bhíonn am saor agat?
What do you do when you have free time?

Sinéad: Is maith liom bheith ag léamh agus tá suim mhór agam sa cheol.
I like to read and I have a lot of interest in music.

Interviewer: An bhfuil ceol agat féin?
Are you musical yourself?

Sinéad: Tá. Seinnim an fhidil agus an fheadóg stáin.
Yes. I play the fiddle and the tin whistle.

Interviewer: Cé chomh maith is atá tú ar an bhfidil?
How good are you on the fiddle?

Sinéad: Tá mé maith go leor. Tá mé ag foghlaim le trí bliana anois.
I'm okay. I'm learning for three years now.

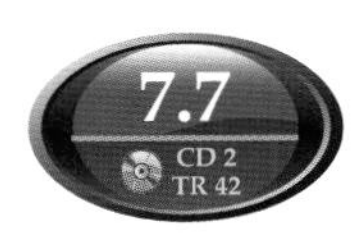

The pronoun sí

In Conversation 7A, when Sinéad was asked if Spanish was difficult, she replied:

> **Tá sí deacair go leor.**
> *It's difficult enough.*

The noun **Spáinnis** (*Spanish*) is feminine, therefore the pronoun **sí** must be used when referring to it.

As we'll see later in this unit, the names of most languages in Irish are feminine.

Nouns which directly follow verbal nouns are usually in the genitive. This is an example from Conversation 7A:

> **Agus tá mé ag foghlaim Spáinnise.**
> *And I'm learning Spanish.*

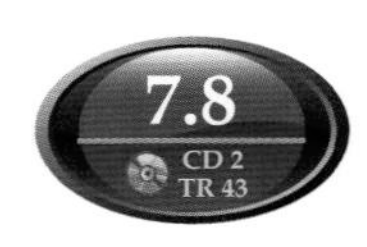

For three years

In Conversation 7B, when Sinéad was asked how good she was on the fiddle, she said:

Tá mé maith go leor. Tá mé ag foghlaim le trí bliana anois.
I'm okay. I'm learning for three years now.

The simple preposition **le** is used to refer to a period of time from the past to the present and to something which is still ongoing:

Tá mé i mo chónaí i Londain le trí bliana.
I've been living in London for three years (i.e. I'm still there).

To find out how long someone has been learning something, you can ask:

Cén fhad atá tú ag foghlaim Gaeilge?
How long have you been learning Irish?

Here are some possible answers below. Note that **anuas** is used to translate *past*:

Le coicís anuas.
For the past fortnight.

Le mí anois.
For a month now.

Le bliain anuas.
For the past year.

Le cúpla bliain.
For a few years.

Le cúig bliana anuas.
For the past five years.

Exercise 7.3: Your turn!

This is your chance to talk now. Pretend you're Sinéad and that you're talking to the interviewer.

Interviewer: Cé chomh maith is atá tú ag clóscríobh?

Say: *I'm reasonably good – I can type fifty words per minute.*

Interviewer: Go breá. Tá Fraincis agat, feicim. Cé chomh maith is atá tú?

Say: *I'm very good. I did French in university. And I'm learning Spanish.*

Interviewer: An bhfuil an Spáinnis deacair?

Say: *It's difficult enough.*

Exercise 7.4: Your turn!

Again, pretend you're Sinéad and that you're talking to the interviewer.

Interviewer: Céard a dhéanann tú nuair a bhíonn am saor agat?

Say: *I like to read and I have a lot of interest in music.*

Interviewer: An bhfuil ceol agat féin?

Say: *Yes. I play the fiddle and the tin whistle.*

Interviewer: Cé chomh maith is atá tú ar an bhfidil?

Say: *I'm okay. I'm learning for three years now.*

Exercise 7.5: Fill in the gaps

Fill in the gaps in these sentences.

1. *Can you type?*
   An bhfuil _______________ agat?

2. *Can you use a computer?*
   An bhfuil tú _________ ríomhaire a _________?

3. *How good are you?*
   Cé chomh maith is _______ tú?

4. *I'm reasonably good.*
   Tá mé _____________ maith.

5. *It's not too easy (use **furasta**).*
   Níl sé _______________.

6. *It's too difficult.*
   Tá sé _______________.

7. *It's very difficult.*
   Tá sé _______________.

8. *And I'm learning Spanish.*
   Agus tá mé ag foghlaim _______________.

9. *Are you musical yourself?*
   An bhfuil ceol _______ _______?

10. *How good are you on the fiddle?*
    Cé chomh maith is _____ tú ar an __________?

Vocabulary: Languages

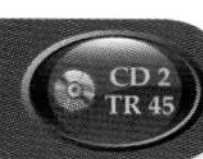

- teanga / an teanga / teangacha — *(a) language / the language / languages*
- Gaeilge / an Ghaeilge — *Irish*
- Béarla / an Béarla — *English*
- Breatnais / an Bhreatnais — *Welsh*
- Gaeilge na hAlban — *Scottish Gaelic*
- Fraincis / an Fhraincis — *French*
- Gearmáinis / an Ghearmáinis — *German*
- Spáinnis / an Spáinnis — *Spanish*
- Iodáilis / an Iodáilis — *Italian*
- Rúisis / an Rúisis — *Russian*
- Sínis / an tSínis — *Chinese*
- Seapáinis / an tSeapáinis — *Japanese*

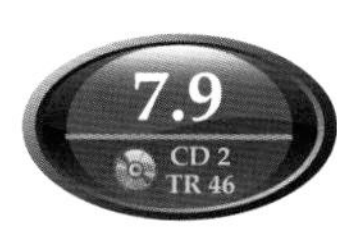

The article an

The definite article **an** is often used in Irish where it wouldn't be in English – when referring to languages in a general sense, for example. You often have a choice whether or not to use the definite article:

Tá an tSeapáinis an-deacair.
Japanese is very difficult.
or
Tá Seapáinis an-deacair.
Japanese is very difficult.

In Irish, the article is used as well before the names of certain countries, days of the week, certain months and festivals, the seasons and titles:

an Iodáil
Italy

an Cháisc
Easter

an Domhnach
Sunday

an samhradh
summer

mí na Bealtaine
May

an Dr Ciarán Ó Gallchóir
Dr Ciarán Ó Gallchóir

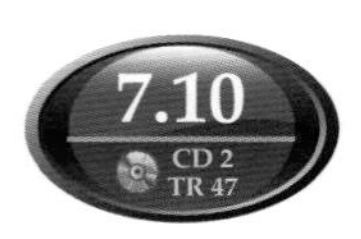

The gender of languages

The names of all the languages are feminine in Irish, with one exception: **Béarla** (*English*).

an Béarla
English

but

an Fhraincis
French

an Iodáilis
Italian

an tSeapáinis
Japanese

Linguistic ability

To find out what languages someone speaks you can ask:

Cad iad na teangacha atá agat?
What languages do you speak?

As we saw earlier, you use the following structure to find out if someone speaks a particular language:

An bhfuil Gearmáinis agat?
Do you speak German?

Tá. Tá mé líofa.
Yes. I'm fluent.

This is how you talk about your knowledge of different languages:

Tá Fraincis líofa agam.
I speak fluent French.

Tá Spáinnis mhaith agam.
I speak good Spanish.

Tá beagán Iodáilise* agam.
I speak some Italian.

Tá cúpla focal Gearmáinise* agam.
I have a few words of German.

* Note that **-e** is added to languages ending in **-is** after words such as **beagán** (*a little/some*) and **cúpla focal** (*a few words*). This is another example of the genitive case, which we mentioned earlier in this unit.

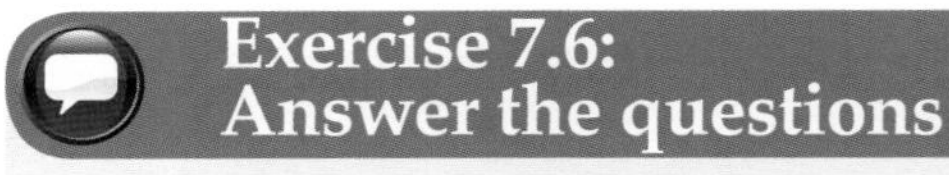

Exercise 7.6: Answer the questions

Answer each of these questions as indicated.

1. Cén fhad atá tú ag foghlaim Gaeilge?
   Say: For a month now.

2. Cén fhad atá tú ag foghlaim Iodáilise?
   Say: For the past three years.

3. Cén fhad atá tú ag foghlaim Gearmáinise?
   Say: For a few years.

4. An bhfuil an Rúisis deacair?
   Say: It's very difficult.

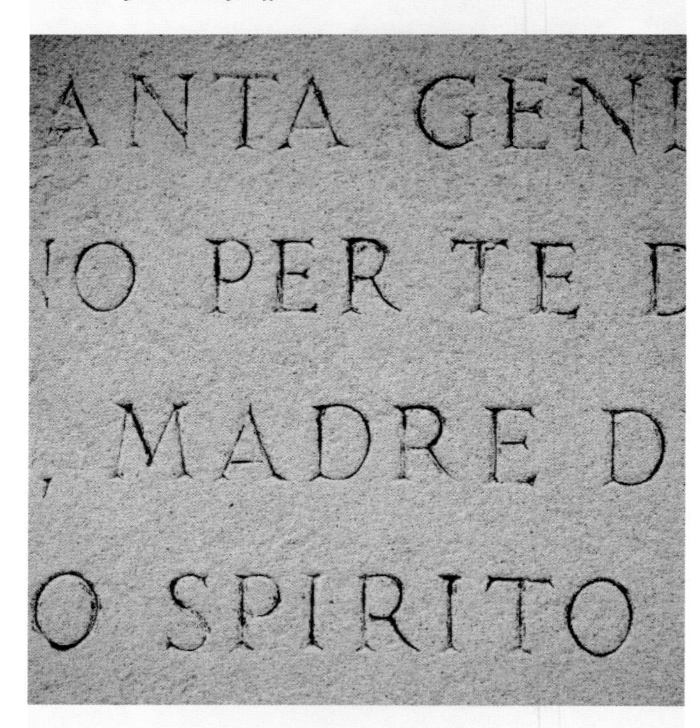

5. An bhfuil Gearmáinis agat?
   Say: Yes. I'm fluent.

6. Cad iad na teangacha atá agat?
   Say: Irish, English and Japanese.

7. An bhfuil Iodáilis agat?
   Say: Yes. I speak some Italian.

8. An bhfuil Fraincis agat?
   Say: I speak fluent French.

Conversation 7C

Colm and Clíona are on their second date and are getting to know more about each other.

Colm:	Cad iad na teangacha atá agat? *What languages do you speak?*
Clíona:	Tá Gearmáinis líofa agam agus beagán Fraincise. *I speak fluent German and some French.*
Colm:	Agus tá Béarla líofa agat, gan amhras! *And you speak fluent English, of course!*
Clíona:	Tá! *Yes!*
Colm:	An bhfuil teanga ar bith eile agat? *Do you speak any other language?*
Clíona:	Bhuel, tá cúpla focal Iodáilise agam. *Well, I have a few words of Italian.*

Conversation 7D

Clíona now asks Colm about his linguistic skills.

Clíona:	Cad iad na teangacha atá agat féin? *What languages do you speak yourself?*
Colm:	Bhuel, is cainteoir dúchais Gaeilge mé. Tógadh le Béarla agus Gaeilge mé. *Well, I'm a native speaker of Irish. I was brought up through English and Irish.*
Clíona:	An-suimiúil. An bhfuil teangacha iasachta ar bith agat? *Very interesting. Do you speak any foreign languages?*
Colm:	Tá mé ag foghlaim Fraincise faoi láthair. Tá mé ag freastal ar chúrsa. *I'm learning French at the moment. I'm attending a course.*
Clíona:	Conas atá ag éirí leat? *How are you getting on?*
Colm:	Maith go leor. *Okay.*

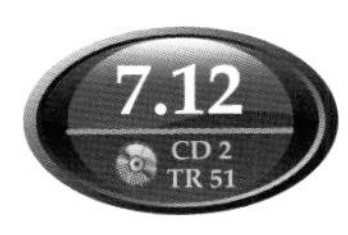

How are you getting on?

In Conversation 7D, when Colm was asked how he was getting on, he said:

Maith go leor.
Okay.

Here are two other possible answers to that question:

Tá ag éirí go maith liom.
I'm getting on well.

Níl ag éirí go rómhaith liom.
I'm not getting on too well.

Exercise 7.7: Your turn!

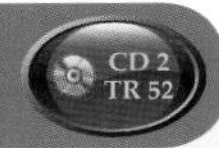

This is your chance to talk now. Pretend you're Colm and that you're talking to Clíona.

Say:	*What languages do you speak?*
Clíona:	Tá Gearmáinis líofa agam agus beagán Fraincise.
Say:	*And you speak fluent English, of course!*
Clíona:	Tá!
Say:	*Do you speak any other language?*
Clíona:	Bhuel, tá cúpla focal Iodáilise agam.

Exercise 7.8: Your turn!

Again, pretend you're Colm and that you're talking to Clíona.

Clíona: Cad iad na teangacha atá agat féin?

Say: *Well, I'm a native speaker of Irish. I was brought up through English and Irish.*

Clíona: An-suimiúil. An bhfuil teangacha iasachta ar bith agat?

Say: *I'm learning French at the moment. I'm attending a course.*

Clíona: Conas atá ag éirí leat?

Say: *Okay.*

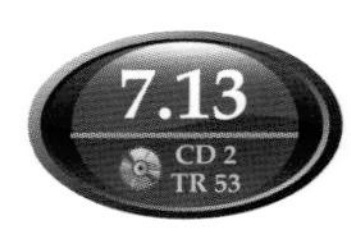

Dealing with communication problems

Here are some sentences you can use when you're having difficulty understanding something in Irish – in a classroom context, for example:

Tá brón orm. Ní thuigim é sin.
I'm sorry. I don't understand that.

Gabh mo leithscéal, an féidir leat é sin a rá arís, le do thoil?
Excuse me, can you say that again, please?

Céard a chiallaíonn ...?
What does ... mean?

An bhféadfá é sin a litriú?
Could you spell that?

An bhféadfá labhairt níos moille, le do thoil?
Could you speak more slowly, please?

Useful tips for learners

Don't be afraid to try out your Irish. It's important to listen to the language and to read it but you will not make proper progress until you're willing to try speaking the language with other people. Remember this: It's usually those who are not afraid to make errors, the so-called "risk-takers", who learn languages the fastest.

Talking heads

Colm Mac Séalaigh
(filmed at the Civic Offices, Dublin)
Tá mé go maith ag ceol agus ag spórt. Níl mé rómhaith ag an gcócaireacht, ar an drochuair.

Tá dhá theanga agam – Gaeilge agus Béarla. Níl agam ach beagán Fraincise.

Meadhbh Ní Eadhra (filmed in An Spidéal, Galway)
Is iriseoir mé agus tá mé go maith ag scríobh, mar sin. Scríobhaim ficsean freisin – scéalta do pháistí agus do dhaoine óga den chuid is mó. Tá suim mhór agam sa cheol agus seinnim an fhidil.

Tá beagán Fraincise agam ach ba bhreá liom tuilleadh teangacha a fhoghlaim. Is féidir liom lámhchleasaíocht a dhéanamh le cúpla liathróid ach go minic titeann siad ar an talamh!

Éamonn Ó Dónaill
(filmed in Dún Laoghaire, County Dublin)
Níl mé go maith ag spórt ar bith, cé gur imir mé sacar nuair a bhí mé ar scoil.

Tá mé réasúnta maith ag canadh ach is annamh a chanaim go poiblí – tá mé róchúthaileach, is dócha!

D'fhoghlaim mé Fraincis nuair a bhí mé ar scoil ach níl mé rólíofa. Tuigim roinnt mhaith Fraincise ach níl mé go maith á labhairt. Tá beagán Iodáilise agam chomh maith.

Translation

Colm Mac Séalaigh
I'm good at music and sport. I'm not too good at cooking, unfortunately.

I speak two languages – Irish and English. I only speak a little French.

Meadhbh Ní Eadhra
I'm a journalist and therefore I'm good at writing. I write fiction as well – stories for children and young people for the most part. I have a lot of interest in music and I play the fiddle.

I speak some French but I'd love to learn more languages. I can juggle with a few balls but they often fall on the ground!

Éamonn Ó Dónaill
I'm not good at any sport, although I played soccer when I was at school.

I'm reasonably good at singing but I seldom sing in public – I'm too shy, I suppose!

I learnt French when I was at school but I'm not too fluent. I understand a good deal of French but I'm not good at speaking it. I speak a little Italian as well.

The audio versions of these excerpts are available on the sound files accompanying this book. The video segments can be seen in the online version of *Gaeilge gan Stró! – Beginners Level*, available on Gaelchultúr's e-learning website, www.ranganna.com.

Exercise 7.9: Review of Unit 7

Have a go at this activity now to see if you know the most important phrases taught in Unit 7.

How would you say the following in Irish?

1. How good are you?
2. I'm reasonably good.
3. It's not too easy (use **furasta**).
4. It's easy enough.
5. It's too difficult.
6. You speak French, I see.
7. Is Spanish difficult?
8. Are you musical yourself?
9. I've been learning for three years now.
10. How long have you been learning Irish?
11. For the past fortnight.
12. For a few years.
13. Japanese is very difficult.
14. I speak some French.
15. I have a few words of Italian.

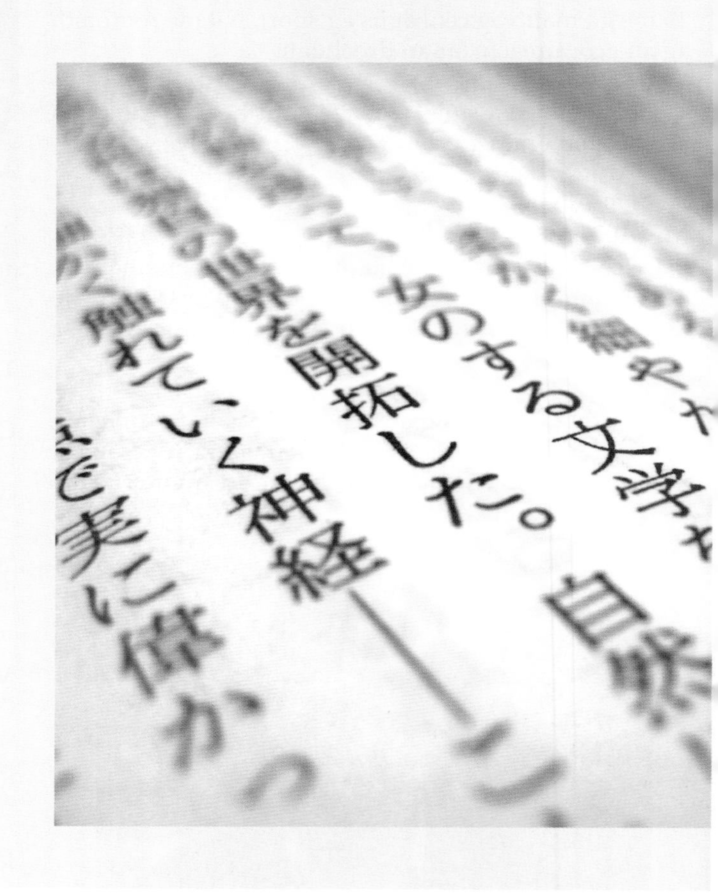

Unit 8: Work

Aonad 8: Cúrsaí Oibre

In this unit you will learn how to:

- ask someone what work he does and answer that question
- name various jobs and places of employment
- ask someone where he works and answer that question
- talk about your work status
- ask someone if he likes his job and answer that question
- ask someone if he has a particular job and answer that question
- describe conditions of employment
- ask someone about his work conditions and answer that question.

San aonad seo foghlaimeoidh tú conas:

- *ceist a chur ar dhuine cén obair a dhéanann sé agus an cheist sin a fhreagairt*
- *poist éagsúla agus áiteanna éagsúla fostaíochta a ainmniú*
- *fiafraí de dhuine cén áit a bhfuil sé ag obair agus an cheist sin a fhreagairt*
- *labhairt faoi do stádas oibre*
- *fiafraí de dhuine an dtaitníonn a phost leis agus an cheist sin a fhreagairt*
- *fiafraí de dhuine an bhfuil post áirithe aige agus an cheist sin a fhreagairt*
- *cur síos a dhéanamh ar choinníollacha fostaíochta*
- *ceist a chur ar dhuine faoina choinníollacha oibre agus an cheist sin a fhreagairt.*

Grammar

- questions and answers in the present tense
- the simple preposition **i(n)**
- dependent forms
- the copula **is** – statements, questions and answers
- the verb **bí** vs. the copula **is**

Gramadach

- *ceisteanna agus freagraí san aimsir láithreach*
- *an réamhfhocal simplí **i(n)***
- *foirmeacha spleácha*
- *an chopail **is** – ráitis, ceisteanna agus freagraí*
- *an briathar **bí** vs. an chopail **is***

Key sounds

CD 2 TR 56

i g**c**omhlacht	(**c** with *urú*)	*in a company*
cén obair a **dh**éanann tú?	(**d** with *séimhiú* followed by slender vowel, **e**)	*what do you work at?*
b**ia**lann	(the vowels **i** and **a**)	*(a) restaurant*
sc**oi**l	(the vowels **o** and **i**)	*(a) school*
ospidéi**l**	(slender **l**)	*hospitals*
ospidéa**l**	(broad **l**)	*(a) hospital*
óstái**n**	(slender **n**)	*hotels*
óstá**n**	(broad **n**)	*(an) hotel*
tiománaí	(slender **t**)	*(a) driver*
tacsaí	(broad **t**)	*(a) taxi*

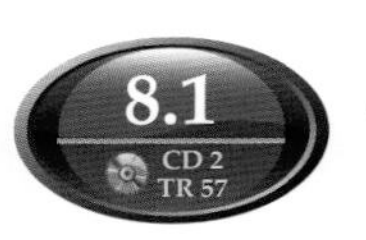

What do you work at?

To find out what work someone does you can ask:

Cén obair a dhéanann tú?
What do you work at?
or
Cén post atá agat?
What job do you have?

To answer those questions, you can use the structure **Is … mé**:

Is múinteoir mé.
I'm a teacher.

Is tiománaí tacsaí mé.
I'm a taxi driver.

As we've already seen, when a question is being repeated in a conversation, you must use **tú féin** or the emphatic form of the pronoun or prepositional pronoun:

Cén obair a dhéanann tú féin?
What do you work at yourself?

Cén obair a dhéanann tusa?
*What do **you** work at?*

Cén post atá agatsa?
*What job do **you** have?*

Vocabulary: Jobs and places of work

- post / an post / poist — *(a) job / the job / jobs*
- múinteoir / an múinteoir / múinteoirí — *(a) teacher / the teacher / teachers*
- léachtóir / an léachtóir / léachtóirí — *(a) lecturer / the lecturer / lecturers*
- iriseoir / an t-iriseoir / iriseoirí — *(a) journalist / the journalist / journalists*
- rúnaí / an rúnaí / rúnaithe — *(a) secretary / the secretary / secretaries*
- altra / an t-altra / altraí — *(a) nurse / the nurse / nurses*
- dochtúir / an dochtúir / dochtúirí — *(a) doctor / the doctor / doctors*
- tiománaí / an tiománaí / tiománaithe — *(a) driver / the driver / drivers*
- freastalaí / an freastalaí / freastalaithe — *(a) waiter / the waiter / waiters*
- meicneoir / an meicneoir / meicneoirí — *(a) mechanic / the mechanic / mechanics*
- tógálaí / an tógálaí / tógálaithe — *(a) builder / the builder / builders*
- cúntóir siopa / an cúntóir siopa / cúntóirí siopa — *(a) shop assistant / the shop assistant / shop assistants*
- búistéir / an búistéir / búistéirí — *(a) butcher / the butcher / butchers*
- gruagaire / an gruagaire / gruagairí — *(a) hairdresser / the hairdresser / hairdressers*
- bainisteoir / an bainisteoir / bainisteoirí — *(a) manager / the manager / managers*
- oifig / an oifig / oifigí — *(an) office / the office / offices*
- monarcha / an mhonarcha / monarchana — *(a) factory / the factory / factories*
- comhlacht / an comhlacht / comhlachtaí — *(a) company / the company / companies*
- ospidéal / an t-ospidéal / ospidéil — *(a) hospital / the hospital / hospitals*
- siopa / an siopa / siopaí — *(a) shop / the shop / shops*
- ollmhargadh / an t-ollmhargadh / ollmhargaí — *(a) supermarket / the supermarket / supermarkets*
- scoil / an scoil / scoileanna — *(a) school / the school / schools*
- bialann / an bhialann / bialanna — *(a) restaurant / the restaurant / restaurants*
- caifé / an caifé / caiféanna — *(a) café / the café / cafés*
- óstán / an t-óstán / óstáin — *(an) hotel / the hotel / hotels*
- teach tábhairne / an teach tábhairne / tithe tábhairne — *(a) pub / the pub / pubs*

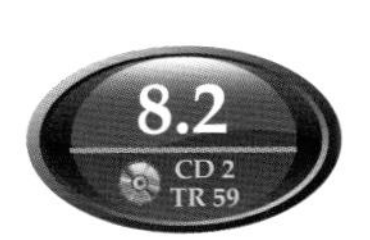

Where do you work?

This is how you say where you work:

Tá mé ag obair …
I work …

i siopa.
in a shop.

i gcomhlacht.
in a company.

in ospidéal.
in a hospital.

i monarcha.
in a factory.

i scoil.
in a school.

in oifig.
in an office.

in óstán.
in an hotel.

i dteach tábhairne.
in a pub.

To find out where someone is working you can ask:

Cén áit a bhfuil tú ag obair?
Where are you working?

When you reply to that question, you can leave out **Tá mé ag obair** … and simply say:

I siopa.
In a shop.

Urú

As we mentioned in Unit 2, the simple preposition **i** (*in*) is used in Irish before words beginning with a consonant:

Tá mé ag obair i mbanc.
I work in a bank.

An *urú* is placed before the consonants **b**, **c**, **d**, **f**, **g**, **p** and **t** after **i**. The other consonants don't change after **i**:

bialann *(a) restaurant* — **i mbialann** *in a restaurant*

caifé *(a) café* — **i gcaifé** *in a café*

but

monarcha *(a) factory* — **i monarcha** *in a factory*

scoil *(a) school* — **i scoil** *in a school*

The form **in** is used before vowels:

oifig
(an) office

Tá mé ag obair in oifig.
I work in an office.

ospidéal
(a) hospital

Tá mé ag obair in ospidéal.
I work in a hospital.

Exercise 8.1: Match the words

Match each Irish word in Column A with its English equivalent in Column B. The first one has been done for you.

	Column A		Column B
1	ospidéal	a	hairdresser
2	gruagaire	b	nurse
3	monarcha	c	hotel
4	comhlacht	e	supermarket
5	bainisteoir	f	restaurant
6	tiománaí	g	hospital
7	ollmhargadh	h	manager
8	bialann	i	company
9	óstán	j	driver
10	altra	k	factory

1	2	3	4	5	6	7	8	9	10
g									

Exercise 8.2: Answer the questions

Answer each of these questions as indicated.

1. Cén post atá agat?
   Say: I'm a manager.
2. Cén obair a dhéanann tú?
   Say: I'm a teacher.
3. Cén post atá agat?
   Say: I'm a secretary.
4. Cén obair a dhéanann tú?
   Say: I'm a waiter.
5. Cén post atá agat?
   Say: I'm a mechanic.
6. Cén obair a dhéanann tú?
   Say: I'm a doctor.
7. Cén áit a bhfuil tú ag obair?
   Say: I'm working in an office.
8. Cén áit a bhfuil tú ag obair?
   Say: I'm working in a company.
9. Cén áit a bhfuil tú ag obair?
   Say: In a supermarket.
10. Cén áit a bhfuil tú ag obair?
    Say: In a restaurant.

Work status

This is how you describe your work status:

Tá mé féinfhostaithe.
I'm self-employed.

Tá mé dífhostaithe.
I'm unemployed.

Tá mé ag lorg oibre faoi láthair.
I'm looking for work at the moment.

Insight

An Caighdeán Oifigiúil (The Official Standard) was developed by Rannóg an Aistriúcháin, the Irish language translation unit in Dáil Éireann. Their final version was published in 1958 and combines elements from the three major dialects. It was introduced to simplify the spelling of Irish and to give a standard written form that was mutually intelligible by speakers of different dialects.

This is the form of the language taught in the Irish education system and used in official or semi-official documents. A revised version of *An Caighdeán Oifigiúil* is due in the coming years.

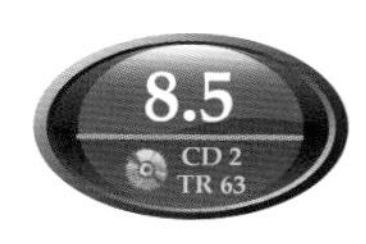

I love my job

This is how you express opinions about your job:

Is maith liom an post.
I like the job.

Is maith liom mo phost.
I like my job.

Tá an post ceart go leor.
The job is okay.

Ní maith liom an post ar chor ar bith.
I don't like the job at all.

To find out if someone likes his job you can ask:

An maith leat do phost?
Do you like your job?

Here are some possible answers:

Is maith.
Yes.

Ní maith.
No.

Tá sé ceart go leor.
It's okay.

Is breá liom é.
I love it.

Ní maith liom ar chor ar bith é.
I don't like it at all.

Is fuath liom é.
I hate it.

Conversation 8A

Alan bumps into his old friend Diarmuid in the pub.

Alan: Cén post atá agat na laethanta seo?
What job do you have these days?

Diarmuid: Is freastalaí mé. Tá mé ag obair i mbialann Iodálach i lár na cathrach.
I'm a waiter. I'm working in an Italian restaurant in the city centre.

Alan: An maith leat an post?
Do you like the job?

Diarmuid: Tá sé ceart go leor. Tá na daoine eile atá ag obair liom go deas.
It's okay. The other people who are working with me are nice.

Alan: An bhfuil an pá go maith?
Is the pay good?

Diarmuid: Níl. Tá sé go dona!
No. It's terrible!

Conversation 8B

Diarmuid now asks Alan about his work.

Diarmuid: Cén áit a bhfuil tú féin ag obair anois?
Where are you working yourself now?

Alan: Tá mé dífhostaithe faoi láthair. Tá mé ag lorg oibre.
I'm unemployed at the moment. I'm looking for work.

Diarmuid: Tá brón orm é sin a chloisteáil. Cén fhad atá tú dífhostaithe?
I'm sorry to hear that. How long have you been unemployed?

Alan: Le sé mhí anuas. Chaill mé mo phost i mí Eanáir.
For the past six months. I lost my job in January.

Diarmuid: Sin tamall fada. Tá mé cinnte go bhfuil tú bréan de bheith as obair.
That's a long time. I'm sure you're sick of being out of work.

Alan: Tá. Is fuath liom é.
Yes. I hate it.

The genitive case

Conversations 8A and 8B contain two examples of the genitive case:

an chathair
the city

i lár na cathrach
in the city centre

obair
work

ag lorg oibre
looking for work

We're not going to focus on the rules of the genitive case in this course, as they're too difficult for this level. We will draw attention to examples of the genitive from time to time, however.

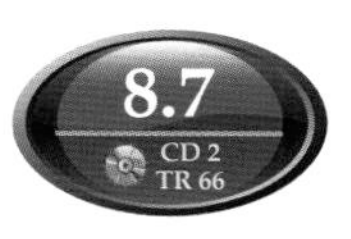

Dependent forms

In Conversation 8B Diarmuid said:

Tá mé cinnte go bhfuil tú bréan de bheith as obair.
I'm sure you're sick of being out of work.

Bhfuil is an example of a dependent form. After certain phrases, or when someone's speech is being reported, verbs in Irish have a special form, known as a dependent form.

This is the negative dependent form:

Cloisim nach bhfuil sí go deas.
I hear she's not nice.

Here are some other examples:

Regular sentence	Dependent form
Tá an obair an-suimiúil. *The work is very interesting.*	**Tá súil agam go bhfuil an obair an-suimiúil.** *I hope the work is very interesting.*
Tá Dónall dífhostaithe. *Dónall is unemployed.*	**Cloisim go bhfuil Dónall dífhostaithe.** *I hear that Dónall is unemployed.*
Tá an post deacair. *The job is difficult.*	**Tá súil agam nach bhfuil an post deacair.** *I hope the job isn't difficult.*

Exercise 8.3: Your turn!

This is your chance to talk now. Pretend you're Diarmuid and that you're talking to Alan.

Alan: Cén post atá agat na laethanta seo?

Say: *I'm a waiter. I'm working in an Italian restaurant in the city centre.*

Alan: An maith leat an post?

Say: *It's okay. The other people who are working with me are nice.*

Alan: An bhfuil an pá go maith?

Say: *No. It's terrible!*

Exercise 8.4: Your turn!

This time, pretend you're Alan and that you're talking to Diarmuid.

Diarmuid: Cén áit a bhfuil tú féin ag obair anois?

Say: *I'm unemployed at the moment. I'm looking for work.*

Diarmuid: Tá brón orm é sin a chloisteáil. Cén fhad atá tú dífhostaithe?

Say: *For the past six months. I lost my job in January.*

Diarmuid: Sin tamall fada. Tá mé cinnte go bhfuil tú bréan de bheith as obair.

Say: *Yes. I hate it.*

Exercise 8.5: Fill in the gaps

Fill in the gaps in these sentences.

1. *What do you work at?*
   Cén obair a ________________ tú?

2. *What job do **you** have?*
   Cén post atá __________?

3. *I'm working in an office in the city centre.*
   Tá mé ag obair in __________ i lár na ________________.

4. *I'm working in a pub on the edge of town.*
   Tá mé ag obair i __________ tábhairne ar ___________ an bhaile.

5. *Where are you working?*
   Cén áit a __________ tú ag obair?

6. *I'm self-employed.*
   Tá mé _________________.

7. *I'm looking for work at the moment.*
   Tá mé ag lorg ___________ faoi láthair.

8. *I don't like the job at all.*
   Ní maith liom an post ar ______ ar ________.

9. *I hate it.*
   Is _________ liom é.

10. *How long have you been unemployed?*
    Cén fhad atá tú ___________________?

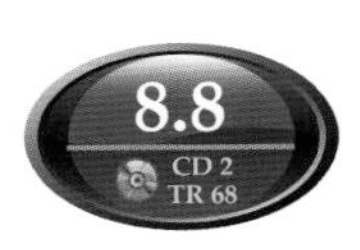

Are you a teacher?

To find out if someone does a particular job, you can ask **An … tú?**. Here are some examples:

An múinteoir tú?
Are you a teacher?
Is ea.
Yes.

An meicneoir tú?
Are you a mechanic?
Ní hea.
No.

An léachtóir tú?
Are you a lecturer?
Is ea.
Yes.

An léachtóir tú?
Are you a lecturer?
Ní hea.
No.

What hours do you work?

This is how you say what hours you work:

Oibrím óna hocht go dtí a ceathair.
I work from eight until four.

To find out what hours someone works you can ask:

Cad iad na huaireanta a oibríonn tú?
What hours do you work?

Here are some possible answers:

Ó leathuair tar éis a hocht go dtí a cúig.
From half past eight until five.

Óna naoi go dtí a cúig.
From nine until five.

Óna sé go dtí meán oíche.
From six until midnight.

8.10 Conditions of employment

These are sentences you can use to describe your conditions of employment:

Is post lánaimseartha é.
It's a full-time job.

Is post páirtaimseartha é.
It's a part-time job.

Is post sealadach é.
It's a temporary job.

Is post buan é.
It's a permanent job.

This is how you make questions of those statements:

An post lánaimseartha é?
Is it a full-time job?

An post páirtaimseartha é?
Is it a part-time job?

An post sealadach é? Is ea.
Is it a temporary job? Yes.

An post buan é? Ní hea.
Is it a permanent job? No.

Useful phrases

- Tá an post strusmhar. — *The job is stressful.*
- Tá an obair deacair / an-deacair. — *The work is difficult / very difficult.*
- Tá an obair furasta / an-fhurasta. — *The work is easy / very easy.*
- Oibrím uaireanta fada. — *I work long hours.*
- Réitím go maith leis na daoine eile. — *I get on well with the other people.*
- Ní réitím go maith leis na daoine eile. — *I don't get on well with the other people.*
- Tá an ceannasaí go deas. — *The boss is nice.*
- Tá an tuarastal go maith / maith go leor. — *The salary is good / okay.*
- Níl an pá go maith. — *The pay isn't good.*

Exercise 8.6: Answer the questions

Answer each of these questions as indicated.

1. An bhfuil tú ag obair i mbialann?
   Say: No. I'm working in a pub.
2. An freastalaí tú?
   Say: Yes.
3. An dochtúir tú?
   Say: No. I'm a nurse.
4. An bainisteoir tú?
   Say: No. I'm a secretary.
5. An freastalaí tú?
   Say: Yes. I'm working in a restaurant.
6. An meicneoir tú?
   Say: No. I'm a driver.
7. An maith leat do phost?
   Say: I don't like it at all.
8. An post lánaimseartha é?
   Say: No. It's a part-time job.
9. An post sealadach é?
   Say: Yes.
10. An post sealadach é?
    Say: No. It's a permanent job.

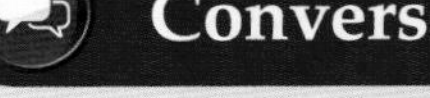

Conversation 8C

Caoimhe and Martin met through an online dating site. They're on their first date and getting to know more about each other.

Caoimhe: Cén obair a dhéanann tú?
What do you work at?

Martin: Is altra mé. Tá mé ag obair in Ospidéal San Séamas.
I'm a nurse. I work in Saint James' Hospital.

Caoimhe: An-suimiúil. An post deacair é?
Very interesting. Is it a difficult job?

Martin: Is ea, tá sé deacair go leor. Oibrím uaireanta fada.
Yes, it's difficult enough. I work long hours.

Caoimhe: An maith leat an post, mar sin féin?
Do you like the job, all the same?

Martin: Is maith – is breá liom é.
Yes – I love it.

Conversation 8D

Martin now asks Caoimhe about her job.

Martin: Cén obair a dhéanann tú féin?
What do you work at yourself?

Caoimhe: Is rúnaí mé. Tá mé ag obair i gcomhlacht beag.
I'm a secretary. I'm working in a small company.

Martin: An post lánaimseartha é?
Is it a full-time job?

Caoimhe: Is ea. Oibrím na gnáthuaireanta.
Yes. I work the usual hours.

Martin: An maith leat é?
Do you like it?

Caoimhe: Ní maith. Tá sé an-leadránach.
No. It's very boring.

Bí vs. is

In Irish, the verb **bí** is often used to talk about something that has less permanent qualities or that could change soon:

Tá lá deas ann inniu.
It's a nice day today.

Tá mé ag obair i mbialann.
I'm working in a restaurant.

The copula **is** is used in the case of more permanent things:

Is Ceanadach mé.	**Is dochtúir mé.**
I'm Canadian.	*I'm a doctor.*

As we've seen in this unit, the copula is also used when referring to the status of a job:

Is post buan é.	**An post sealadach é?**
It's a permanent job.	*Is it a temporary job?*

Exercise 8.7: Your turn!

This is your chance to talk now. Pretend you're Martin and that you're talking to Caoimhe.

Caoimhe: Cén obair a dhéanann tú?

Say: *I'm a nurse. I work in Saint James' Hospital.*

Caoimhe: An-suimiúil. An post deacair é?

Say: *Yes, it's difficult enough. I work long hours.*

Caoimhe: An maith leat an post, mar sin féin?

Say: *Yes – I love it.*

Exercise 8.8: Your turn!

This time, pretend you're Caoimhe and that you're talking to Martin.

Martin: Cén obair a dhéanann tú féin?

Say: *I'm a secretary. I'm working in a small company.*

Martin: An post lánaimseartha é?

Say: *Yes. I work the usual hours.*

Martin: An maith leat é?

Say: *No. It's very boring.*

Useful tips for learners

It's important to think about grammar as you learn Irish, but don't overdo it! Learn the gender and plural of nouns, for example, or how to ask and answer questions, but don't focus too much on grammar. Remember that you'll learn a lot of rules subconsciously if you listen to the language and read it on a regular basis.

At this stage, there's no need for you to learn the more complex grammatical rules (those governing the genitive case, for example): you'll have plenty of opportunities to master those rules as you become more proficient in the language.

Talking heads

Siobhán Patten (filmed in Temple Bar, Dublin)
Tá mé ag obair le Gaelchultúr i mBaile Átha Cliath le trí bliana anois. Eagraím cúrsaí Gaeilge agus bím ag múineadh go minic freisin.

Tosaím ag obair gach maidin ag leathuair tar éis a naoi agus críochnaím idir leathuair tar éis a cúig agus a sé de ghnáth. Is maith liom an post go mór. Bím faoi bhrú anois is arís ach bainim an-sásamh as an obair.

Tadhg Mac Dhonnagáin (filmed in An Spidéal, Galway)
Is foilsitheoir mé agus tá leabhair do pháistí agus do dhéagóirí foilsithe agam le roinnt blianta anuas.

Scríobhaim scripteanna teilifíse freisin agus tá gradaim IFTA buaite ag cláracha a raibh baint agam leo: an tsraith do dhéagóirí *Aifric* agus an clár cultúir *Cúrsaí Ealaíne*.

Is ceoltóir mé chomh maith. Cumaim amhráin agus casaim ceol Gaelach ag seisiúin thart ar Chonamara le cairde liom.

Caoimhe Ní Chonchoille (filmed in An Spidéal, Galway)
Tá mé ag obair mar iriseoir le Nuacht TG4 le ceithre bliana anois. Is breá liom an post – bíonn éagsúlacht ag baint le mo chuid oibre, castar gach cineál duine orm agus ní bhíonn dhá lá ar bith cosúil le chéile.

Is post lánaimseartha é. Oibrím deich n-uaire sa lá ar feadh ceithre lá agus ansin bíonn trí lá saor agam.

Translation

Siobhán Patten
I've been working with Gaelchultúr in Dublin for three years now. I organise Irish language courses and I often teach as well.

I start work each morning at half past nine and I usually finish between half past five and six. I like the job a lot. I'm under pressure now and again but I get a lot of satisfaction from the work.

Tadhg Mac Dhonnagáin
I'm a publisher and I've published books for children and for teenagers in the past few years.

I also write television scripts and programmes in which I was involved have won IFTA awards: the series for teenagers *Aifric* and the culture programme *Cúrsaí Ealaíne*.

I'm also a musician. I compose songs and I play Irish music at sessions around Conamara with friends of mine.

Caoimhe Ní Chonchoille
I'm working as a journalist with TG4 News for four years now. I love the job – my work is varied, I meet all sorts of people and no two days are the same.

It's a full-time job. I work ten hours a day for four days and then I have three days free.

Exercise 8.9: Review of Unit 8

Have a go at this activity now to see if you know the most important phrases taught in Unit 8.

How would you say the following in Irish?

1. What do you work at?
2. What do you work at yourself?
3. I'm a butcher.
4. I'm a builder.
5. Where are you working?
6. I work in a factory.
7. I work in an hotel.
8. I'm self-employed.
9. I'm unemployed at the moment.
10. Do you like your job? No.
11. Are you a secretary? Yes.
12. What hours do you work?
13. I work long hours.
14. Is it a permanent job? No.
15. It's a temporary job.

Unit 9: Food and Drink

Aonad 9: Bia agus Deoch

In this unit you will learn how to:

- say you're hungry or thirsty
- name different kinds of food and drink
- say what kind of food you eat and what you like to drink
- ask someone if he eats a particular kind of food
- express opinions on food
- offer someone a drink and accept or reject an offer of a drink
- order a drink
- ask how much something costs and answer that question
- ask for the bill.

Grammar

- the present tense
- emphatic suffixes
- **is maith** vs. **ba mhaith**
- counting euros

San aonad seo foghlaimeoidh tú conas:

- *a rá go bhfuil ocras nó tart ort*
- *cineálacha éagsúla bia agus deochanna a ainmniú*
- *a rá cén cineál bia a itheann tú agus cad is maith leat a ól*
- *ceist a chur ar dhuine an itheann sé cineál ar leith bia*
- *tuairimí a chur in iúl maidir le bia*
- *deoch a thairiscint do dhuine agus glacadh le tairiscint dí nó diúltú di*
- *deoch a ordú*
- *ceist a chur cé mhéad atá rud éigin agus an cheist sin a fhreagairt*
- *an bille a lorg.*

Gramadach

- *an aimsir láithreach*
- *iarmhíreanna treise*
- ***is maith** vs. **ba mhaith***
- *euronna a chomhaireamh*

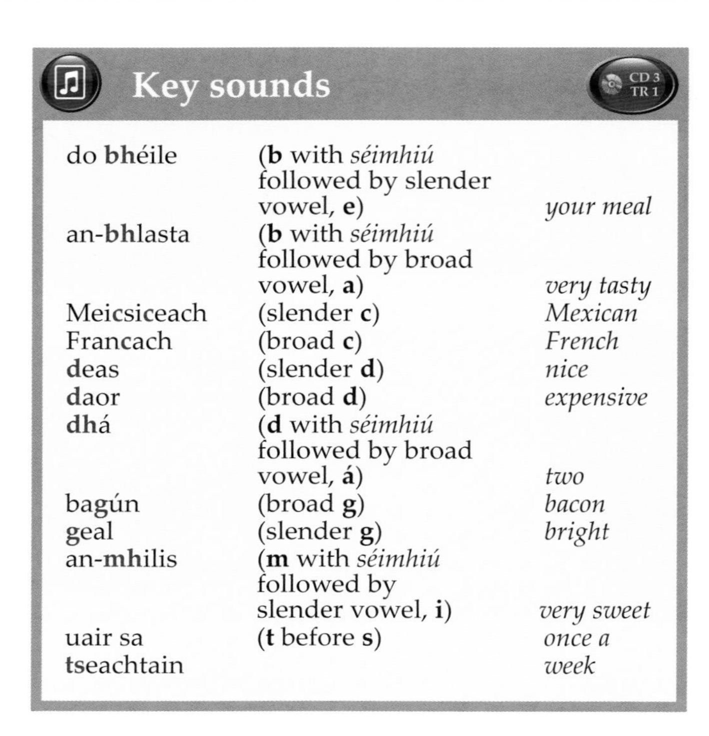

Key sounds

CD 3 TR 1

do **bh**éile	(**b** with *séimhiú* followed by slender vowel, **e**)	*your meal*
an-**bh**lasta	(**b** with *séimhiú* followed by broad vowel, **a**)	*very tasty*
Meicsi**c**each	(slender **c**)	*Mexican*
Fran**c**ach	(broad **c**)	*French*
deas	(slender **d**)	*nice*
daor	(broad **d**)	*expensive*
dhá	(**d** with *séimhiú* followed by broad vowel, **á**)	*two*
ba**g**ún	(broad **g**)	*bacon*
geal	(slender **g**)	*bright*
an-**mh**ilis	(**m** with *séimhiú* followed by slender vowel, **i**)	*very sweet*
uair sa **ts**eachtain	(**t** before **s**)	*once a week*

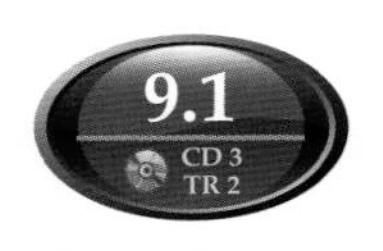

I'm hungry

This is how you say you're hungry:

Tá ocras orm.
I'm hungry.

And this is how you say you're thirsty:

Tá tart orm.
I'm thirsty.

To find out if someone is hungry or thirsty you ask:

An bhfuil ocras ort?
Are you hungry?
Tá.
Yes.

An bhfuil tart ort?
Are you thirsty?
Níl.
No.

Vocabulary 1: Food and drink 1

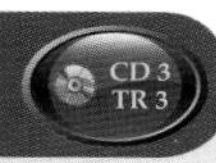

- sú oráiste — *orange juice*
- ubh / an ubh — *(an) egg / the egg*
- calóga arbhair — *cornflakes*
- putóg / an phutóg — *pudding / the pudding*
- ispín / an t-ispín / ispíní — *(a) sausage / the sausage / sausages*
- bagún / an bagún — *bacon / the bacon*
- arán bán / an t-arán bán — *white bread / the white bread*
- arán donn / an t-arán donn — *brown bread / the brown bread*
- tósta / an tósta — *toast / the toast*
- im / an t-im — *butter / the butter*
- cupán tae / an cupán tae — *(a) cup of tea / the cup of tea*
- caife / an caife — *(a) coffee / the coffee*
- siúcra / an siúcra — *sugar / the sugar*
- gloine bainne — *(a) glass of milk*
- spúnóg amháin, dhá spúnóg, trí spúnóg — *one spoon, two spoons, three spoons*
- anraith / an t-anraith — *soup / the soup*
- milseog / an mhilseog — *(a) dessert / the dessert*
- briosca / an briosca / brioscaí — *(a) biscuit / the biscuit / biscuits*
- torthaí — *fruit*
- sailéad torthaí — *fruit salad*
- feoil / an fheoil — *meat / the meat*
- sicín rósta / an sicín rósta — *(a) roast chicken / the roast chicken*
- bia mara / an bia mara — *seafood / the seafood*
- iasc / an t-iasc — *fish / the fish*
- glasraí — *vegetables*

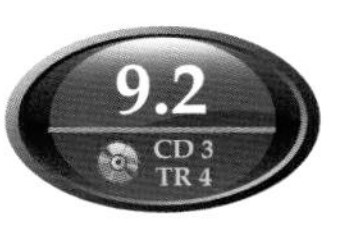

9.2 I eat all kinds of food

CD 3 TR 4

Here are some useful sentences you can use to talk about things you eat and don't eat, and drink and don't drink:

Ithim gach cineál bia.
I eat all kinds of food.

Ní ithim feoil. Is veigeatóir mé.
I don't eat meat. I'm a vegetarian.

Ní ithim bia mara.
I don't eat seafood.

Ólaim fíon geal.
I drink white wine.

Ní ólaim fíon dearg.
I don't drink red wine.

9.3 Do you eat fish?

CD 3 TR 5

This is how you find out if someone eats a particular kind of food or drinks a particular kind of drink:

An itheann tú iasc?
Do you eat fish?
Ithim.
Yes.

An itheann tú feoil?
Do you eat meat?
Ní ithim.
No.

An ólann tú fíon dearg?
Do you drink red wine?
Ólaim.
Yes.

Exercise 9.1: Match the words

Match each Irish word in Column A with its English equivalent in Column B. The first one has been done for you.

	Column A		Column B
1	siúcra	a	brown bread
2	gloine bainne	b	soup
3	arán donn	c	dessert
4	arán bán	e	meat
5	torthaí	f	sugar
6	im	g	seafood
7	iasc	h	biscuit
8	bia mara	i	fish
9	feoil	j	glass of milk
10	milseog	k	fruit
11	briosca	l	butter
12	anraith	m	white bread

1	2	3	4	5	6	7	8	9	10	11	12
f											

Exercise 9.2: Give the Irish version

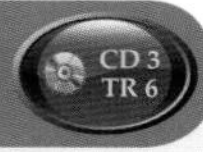

Give the Irish version of each of the following words:

1. orange juice
2. white bread
3. a cup of tea
4. sugar
5. cornflakes
6. fish
7. dessert
8. biscuits
9. fruit salad
10. a glass of milk

I like Italian food

In Unit 2, you learnt how to name different nationalities, e.g. **Francach** (*a French person*), **Rúiseach** (*a Russian person*).

Those words can also be used as adjectives, to describe something from a particular country:

Is maith liom bia Francach.
I like French food.

Here are some other useful sentences that you can use to give your opinion of various cuisines:

Is breá liom bia Meicsiceach.
I love Mexican food.

Is breá liom bia Iodálach.
I love Italian food.

Ní maith liom bia Síneach.
I don't like Chinese food.

Ní maith liom bia Spáinneach.
I don't like Spanish food.

Ceapaim go bhfuil bia Seapánach go deas.
I think Japanese food is nice.

Do you like French food?

To find out if someone likes a particular cuisine you can ask:

An maith leat bia Francach?
Do you like French food?

Here are some possible answers:

Is maith./Ní maith.
Yes./No.

Is breá liom é.
I love it.

Ceapaim go bhfuil sé go deas.
I think it's nice.

Insight

The most commonly used toast in Irish is **sláinte!** (*health!*). Here are some other toasts:

Sláinte mhór.
Good health (literally, *big health).*

Sláinte mhaith agat i bhfad ó bhrón.
Good health to you far from sorrow.

Sláinte na bhfear agus go maire na mná go deo.
Health to the men and may the women live forever.

Fad saoil agat, gob fliuch agus bás in Éirinn.
May you have a long life, a wet mouth and death in Ireland.

Numerous Irish proverbs refer to drinking, including the following:

Is túisce deoch ná scéal.
(*A drink precedes a story*, i.e. one should offer a drink before asking for news.)

Doirt do dheoch is beidh tart ort.
(*Spill your drink and you'll be thirsty*, i.e. wilful waste makes woeful want.)

Nuair a bhíos an braon istigh bíonn an chiall amuigh.
(*When the drop is inside sense is outside*, i.e. drink makes people act foolishly.)

Conversation 9A

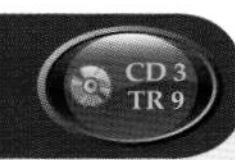

Fiona and Aoife have been working late and now they're about to go to a restaurant to have a bite to eat before going home.

Fiona: An itheann tú feoil?
Do you eat meat?

Aoife: Ithim, cinnte. Ithim gach cineál bia.
Yes, indeed. I eat all kinds of food.

Fiona: Ithimse feoil freisin ach ní ithim bia mara.
***I** eat meat as well but I don't eat seafood.*

Aoife: An maith leat bia Indiach? Tá bialann Indiach gar do lár an bhaile.
Do you like Indian food? There's an Indian restaurant near the centre of town.

Fiona: An bhfuil sé daor?
Is it expensive?

Aoife: Níl, agus tá an bia an-bhlasta.
No, and the food is very tasty.

Conversation 9B

Fiona and Aoife are eating their main course in the Indian restaurant.

Fiona: Conas atá an sicín?
How's the chicken?

Aoife: Tá sé an-spíosrach ach an-deas. Conas atá do bhéile féin?
It's very spicy but very nice. How is your own meal?

Fiona: Tá sé an-bhlasta ach rud beag fuar.
It's very tasty but a little bit cold.

Aoife: Is mór an trua sin. An bhfuil an t-arán naan go deas?
That's a pity. Is the naan bread nice?

Fiona: Tá, tá sé deas úr. Ar mhaith leat píosa?
Yes, it's nice and fresh. Would you like a piece?

Aoife: Níor mhaith, go raibh maith agat. Tá mé lán!
No, thanks. I'm full!

Emphatic suffix

In Conversation 9A, Fiona said:

Ithimse feoil freisin ach ní ithim bia mara.
***I** eat meat as well but I don't eat seafood.*

The **-se** at the end of **ithim** is an emphatic suffix, used to add emphasis. Here are some more examples of the same thing:

Máire: **Téim go Béal Feirste gach Nollaig.**
I go to Belfast every Christmas.

Fionn: **Téimse ansin freisin.**
***I** go there as well.*

Molly: **Imrím leadóg cúpla uair sa tseachtain.**
I play tennis a few times a week.

Pól: **Imrímse leadóg go minic freisin.**
***I** play tennis often as well.*

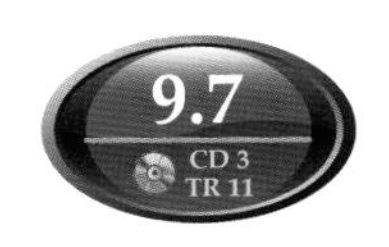

It's very spicy

You heard different opinions expressed in Conversation 9B regarding the food:

Tá sé an-spíosrach ach an-deas.
It's very spicy but very nice.

Tá sé an-bhlasta ach rud beag fuar.
It's very tasty but a little bit cold.

Tá sé deas úr.
It's nice and fresh.

Here are a few other useful sentences:

Tá an t-anraith seo an-te.
This soup is very hot.

Tá an mhilseog seo an-mhilis.
This dessert is very sweet.

Tá sé róthe.
It's too hot.

Tá sé rómhilis.
It's too sweet.

Exercise 9.3: Your turn!

This is your chance to talk now. Pretend you're Aoife and that you're talking to Fiona.

Fiona: An itheann tú feoil?

Say: *Yes, indeed. I eat all kinds of food.*

Fiona: Ithimse feoil freisin ach ní ithim bia mara.

Say: *Do you like Indian food? There's an Indian restaurant near the centre of town.*

Fiona: An bhfuil sé daor?

Say: *No, and the food is very tasty.*

Exercise 9.4: Your turn!

Again, pretend you're Aoife and that you're talking to Fiona.

Fiona: Conas atá an sicín?

Say: *It's very spicy but very nice. How is your own meal?*

Fiona: Tá sé an-bhlasta ach rud beag fuar.

Say: *That's a pity. Is the naan bread nice?*

Fiona: Tá, tá sé deas úr. Ar mhaith leat píosa?

Say: *No, thanks. I'm full!*

Exercise 9.5: Fill in the gaps

Fill in the gaps in these sentences.

1. *I'm hungry.*
   Tá ________ orm.
2. *Are you thirsty?*
   An bhfuil ________ ort?
3. *I don't eat meat. I'm a vegetarian.*
   Ní __________ feoil. ____ veigeatóir mé.

4. *I don't drink red wine.*
   Ní ólaim fíon ____________.
5. *Do you eat meat?*
   An ____________ tú feoil?
6. *I love Italian food.*
   Is breá liom bia ______________.
7. *I think Japanese food is nice.*
   Ceapaim go __________ bia Seapánach go deas.
8. *It's very spicy but very nice.*
   Tá sé ________________ ach an-deas.
9. *It's nice and fresh.*
   Tá sé deas ______.
10. *Would you like a piece?*
    Ar __________ leat píosa?

Vocabulary 2: Food and drink 2

- uisce mianraí — *mineral water*
- deoch bhog / deochanna boga — *(a) soft drink / soft drinks*
- beoir / an bheoir — *(a) beer / the beer*
- pionta beorach — *a pint of beer*
- gloine beorach — *a glass of beer*
- fíon / an fíon — *wine / the wine*
- buidéal fíona — *a bottle of wine*
- gloine fíona — *a glass of wine*
- uisce beatha / an t-uisce beatha — *whiskey / the whiskey*
- freastalaí / an freastalaí / freastalaithe — *(a) waiter / the waiter / waiters*
- biachlár / an biachlár — *(a) menu / the menu*
- an chéad chúrsa — *the first course / the starter*
- an príomhchúrsa — *the main course*

Buying someone a drink

To find out if someone would like a drink, you can ask:

An mbeidh deoch agat?
Will you have a drink?

You can begin your reply with the future tense form of the verb **bí**:

Beidh gloine fíona agam, le do thoil.
I'll have a glass of wine, please.

Ní bheidh, go raibh maith agat.
No, thank you.

To find out what someone would like to drink you can ask:

Cad ba mhaith leat?
What would you like?

To reply, you can simply say the name of the drink:

Caife dubh, le do thoil.
A black coffee, please.

Ordering drinks

If you go to the counter in a bar to order drinks you might be asked:

Cad ba mhaith leat?
What would you like?

In reply, you can simply name the drinks you want:

Fíon dearg, sú oráiste agus cupán caife, le do thoil.
A red wine, an orange juice and a cup of coffee, please.

When you've finished having drinks or a meal and you would like the bill, you can say:

An bille, le do thoil.
The bill, please.

Paying for drinks

To find out how much you owe you can say:

Cé mhéad sin?
How much is that?

Here are some possible answers:

€2	**dhá euro**
€2.10	**dhá euro deich cent**
€2.20	**dhá euro fiche cent**
€2.30	**dhá euro tríocha cent**
€2.40	**dhá euro ceathracha cent**
€2.50	**dhá euro caoga cent**
€3	**trí euro**
€4.60	**ceithre euro seasca cent**
€5.70	**cúig euro seachtó cent**
€6.80	**sé euro ochtó cent**
€7.90	**seacht euro nócha cent**
€8	**ocht euro**
€9	**naoi euro**
€10	**deich euro**

Exercise 9.6: Answer the questions

Answer each of these questions as indicated.

1. An maith leat bia Meicsiceach?
   Say: I love it.
2. An maith leat bia Seapánach?
   Say: Yes. I think it's nice.
3. Conas atá an sicín?
   Say: It's very spicy but very nice.
4. An mbeidh deoch agat?
   Say: I'll have a black coffee, please.
5. Cad ba mhaith leat?
   Say: Red wine, please.
6. Cé mhéad sin?
   Say: Four euro seventy cent.
7. Cé mhéad sin?
   Say: Eight euro thirty cent.
8. Cé mhéad sin?
   Say: Ten euro twenty cent.

Conversation 9C

Cormac arrives for a meeting in an Irish language company in Galway and is offered a drink by one of the employees.

Gearóidín: Ar mhaith leat tae nó caife? Nó arbh fhearr leat gloine uisce?
Would you like tea or coffee? Or would you prefer a glass of water?

Cormac: Beidh cupán caife agam, le do thoil.
I'll have a cup of coffee, please.

Gearóidín: An dtógann tú siúcra?
Do you take sugar?

Cormac: Tógaim. Dhá spúnóg, le do thoil.
Yes. Two spoons, please.

Gearóidín: Agus bainne?
And milk?

Cormac: Ní thógaim bainne. Go raibh maith agat.
I don't take milk. Thank you.

Gearóidín: Go ndéana a mhaith duit.
You're welcome.

Conversation 9D

Seosamh and Peadar are having a drink together after work.

Seosamh: Cad ba mhaith leat?
What would you like?

Peadar: Pionta Guinness, le do thoil. Cad a bheidh agatsa?
*A pint of Guinness, please. What will **you** have?*

Seosamh: Beidh pionta agamsa freisin.
I'll have a pint as well.

Peadar: Ar mhaith leat rud éigin a ithe?
Would you like to eat something?

Seosamh: Ba mhaith. Tá an-ocras orm.
Yes. I'm really hungry.

Like vs. would like

Learners of Irish often confuse **is maith liom** (*I like*) and **ba mhaith liom** (*I would like*). You should try and avoid that mistake!

Is maith liom (*I like*)	**Ba mhaith liom** (*I would like*)
Is maith liom bia Spáinneach. *I like Spanish food.*	**Ba mhaith liom cupán caife a ól.** *I'd like to drink a cup of coffee.*
Ní maith liom fíon dearg. *I don't like red wine.*	**Níor mhaith liom fíon a ól.** *I wouldn't like to drink wine.*
An maith leat bia Spáinneach? Is maith. *Do you like Spanish food? Yes.*	**Ar mhaith leat gloine fíona? Ba mhaith.** *Would you like a glass of wine? Yes.*
An maith leat fíon dearg? Ní maith. *Do you like red wine? No.*	**Ar mhaith leat pionta a ól? Níor mhaith.** *Would you like to drink a pint? No.*

Exercise 9.7: Your turn!

This is your chance to talk now. Pretend you're Cormac and that you're talking to Gearóidín.

Gearóidín: Ar mhaith leat tae nó caife? Nó arbh fhearr leat gloine uisce?

Say: *I'll have a cup of coffee, please.*

Gearóidín: An dtógann tú siúcra?

Say: *Yes. Two spoons, please.*

Gearóidín: Agus bainne?

Say: *I don't take milk. Thank you.*

Gearóidín: Go ndéana a mhaith duit.

Exercise 9.8: Your turn!

This time, pretend you're Seosamh and that you're talking to Peadar.

Say: *What would you like?*

Peadar: Pionta Guinness, le do thoil. Cad a bheidh agatsa?

Say: *I'll have a pint as well.*

Peadar: Ar mhaith leat rud éigin a ithe?

Say: *Yes. I'm really hungry.*

Exercise 9.9: Masculine & feminine

Write the correct version of each noun in the gap after the article and change the noun if necessary. If you can't remember the rules, have a look again at the table in 4.4 on page 38 as a guide.

1. putóg (feminine) (*pudding*)

   an ________________

2. arán (masculine) (*bread*)

   an ________________

3. siúcra (masculine) (*sugar*)

   an ________________

4. milseog (feminine) (*dessert*)

   an ________________

5. anraith (masculine) (*soup*)

   an ________________

6. beoir (feminine) (*beer*)

   an ________________

7. ubh (feminine) (*egg*)

   an ________________

8. fíon (masculine) (*wine*)

   an ________________

9. bia (masculine) (*food*)

   an ________________

10. bialann (feminine) (*restaurant*)

    an ________________

Useful tips for learners

Learners often find it frustrating not being able to express complex ideas in Irish; they find that they're not as fluent as they are in their mother tongue and their vocabulary is a lot more limited. It's important to say things as simply as you can in Irish, using the words and structures you already know; think of what you want to say in Irish itself, rather than translating from your mother tongue. You'll gradually learn more complicated structures and your frustration will lessen.

Talking heads

Cóilín Ó Floinn (filmed in Temple Bar, Dublin)
Ithim gach cineál bia, seachas bia mara. Is breá liom bia Iodálach agus bia Francach. Ithim mo lón i gcaifé nó i mbialann go minic, ach ithim an dinnéar sa bhaile.

Ólaim Guinness agus fíon dearg ach ní maith liom fíon geal ar chor ar bith.

Dairíne Ní Dhonnchú
(filmed in Temple Bar, Dublin)
Ithim gach cineál bia ach ní ithim mórán seacláide. Is maith liom bia folláin a ithe agus is breá liom torthaí agus glasraí.

Ólaim tae glas le mo bhricfeasta agus arís ag am lóin. Bíonn fíon dearg agam le mo dhinnéar uaireanta.

Meadhbh Ní Eadhra
(filmed in Merrion Square Park, Dublin)
Is maith liom sicín rósta le prátaí agus cairéid. Is béile blasta é sin.

Is breá liom bheith ag ól uisce – bíonn buidéal agam i mo mhála i gcónaí.

Ní maith liom brocailí, cabáiste ná iasc de chineál ar bith. Tá siad lofa!

Bia Iodálach an cineál bia is fearr liom. Bíonn sé go hálainn i gcónaí, ach ní féidir bia mo mhamaí a shárú!

Páidí Ó Lionáird (filmed in An Spidéal, Galway)
Is breá liom bia Iodálach agus bia Síneach. Ní feoilséantóir mé – ithim feoil agus is breá liom bia mara.

Téim go Gaillimh chuig na bialanna go minic. Is é Buon Appetito an bhialann is fearr liom – tá an bia blasta ann agus tá sé an-réasúnta.

Translation

Cóilín Ó Floinn
I eat all sorts of food, except seafood. I love Italian food and French food. I often eat my lunch in a café or restaurant, but I eat dinner at home.

I drink Guinness and red wine but I don't like white wine at all.

Dairíne Ní Dhonnchú
I eat all sorts of food but I don't eat much chocolate. I like to eat healthy food and I love fruit and vegetables.

I drink green tea with my breakfast and again at lunchtime. I sometimes have red wine with my dinner.

Meadhbh Ní Eadhra
I like roast chicken with potatoes and carrots. That's a tasty meal.

I love drinking water – I always have a bottle in my bag.

I don't like broccoli, cabbage or any kind of fish. They're rotten!

Italian food is my favourite food. It's always lovely, but you can't beat my mum's cooking!

Páidí Ó Lionáird
I love Italian food and Chinese food. I'm not a vegetarian – I eat meat and I love seafood.

I often go to Galway to the restaurants. Buon Appetito is my favourite restaurant – the food there is tasty and it's very reasonable.

The audio versions of these excerpts are available on the sound files accompanying this book. The video segments can be seen in the online version of *Gaeilge gan Stró! – Beginners Level*, available on Gaelchultúr's e-learning website, www.ranganna.com.

Exercise 9.10: Review of Unit 9

Have a go at this activity now to see if you know the most important phrases taught in Unit 9.

How would you say the following in Irish?

1. I'm hungry.
2. Are you thirsty?
3. I don't eat meat. I'm a vegetarian.
4. I don't drink red wine.
5. Do you drink white wine? Yes.
6. I love Japanese food.
7. I think Chinese food is nice.
8. Do you like Italian food? Yes.
9. Do you like French food? No.
10. It's very tasty.
11. It's very spicy but very nice.
12. Will you have a drink? No, thanks.
13. I'll have a glass of wine, please.
14. What would you like?
15. How much is that? Three euro fifty cent.

Unit 10: Health Matters
Aonad 10: Cúrsaí Sláinte

In this unit you will learn how to:

- say you don't feel well
- ask someone what's wrong with him and answer that question
- empathise with someone
- ask someone how long he's been ill and answer that question
- ask someone if he feels better and answer that question
- name various parts of the body
- give information about an illness or injury
- refer to another person's illness or appearance.

San aonad seo foghlaimeoidh tú conas:

- *a rá nach bhfuil tú ag mothú go maith*
- *ceist a chur ar dhuine cad atá air agus an cheist sin a fhreagairt*
- *comhbhá a léiriú le duine*
- *fiafraí de dhuine cén fhad atá sé tinn agus an cheist sin a fhreagairt*
- *ceist a chur ar dhuine an mothaíonn sé níos fearr agus an cheist sin a fhreagairt*
- *baill bheatha éagsúla a ainmniú*
- *eolas a thabhairt faoi thinneas nó faoi ghortú*
- *tagairt a dhéanamh do thinneas nó do chuma duine eile.*

Grammar

- the prepositional pronouns **ar** and **ag**
- comparative forms of the adjective
- adjectives in the plural
- possessive adjectives

Gramadach

- *na forainmneacha réamhfhoclacha* ***ar*** *agus* ***ag***
- *céimeanna comparáide na haidiachta*
- *aidiachtaí san uimhir iolra*
- *aidiachtaí sealbhacha*

Key sounds

CD 3 TR 23

mo **bh**olg	(**b** with *séimhiú* followed by broad vowel, **o**)	*my stomach*
droch-**ch**asachtach	(**c** with *séimhiú* followed by broad vowel, **a**)	*a bad cough*
déarfainn é	(slender **d**)	*I'd say so*
go **d**ona	(broad **d**)	*terrible*
gruaig **fh**ada	(**f** with *séimhiú*)	*long hair*
ghortaigh mé	(**g** with *séimhiú* followed by broad vowel, **o**)	*I hurt*
ó **mh**aidin	(**m** with *séimhiú* followed by broad vowel, **a**)	*since this morning*
a **Sh**éamais	(**s** with *séimhiú*)	*Séamas*
tinneas cinn	(slender **t**)	*(a) headache*
tú	(broad **t**)	*you*
scornach **th**inn	(**t** with *séimhiú*)	*(a) sore throat*

I don't feel well

You can use the following sentences when you don't feel well:

Níl mé ag mothú go maith.
I don't feel well.

Tá mé tinn.
I'm sick.

Tá mé an-tinn.
I'm very sick.

What's wrong with you?

To find out if someone is ill, you can ask:

An bhfuil tú tinn?
Are you sick?

Tá. Tá fliú orm.
Yes. I have the flu (literally, *there's flu on me*).

To find out what's wrong with someone, you can ask:

Cad atá ort?
What's wrong with you (literally, *what's on you*)?

Here are some possible answers:

Tá tinneas cinn orm.
I have a headache.

Tá pian i mo bholg.
I have a pain in my stomach.

Tá slaghdán orm.
I have a cold.

Tá scornach thinn orm.
I have a sore throat.

Tá casachtach orm.
I have a cough.

Tá tinneas fiacaile orm.
I have a toothache.

You poor thing!

To empathise with someone you can say:

Is mór an trua sin.
That's a pity.

A chréatúir!
You poor thing!

Mo ghraidhin thú!
You poor thing!

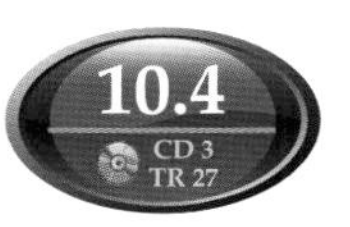

How long have you been sick?

To find out how long someone has been sick, you can ask:

Cén fhad atá tú tinn?
How long have you been sick?

Cén fhad atá sé sin ort?
How long have you had that?

Here are some possible answers:

Ó mhaidin.
Since this morning.

Ó bhí inné ann.
Since yesterday.

Le dhá lá anuas.
For the past two days.

Le cúpla lá anuas.
For the past few days.

Le seachtain anois.
For a week now.

Exercise 10.1: Answer the questions

Answer each of these questions as indicated.

1. An bhfuil tú tinn?
   Say: Yes. I have the flu.
2. An bhfuil tú tinn?
   Say: Yes. I have a pain in my stomach.
3. An bhfuil tú tinn?
   Say: Yes. I'm very sick.
4. Cad atá ort?
   Say: I have a headache.
5. Cad atá ort?
   Say: I have a cold.
6. Cad atá ort?
   Say: I have a toothache.
7. Cad atá ort?
   Say: I have a cough.
8. Cad atá ort?
   Say: I have a sore throat.

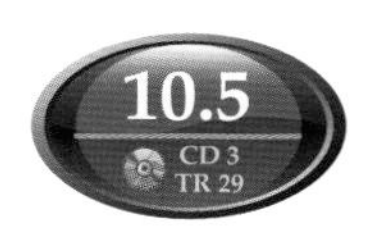

Are you better?

To find out if someone's condition is improving, you can ask:

An bhfuil tú níos fearr?
Are you better?

or

An bhfuil biseach ag teacht ort?
Are you recovering?

Here are some possible answers:

Tá, go raibh maith agat.
Yes, thank you.

Tá mé rud beag níos fearr.
I'm a little bit better.

Tá mé i bhfad níos fearr.
I'm much better.

Níl, tá mé níos measa.
No, I'm worse.

Insight

Ireland is considered one of the most densely named countries in Europe. Most place names in the country are anglicisations, or phonetic spellings, of Irish language names, although some come directly from the English language and from Old Norse. The process of anglicisation began in the seventeenth century; place names were written according to the spelling conventions of the English language and these new forms were used by the colonial rulers. The Irish-speaking population continued to use the Irish language versions, but these were ignored in official documents.

The Placenames Database of Ireland can be found online at www.logainm.ie. It contains thousands of place names, including names of centres of population (townlands, towns, villages, districts), physical features (rivers, lakes, islands, mountains, hills), and man-made features (castles, churches, monasteries, graveyards, bridges, streets).

Here are some of the most common elements found in Irish place names:

Irish word	Meaning	Examples of place names
baile	town, townland	Ballymena, Ballymoney
carraig	rock	Carrickfergus, Carrickmacross
cill	church	Kildare, Kilkenny Killarney
cnoc	hill	Knock, Knocklyon
doire	oak-wood, grove	Derry, Derrynane
domhnach	church	Donaghadee, Donnybrook
dún	fort, palace	Dundrum, Dungloe
leitir	hillside	Letterkenny, Letterfrack
mullach	summit	Malahide, Mullaghmore
ráth	circular fort, earth mound	Rathmines, Rathmullan

Conversation 10A

CD 3 TR 30

Méabh tells her friend Siobhán that she's not feeling too well at the moment.

Méabh: Níl mé ag mothú go maith ar chor ar bith.
I don't feel well at all.

Siobhán: Cad atá ort?
What's wrong with you?

Méabh: Tá scornach thinn orm agus droch-chasachtach.
I have a sore throat and a bad cough.

Siobhán: A chréatúir! Seans go bhfuil fliú ag teacht ort.
You poor thing! There's a chance you're getting the flu.

Méabh: Déarfainn é. Tá mé ag mothú go dona.
I'd say so. I feel terrible.

Siobhán: Téigh go dtí do leaba agus beidh tú níos fearr amárach.
Go to your bed and you'll be better tomorrow.

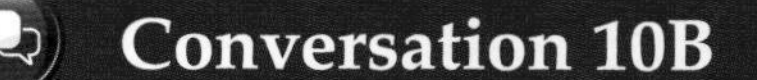

Conversation 10B

CD 3 TR 30

Séamas is at work and not feeling well. His colleague Máirín advises him to go home.

Máirín: An bhfuil tú ceart go leor, a Shéamais? Tá cuma thinn ort.
Are you okay, Séamas? You look sick.

Séamas: Níl mé ag mothú go maith ar chor ar bith.
I don't feel well at all.

Máirín: Cad atá ort?
What's wrong with you?

Séamas: Tá pian uafásach i mo bholg.
I have a terrible pain in my stomach.

Máirín: Cén fhad atá sé sin ort?
How long have you had that?

Séamas: Tá sé orm ó mhaidin. Agus tá sé ag éirí níos measa.
I've had it since this morning. And it's getting worse.

Máirín: Imigh leat abhaile. Beidh biseach ort ar maidin, tá mé cinnte.
Go on home. You'll have recovered by the morning, I'm sure.

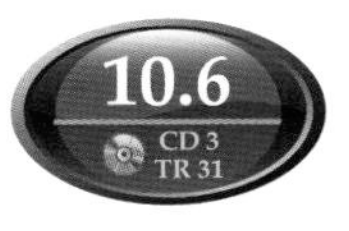

Nouns and adjectives

In Irish, adjectives (with a few exceptions) follow the noun and agree with it in gender, number and case. A *séimhiú* is added to the beginning of adjectives when they qualify nouns that are feminine, in most cases in the singular. Here is an example from Conversation 10A:

> **Tá scornach thinn orm.**
> *I have a sore throat.*

We'll be returning to adjectives later in this unit and in the next unit.

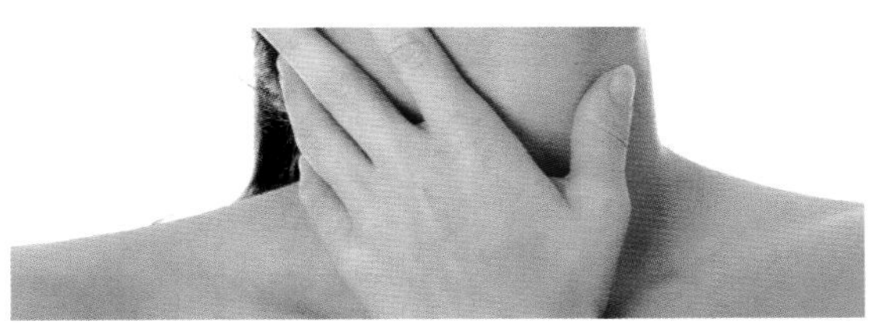

Better and worse

To say that something is better, worse, bigger, etc. you use the word **níos**, followed by the adjective. This is known as the comparative. Here are two examples from Conversations 10A and 10B:

> **níos fearr** (*better*)
> **níos measa** (*worse*)

Some of the most commonly used comparatives are listed below. You'll notice that most of the comparative forms are very different from the basic forms of the adjective.

Adjective	Comparative
maith (*good*)	**níos fearr** (*better*)
olc (*bad*)	**níos measa** (*worse*)
mór (*big*)	**níos mó** (*bigger*)
beag (*small*)	**níos lú** (*smaller*)
deas (*nice*)	**níos deise** (*nicer*)
óg (*young*)	**níos óige** (*younger*)
sean (*old*)	**níos sine** (*older*)

Exercise 10.2: Your turn!

This is your chance to talk now. Pretend you're Méabh and that you're talking to Siobhán.

Say: *I don't feel well at all.*

Siobhán: Cad atá ort?

Say: *I have a sore throat and a bad cough.*

Siobhán: A chréatúir! Seans go bhfuil fliú ag teacht ort.

Say: *I'd say so. I feel terrible.*

Siobhán: Téigh go dtí do leaba agus beidh tú níos fearr amárach.

Exercise 10.3: Your turn!

This time, pretend you're Máirín and that you're talking to Séamas.

Say: *Are you okay, Séamas? You look sick.*

Séamas: Níl mé ag mothú go maith ar chor ar bith.

Say: *What's wrong with you?*

Séamas: Tá pian uafásach i mo bholg.

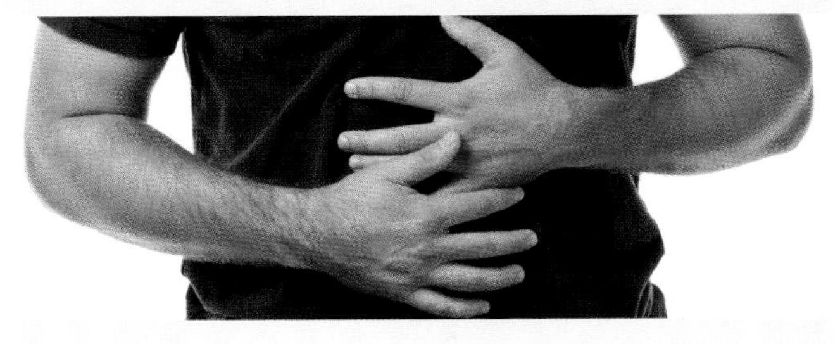

Say: *How long have you had that?*

Séamas: Tá sé orm ó mhaidin. Agus tá sé ag éirí níos measa.

Say: *Go on home. You'll have recovered by the morning, I'm sure.*

Exercise 10.4: Fill in the gaps

Fill in the gaps in these sentences.

1. *I don't feel well.*
   Níl mé ag __________ go maith.
2. *I have a sore throat.*
   Tá scornach ________ orm.
3. *I have a toothache.*
   Tá ___________ ___________ orm.
4. *That's a pity.*
   Is mór an _________ sin.
5. *How long have you had that?*
   Cén ________ atá sé sin ort?
6. *For the past few days.*
   Le cúpla lá __________.
7. *For a week now.*
   Le ______________ anois.
8. *Are you recovering?*
   An bhfuil ____________ ag teacht ort?
9. *Are you better?*
   An bhfuil tú níos __________?
10. *No, I'm worse.*
    Níl, tá mé níos ____________.

Vocabulary: Parts of the body

- ceann — *(a) head*
- gruaig — *hair*
- aghaidh — *(a) face*
- cluas / cluasa — *(an) ear / ears*
- súil / súile — *(an) eye / eyes*
- srón — *(a) nose*
- muineál — *(a) neck*
- bolg — *(a) stomach*
- brollach — *(a) breast*
- lámh / lámha — *(a) hand / hands* or *(an) arm / arms*
- méar / méara — *(a) finger / fingers*
- cos / cosa — *(a) foot / feet* or *(a) leg / legs*
- glúin / glúine — *(a) knee / knees*
- tóin — *(a) backside*

Exercise 10.5: Give the Irish version

Give the Irish version of each of these words.

1. breast
2. face
3. hands
4. eyes
5. hair
6. backside
7. nose
8. neck
9. fingers
10. leg
11. legs
12. stomach

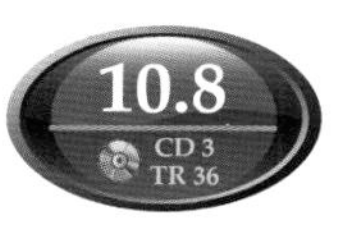

The prepositional pronoun ar

As we've seen in this unit, the prepositional pronoun **ar** is used when illnesses are being referred to:

Tá tinneas cinn orm.
I have a headache (literally, *there's a headache on me*).

It's also used to describe external parts of the body:

Tá gruaig fhada orm.
I have long hair.

Here are the different forms of **ar**:

Singular		Plural	
1	**orm** *on me*	1	**orainn** *on us*
2	**ort** *on you*	2	**oraibh** *on you*
3	**air** *on him* **uirthi** *on her*	3	**orthu** *on them*

Here, then, is how you refer to other people's illnesses and appearance:

Tá slaghdán air.
He has a cold.

Tá casachtach uirthi.
She has a cough.

Tá scornach thinn orthu.
They have sore throats.

Tá gruaig fhada uirthi.
She has long hair.

This is how you ask what someone looks like:

Cén chuma atá air?
What does he look like?

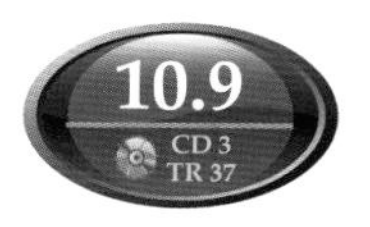

The prepositional pronoun ag

The prepositional pronoun **ag** is used to describe internal parts of the body:

Tá súile gorma agam.
I have blue eyes (literally, *there are blue eyes at me*).

Tá fiacla deasa agam.
I have nice teeth.

Here are the different forms of **ag**:

Singular		Plural	
1	**agam** *at me*	1	**againn** *at us*
2	**agat** *at you*	2	**agaibh** *at you*
3	**aige** *at him* **aici** *at her*	3	**acu** *at them*

Here is how you use **ag** when referring to other people:

Tá súile gorma aige.
He has blue eyes.

Tá súile glasa aici.
She has green eyes.

Tá fiacla deasa agaibh.
You have nice teeth.

Tá fiacla deasa acu.
They have nice teeth.

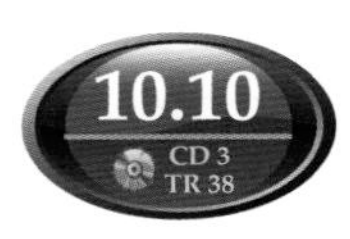

Adjectives in the plural

As we mentioned earlier, adjectives agree with the noun in gender, number and case. Therefore, when an adjective is used with the plural form of **súil**, i.e. **súile**, that adjective must be in the plural as well.

Tá súile gorma agam.
I have blue eyes.

Here are the changes undergone by various adjectives in the plural:

Singular	Plural
gorm *blue*	**gorma**
donn *brown*	**donna**
glas *green*	**glasa**
deas *nice*	**deasa**

Conversation 10C

Niamh tells Nollaig what the new manager looks like.

Nollaig: Cén chuma atá ar an mbainisteoir nua?
What does the new manager look like?

Niamh: Tá sí an-dathúil. Tá gruaig fhada dhonn uirthi …
She's very good-looking. She has long brown hair …

Nollaig: Go deas!
Very nice!

Niamh: … agus tá súile gorma aici.
… and she has blue eyes.

Nollaig: An bhfuil sí cairdiúil?
Is she friendly?

Niamh: Tá. Tá sí an-chairdiúil. Ó, agus ró-óg duitse.
Yes. She's very friendly. Oh, and too young for ***you****.*

Conversation 10D

Rebecca hears that her colleague Deirbhile has had an accident. She rings her to see if she's okay.

Rebecca: An bhfuil tú ceart go leor? Cad a tharla?
Are you okay? What happened?

Deirbhile: Thit mé de mo rothar inné agus ghortaigh mé mo chos.
I fell off my bike yesterday and hurt my leg.

Rebecca: Níl sí briste?
It's not broken?

Deirbhile: Níl, buíochas le Dia.
No, thank God.

Rebecca: Bhí an t-ádh leat. An bhfuil sí tinn?
You were lucky. Is it sore?

Deirbhile: Níl sí ró-olc. Chuaigh mé chuig an dochtúir agus thug sé táibléid dom don phian.
It's not too bad. I went to the doctor and he gave me tablets for the pain.

Rebecca: Is maith sin. Thit mise agus mé ag sciáil anuraidh agus bhris mé mo lámh.
That's good. ***I*** *fell while skiing last year and I broke my arm.*

Sí

In Conversation 10D, the pronoun **sí** (*it*) is used when reference is made to Deirbhile's leg. For example:

An bhfuil sí tinn?
Is it sore?

The pronoun **sí** is used because the noun it's replacing, **cos**, is feminine.

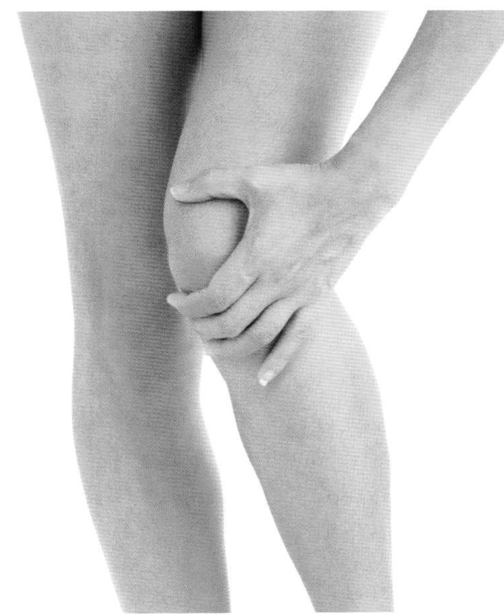

The past tense

The past tense forms of various verbs are used in Conversation 10D:

Thit mé de mo rothar inné agus ghortaigh mé mo chos.
I fell off my bike yesterday and hurt my leg.

Chuaigh mé chuig an dochtúir agus thug sé táibléid dom don phian.
I went to the doctor and he gave me tablets for the pain.

Thit mise agus mé ag sciáil anuraidh agus bhris mé mo lámh.
I fell while skiing last year and I broke my arm.

We'll be looking at the past tense in more detail in Units 13 and 14.

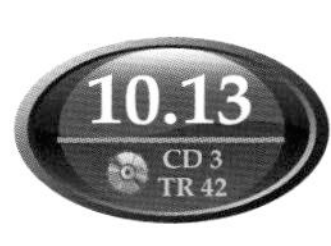

Possessive adjectives

We focused on possessive adjectives in Unit 3, in the context of the family. They're also used when describing injuries. A *séimhiú* is added to nouns beginning with a consonant which follow **mo** (*my*) and **do** (*your*):

Ghortaigh mé mo chos.
I hurt my leg.

Bhris tú do chos, cloisim.
You broke your leg, I hear.

Here are some other examples:

bolg *stomach*	**Tá pian i mo bholg.** *I have a pain in my stomach.*
ceann *head*	**Seachain do cheann.** *Mind your head.*
gruaig *hair*	**Is breá liom do ghruaig.** *I love your hair.*
muineál *neck*	**mo mhuineál** *my neck*
súile *eyes*	**do shúile** *your eyes*
tóin *backside*	**mo thóin** *my backside*

As we saw in Unit 3, **mo** and **do** are shortened when they precede a noun beginning with a vowel:

aghaidh *face*	**m'aghaidh** *my face*

Exercise 10.6 Your turn!

This is your chance to talk now. Pretend you're Niamh and that you're talking to Nollaig.

Nollaig: Cén chuma atá ar an mbainisteoir nua?

Say: *She's very good-looking. She has long brown hair …*

Nollaig: Go deas!

Say: *… and she has blue eyes.*

Nollaig: An bhfuil sí cairdiúil?

Say: *Yes. She's very friendly. Oh, and too young for **you**.*

Exercise 10.7: Your turn!

This time, pretend you're Rebecca and that you're talking to Deirbhile.

Say: *Are you okay? What happened?*

Deirbhile: Thit mé de mo rothar inné agus ghortaigh mé mo chos.

Say: *It's not broken?*

Deirbhile: Níl, buíochas le Dia.

Say: *You were lucky. Is it sore?*

Deirbhile: Níl sí ró-olc. Chuaigh mé chuig an dochtúir agus thug sé táibléid dom don phian.

Say: *That's good. **I** fell while skiing last year and I broke my arm.*

Exercise 10.8: Give the Irish version

Give the Irish version of each of these words.

1. my breast
2. your face
3. your hands
4. my eyes
5. your hair
6. my backside
7. my nose
8. your neck
9. your fingers
10. my leg
11. your legs
12. my stomach

Useful tips for learners

Listen to Irish as much as you can, even if you only manage to understand the odd word or phrase. Use the audio files that accompany this book, watch Irish language programmes on TG4 (http://live.tg4.ie) and listen to Raidió na Gaeltachta (www.rte.ie/rnag) regularly. The programme *Camchuairt*, which is a round-up of news and events from the various *Gaeltacht* regions, is broadcast from Monday to Friday on Raidió na Gaeltachta and is worth listening to as the same type of language (e.g. days of the week) tends to be repeated often.

It's important to develop the skill of being able to get the gist of what is being said by understanding a word here and there.

Talking heads

Colm Mac Séalaigh
(filmed at the Civic Offices, Dublin)
Ghortaigh mé mo lámh uair amháin nuair a bhí mé óg. Bhí mé ag rothaíocht nuair a thit mé agus bhris mé mo lámh. Bhí sé pianmhar go leor ar feadh cúpla lá, is cuimhin liom.

Tadhg Mac Dhonnagáin
(filmed in An Spidéal, Galway)
Is duine sláintiúil go leor mé agus is annamh a thagann fliú ná slaghdán orm i gcaitheamh an gheimhridh. Déanaim go leor aclaíochta – imrím leadóg sa samhradh agus téim ag siúl cois na farraige cúig lá sa tseachtain.

Bhris mé mo laidhricín agus mé ag sleamhnú sa sneachta nuair a bhí mé sa bhunscoil.

Éamonn Ó Dónaill
(filmed in Dún Laoghaire, County Dublin)
Tá mé réasúnta sláintiúil. Ólaim alcól, ceart go leor, ach níor chaith mé tobac riamh agus tá áthas orm faoi sin.

Níor bhris mé cos ná lámh riamh ach ghearr mé mo chos go dona i dtimpiste gluaisrothair. Bhí mé aon bhliain déag ag an am agus is cuimhin liom go raibh an phian go dona ar fad.

Translation

Colm Mac Séalaigh
I hurt my arm once when I was young. I was cycling when I fell and broke my arm. It was quite painful for a few days, I remember.

Tadhg Mac Dhonnagáin
I'm quite a healthy person and I seldom get the flu or a cold during the winter. I do plenty of exercise – I play tennis in the summer and I go walking by the seaside five days a week.

I broke my little finger when sliding in the snow when I was in primary school.

Éamonn Ó Dónaill
I'm reasonably healthy. I drink alcohol, alright, but I never smoked and I'm happy about that.

I never broke a leg or arm but I cut my foot badly in a motorcycle accident. I was eleven years (old) at the time and I remember that the pain was really bad.

The audio versions of these excerpts are available on the sound files accompanying this book. The video segments can be seen in the online version of *Gaeilge gan Stró! – Beginners Level*, available on Gaelchultúr's e-learning website, www.ranganna.com.

Exercise 10.9: Review of Unit 10

Have a go at this activity now to see if you know the most important phrases taught in Unit 10.

How would you say the following in Irish?

1. I don't feel well.
2. I'm very sick.
3. What's wrong with you?
4. I have a cold.
5. I have a sore throat.
6. How long have you been sick?
7. Are you better?
8. Are you recovering?
9. I'm much better.
10. She has a cough.
11. He has long hair.
12. What does he look like?
13. He has blue eyes.
14. She has nice teeth.
15. I hurt my leg.

Unit 11: Clothes and Shopping
Aonad 11: Éadaí agus Siopadóireacht

In this unit you will learn how to:

- seek and express opinions about items of clothing
- name different items of clothing
- refer to colour, length and size
- differentiate between different goods
- ask about cost and give information about cost.

San aonad seo foghlaimeoidh tú conas:

- *tuairimí a lorg agus a chur in iúl faoi bhaill éadaí*
- *baill éagsúla éadaí a ainmniú*
- *tagairt a dhéanamh do dhath, fad agus toise*
- *idirdhealú a dhéanamh idir earraí éagsúla*
- *fiafraí faoi chostas agus eolas a thabhairt faoi chostas.*

Grammar

- demonstrative adjectives
- personal pronouns
- the prefixes **an-** and **ró-**
- counting euros
- adjectives in the singular and plural

Gramadach

- *aidiachtaí taispeántacha*
- *forainmneacha pearsanta*
- *na réimíreanna **an-** agus **ró-***
- *euronna a chomhaireamh*
- *aidiachtaí san uimhir uatha agus uimhir iolra*

Key sounds

CD 3 TR 47

dhá **ch**éad	(**c** with *séimhiú* followed by slender vowel, **e**)	*two hundred*
deas, mui**d**	(slender **d**)	*nice, we/us*
dath, sia**d**	(broad **d**)	*(a) colour, they*
ró**dh**aor	(**d** with *séimhiú* followed by broad vowel, **a**)	*too expensive*
ró**dh**orcha	(**d** with *séimhiú* followed by broad vowel, **o**)	*too dark*
geansaí	(slender **g**)	*(a) sweater*
gorm	(broad **g**)	*blue*
ró**gh**earr	(**g** with *séimhiú* followed by slender vowel, **e**)	*too short*
dú**gh**orm	(**g** with *séimhiú* followed by broad vowel, **o**)	*navy*
siopa	(slender **s**)	*(a) shop*
crio**s**	(broad **s**)	*(a) belt*

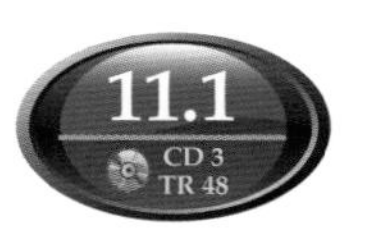

11.1 That shirt is nice

CD 3 TR 48

Here are some useful sentences for expressing opinions on clothes and shoes:

Is maith liom an bríste dearg seo.
I like these red trousers.

Is breá liom na bróga seo.
I love these shoes.

Tá an léine sin go deas.
That shirt is nice.

Tá an geansaí sin go hálainn.
That sweater is lovely.

Tá an sciorta seo rómhór agam.
This skirt is too big for me.

Tá an cóta seo rótheann.
This coat is too tight.

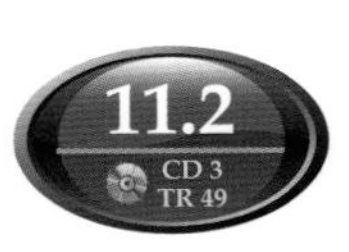

11.2 Do you like this sweater?

CD 3 TR 49

We've already looked at how to ask someone whether or not he likes something and how to answer such a question. The same structures can be used in the context of clothes and shopping:

An maith leat an geansaí seo?
Do you like this sweater?
Is maith.
Yes.

An maith leat an dath sin?
Do you like that colour?
Ní maith.
No.

Here are some other possible answers:

Is breá liom é.
I love it.

Ní maith liom ar chor ar bith é.
I don't like it at all.

Ceapaim go bhfuil sé gránna.
I think it's ugly.

11.3 Seo and sin

CD 3 TR 50

When the demonstrative adjectives **seo** (*this*) and **sin** (*that*) are used in speech, the stress is placed on the preceding noun. It's incorrect to stress the words **seo** and **sin**. Have a look at these examples:

An *cóta* seo.
***This** coat.*

An *léine* sin.
***That** shirt.*

11.4 Personal pronouns as object

CD 3 TR 51

We already looked at the personal pronouns in Unit 1, but let's look again at the various forms:

Singular	Plural
mé *I, me*	**muid** *us, we*
tú *you*	**sibh** *you*
sé *he, it*	**siad** *they*
sí *she, it*	

When personal pronouns in the third person, singular and plural, are the object of a sentence, the initial **s** in those pronouns is lost. Here are some examples:

sé *he, it*	**An maith leat an geansaí seo?** *Do you like this sweater?* **Is breá liom é.** *I love it.*	**é** *he, him, it*
sí *she, it*	**An maith leat an léine seo?** *Do you like this shirt?* **Is breá liom í.** *I love it.*	**í** *she, her, it*
siad *they*	**An maith leat na bróga seo?** *Do you like these shoes?* **Is breá liom iad.** *I love them.*	**iad** *they, them*

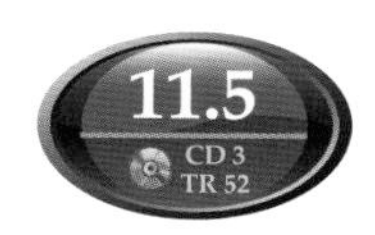

11.5 The appropriate pronoun 1

CD 3 TR 52

As we've already seen, all nouns in Irish are either masculine or feminine. The pronoun you use in place of a noun is determined by the gender of the noun and whether it's in the singular or plural. Let's look at some examples.

The noun **geansaí** (*sweater*) is masculine, therefore the pronoun **é** is used in place of that noun in cases like this:

An maith leat an geansaí sin?
Do you like that sweater?

Is breá liom é.
I love it.

The noun **léine** (*shirt*) is feminine, therefore the pronoun **í** is used in place of that noun in cases like this:

An maith leat an léine seo?
Do you like this shirt?

Is breá liom í.
I love it.

The noun **bróga** (*shoes*) is in the plural, therefore the pronoun **iad** is used in place of that noun in cases like this:

An maith leat na bróga dubha?
Do you like the black shoes?

Is breá liom iad.
I love them.

Vocabulary 1: Shopping and clothes

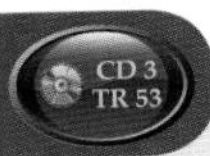

- siopa éadaí / an siopa éadaí / siopaí éadaí — *(a) clothes shop / the clothes shop / clothes shops*
- siopa bróg / an siopa bróg / siopaí bróg — *(a) shoe shop / the shoe shop / shoe shops*
- gúna / an gúna / gúnaí — *(a) dress / the dress / dresses*
- sciorta / an sciorta / sciortaí — *(a) skirt / the skirt / skirts*
- culaith / an chulaith / cultacha — *(a) suit / the suit / suits* or *(a) dress / the dress / dresses*
- léine / an léine / léinte — *(a) shirt / the shirt / shirts*
- carbhat / an carbhat / carbhait — *(a) tie / the tie / ties*
- bríste / an bríste / brístí — *trousers / the trousers / trousers*
- crios / an crios / criosanna — *(a) belt / the belt / belts*
- geansaí / an geansaí / geansaithe — *(a) sweater / the sweater / sweaters*
- cóta báistí / an cóta báistí / cótaí báistí — *(a) raincoat / the raincoat / raincoats*
- seaicéad / an seaicéad / seaicéid — *(a) jacket / the jacket / jackets*
- fo-éadaí — *underwear*
- cíochbheart / an cíochbheart / cíochbhearta — *(a) bra / the bra / bras*
- bróg / an bhróg / bróga — *(a) shoe / the shoe / shoes*
- buatais / an bhuatais / buataisí — *(a) boot / the boot / boots*
- riteoga — *tights*
- stoca / an stoca / stocaí — *(a) stocking / the stocking / stockings*

Exercise 11.1: Answer the questions

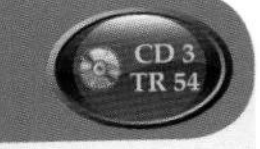

Answer each of these questions as indicated. When a pronoun is required in an answer, make sure you use the correct one. The nouns in numbers 2 and 4 are feminine. The rest are masculine or in the plural.

1. An maith leat an geansaí sin?
   Say: Yes.
2. An maith leat an léine seo?
   Say: No.
3. An maith leat an cóta seo?
   Say: I love it.
4. An maith leat an chulaith sin?
   Say: I don't like it at all.
5. An maith leat na bróga sin?
   Say: I don't like them at all.
6. An maith leat an carbhat seo?
   Say: Yes. I love it.
7. An maith leat na riteoga sin?
   Say: I love them.
8. An maith leat na stocaí seo?
   Say: I don't like them at all.
9. An maith leat na buataisí seo?
   Say: No.
10. An maith leat an gúna seo?
    Say: I love it.

Exercise 11.2: Match the words

Match each Irish word in Column A with its English equivalent in Column B. The first one has been done for you.

	Column A		Column B
1	bróga	a	bra
2	crios	b	underwear
3	gúnaí	c	sweater
4	culaith	e	shoe
5	cóta báistí	f	tights
6	geansaí	g	tie
7	bróg	h	suit / dress
8	fo-éadaí	i	shoes
9	riteoga	j	raincoat
10	carbhat	k	belt
11	geansaithe	l	sweaters
12	cíochbheart	m	dresses

1	2	3	4	5	6	7	8	9	10	11	12
i											

Insight

Schools outside the *Gaeltacht* in which Irish is used by pupils and teachers and in which all subjects are taught through Irish are known as *Gaelscoileanna*. In 1970, there were fewer than ten such schools in Ireland, but due to the efforts of parents in various communities throughout the country, the numbers have increased greatly since then. There are now 172 primary schools (including 33 in Northern Ireland) and 39 post-primary schools (including three in Northern Ireland) in which Irish is the language of instruction. These cater for around 40,000 pupils.

In the Irish Republic, Irish is a compulsory subject in the final school exam, the Leaving Certificate. The majority of Irish people are in favour of this policy, although it's opposed by certain prominent politicians and media commentators. Those who favour the present policy feel that making Irish an optional subject would have an adverse effect on the language.

Conversation 11A

CD 3 TR 55

Helen and Martina are shopping together.

Helen: An maith leat an T-léine seo?
Do you like this T-shirt?

Martina: Ní maith. Ceapaim go bhfuil sí gránna.
No. I think it's ugly.

Helen: Dáiríre! Ceapaimse go bhfuil sí go deas.
*Really! **I** think it's nice.*

Martina: Tá an ceann dearg sin níos deise.
That red one is nicer.

Helen: Tá sí an-daor: tríocha a cúig euro.
It's very expensive: thirty-five euro.

Martina: Tá sin i bhfad ródhaor.
That's far too expensive.

Conversation 11B

Derek is shopping with his girlfriend Eithne and finding that she's hard to please when it comes to clothes!

Derek: An maith leat na bróga seo?
Do you like these shoes?

Eithne: Ní maith liom ar chor ar bith iad. Tá siad gránna.
I don't like them at all. They're ugly.

A little later

Derek: Tá an seaicéad seo go deas, nach bhfuil?
This jacket is nice, isn't it?

Eithne: Níl. Ní maith liom an dath – tá sé ró-éadrom.
No. I don't like the colour – it's too light.

Later still

Derek: An maith leat an cóta seo?
Do you like this coat?

Eithne: Ní maith – tá sé ródhorcha. Agus ródhaor: dhá chéad euro!
No – it's too dark. And too expensive: two hundred euro!

Derek: Tá mise ag dul abhaile …
***I**'m going home …*

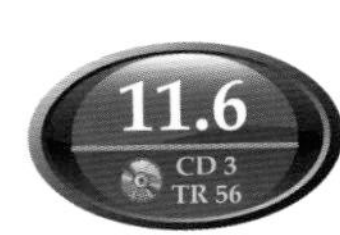

The prefixes an- and ró-

In Unit 7, we looked at the prefixes **an-** (*very*) and **ró-** (*too*). Here is a reminder of the rules:

There is a *séimhiú* on consonants (other than **d**, **t**, **s**) that follow **an-**; vowels that follow it remain unchanged.

There is a *séimhiú* on consonants that follow **ró-**; again, vowels that follow it remain unchanged.

Here are some examples:

fada / an-fhada / rófhada
long / very long / too long

gearr / an-ghearr / róghearr
short / very short / too short

mór / an-mhór / rómhór
big / very big / too big

éadrom / an-éadrom / ró-éadrom
light / very light / too light

dorcha / an-dorcha / ródhorcha
dark / very dark / too dark

The appropriate pronoun 2

As we saw earlier, when personal pronouns in the third person, singular and plural, are the object of a sentence, the initial **s** in those pronouns is lost.

When the pronoun is the subject of the sentence, however, the forms **sé**, **sí** and **siad** are used:

Tá sé go deas.
It's nice.

Tá siad go deas.
They're nice.

As we mentioned earlier, the pronoun you use in place of a noun is determined by the gender of the noun and whether it's in the singular or plural. Let's look at some examples:

The noun **geansaí** (*sweater*) is masculine, therefore the pronoun **sé** is used in place of that noun in cases like this:

An maith leat an geansaí sin?
Do you like that sweater?

Tá sé go deas.
It's nice.

The noun **léine** (*shirt*) is feminine, therefore the pronoun **sí** is used in place of that noun in cases like this:

An maith leat an léine seo?
Do you like this shirt?

Tá sí go hálainn.
It's lovely.

The noun **bróga** (*shoes*) is in the plural, therefore the pronoun **siad** is used in place of that noun in cases like this:

An maith leat na bróga dubha?
Do you like the black shoes?

Tá siad an-deas.
They're very nice.

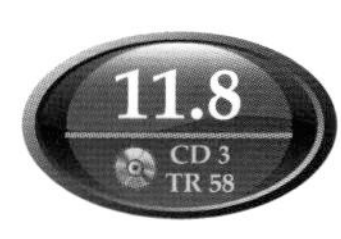

Counting euros

To find out how much something costs, you ask:

Cé mhéad atá sé?
How much is it?
or
Cé mhéad atá siad?
How much are they?
or
Cé mhéad atá an léine sin?
How much is that shirt?

In Units 4 and 9, we looked at counting euros. Let's look at some more prices now:

€20	**fiche euro**
€25	**fiche a cúig euro**
€30	**tríocha euro**
€40	**ceathracha euro**
€50	**caoga euro**
€60	**seasca euro**
€70	**seachtó euro**
€80	**ochtó euro**
€90	**nócha euro**
€100	**céad euro**
€110	**céad is a deich euro**
€220	**dhá chéad fiche euro**
€330	**trí chéad tríocha euro**
€440	**ceithre chéad ceathracha euro**
€550	**cúig chéad caoga euro**

Exercise 11.3: Your turn!

This is your chance to talk now. Pretend you're Martina and that you're talking to Helen.

Helen: An maith leat an T-léine seo?

Say: *No. I think it's ugly.*

Helen: Dáiríre! Ceapaimse go bhfuil sí go deas.

Say: *That red one is nicer.*

Helen: Tá sí an-daor: tríocha a cúig euro.

Say: *That's far too expensive.*

Exercise 11.4: Your turn!

This time, pretend you're Eithne and that you're talking to Derek.

Derek: An maith leat na bróga seo?

Say: *I don't like them at all. They're ugly.*

Derek: Tá an seaicéad seo go deas, nach bhfuil?

Say: *No. I don't like the colour – it's too light.*

Derek: An maith leat an cóta seo?

Say: *No – it's too dark. And too expensive: two hundred euro!*

Derek: Tá mise ag dul abhaile …

Exercise 11.5: Fill in the gaps

Fill in the gaps in these sentences.

1. *I love these shoes.*
   Is breá liom na __________ seo.
2. *That sweater is lovely.*
   Tá an geansaí sin go ______________.
3. *This skirt is too big for me.*
   Tá an sciorta seo _____________ agam.
4. *This coat is too tight.*
   Tá an cóta seo ______________.
5. *I think it's ugly.*
   Ceapaim go __________ sé gránna.
6. *Do you like them?*
   An maith leat _______?
7. *Do you like this shirt? I love it.*
   An maith leat an léine seo? Is breá liom ____.
8. *I don't like it at all.*
   Ní maith liom ar ________ ar bith é.
9. *This jacket is nice, isn't it?*
   Tá an seaicéad seo go deas, nach __________?
10. *It's too dark.*
    Tá sé _________________.

Exercise 11.6: Answer the questions

Answer each of these questions as indicated.

1. Tá an sciorta seo go deas, nach bhfuil?
   Say: No. It's too short.
2. An maith leat an gúna seo?
   Say: No. It's very long.
3. An maith leat na stocaí seo?
   Say: No. They're very dark.
4. An maith leat na bróga seo?
   Say: Yes. They're lovely.
5. Cé mhéad atá sé?
   Say: Fifty euro.
6. Cé mhéad atá an cóta sin?
   Say: Two hundred and twenty euro.
7. Cé mhéad atá an léine sin?
   Say: Sixty euro.
8. Cé mhéad atá siad?
   Say: Twenty-five euro.

Vocabulary 2: Colours, length and size

CD 3 TR 61

- glas — *green*
- gorm — *blue*
- dúghorm — *navy*
- dearg — *red*
- donn — *brown*
- buí — *yellow*
- dubh — *black*
- bán — *white*
- liath — *grey*
- bándearg — *pink*
- corcra — *purple*
- geal — *bright*
- dorcha — *dark*
- fada — *long*
- gearr — *short*
- mór — *big*
- beag — *small*

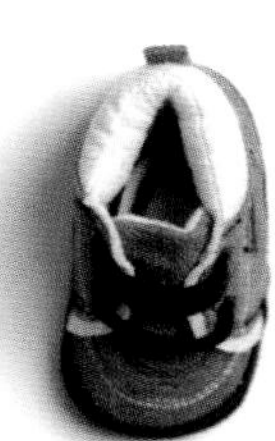

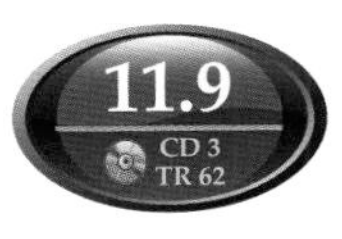

11.9 Which one?

CD 3 TR 62

We came across the word **ceann** (*one*, of things, animals) already, in Unit 4. This word is also used to differentiate between things.

Sinéad: **An maith leat an cóta seo?**
Do you like this coat?

Peadar: **Cé acu ceann?**
Which one?

Sinéad: **An ceann seo.**
This one.

11.10 Adjectives in the plural

CD 3 TR 63

As we saw in the previous unit, adjectives agree with the noun in gender, number and case. When an adjective is used with the plural form of **bróg**, i.e. **bróga**, for example, that adjective must be in the plural as well:

Tá na bróga dubha sin go deas.
Those black shoes are nice.

In the plural, **-e** is added to adjectives ending in a slender consonant (i.e. a consonant preceded by **i** or **e**):

Singular	Plural
maith *good*	**maithe**
binn *sweet (of sound)*	**binne**

An -**a** is added to adjectives ending in a broad consonant (i.e. a consonant preceded by **a**, **o** or **u**):

Singular	Plural
bán *white*	**bána**
dearg *red*	**dearga**
geal *bright*	**geala**
mór *big*	**móra**
beag *small*	**beaga**
deas *nice*	**deasa**

Adjectives ending in a vowel don't undergo any change:

Singular	Plural
gránna *ugly*	**gránna**
dorcha *dark*	**dorcha**
fada *long*	**fada**

Conversation 11C

Helen and Martina are still shopping!

Martina: An maith leat an hata sin?
Do you like that hat?

Helen: Cé acu ceann?
Which one?

Martina: An ceann dubh agus dearg sin.
That black and red one.

Helen: Tá sé an-mhór. Agus an-daor, déarfainn.
It's very big. And very expensive, I'd say.

Martina: Tá sé daor go leor: ochtó euro.
It's expensive enough: eighty euro.

Conversation 11D

Caitríona and her friend Janice talk about their recent purchases.

Caitríona: Cheannaigh mé sciorta nua inné.
I bought a new skirt yesterday.

Janice: Ó? An bhfuil sé go deas?
Oh? Is it nice?

Caitríona: Tá sé go hálainn. Tá dath deas gorm air agus tá sé an-ghearr.
It's lovely. It's a nice blue colour and it's very short.

Janice: Cheannaigh mé féin buataisí dubha ag an deireadh seachtaine.
I bought black boots myself at the weekend.

Caitríona: Bhí siad an-daor, is dócha!
They were very expensive, I suppose!

Janice: Bhí, ach is cuma liom!
Yes, but I don't care!

11.11 Nouns and adjectives

As we saw in Unit 10, a *séimhiú* is added to the beginning of adjectives when they qualify nouns that are feminine, in most cases in the singular.

The noun **ceann**, which was used in Conversation 11C, is masculine, however, and therefore no change is made to the initial consonant of the adjective which follows it:

An ceann dubh agus dearg sin.
That black and red one.

Here are some more examples of nouns followed by an adjective:

Masculine noun + adjective	Feminine noun + adjective
gúna glas *a green dress*	**léine ghlas** *a green shirt*
geansaí gorm *a blue sweater*	**culaith ghorm** *a blue suit*
cóta dearg *a red coat*	**léine dhearg** *a red shirt*
seaicéad donn *a brown jacket*	**culaith dhonn** *a brown suit*
gúna buí *a yellow dress*	**léine bhuí** *a yellow shirt*
geansaí dubh *a black sweater*	**culaith dhubh** *a black suit*
cóta geal *a bright coat*	**léine gheal** *a bright shirt*
seaicéad corcra *a purple jacket*	**culaith chorcra** *a purple suit*
sciorta gearr *a short skirt*	**léine ghearr** *a short shirt*
cóta fada *a long coat*	**culaith fhada** *a long dress*
geansaí mór *a big sweater*	**léine mhór** *a big shirt*
cóta beag *a small coat*	**culaith bheag** *a small dress*

Exercise 11.7: Your turn!

This is your chance to talk now. Pretend you're Martina and that you're talking to Helen.

Say: *Do you like that hat?*

Helen: Cé acu ceann?

Say: *That black and red one.*

Helen: Tá sé an-mhór. Agus an-daor, déarfainn.

Say: *It's expensive enough: eighty euro.*

Exercise 11.8: Your turn!

This time, pretend you're Janice and that you're talking to Caitríona.

Caitríona: Cheannaigh mé sciorta nua inné.

Say: *Oh? Is it nice?*

Caitríona: Tá sé go hálainn. Tá dath deas gorm air agus tá sé an-ghearr.

Say: *I bought black boots myself at the weekend.*

Caitríona: Bhí siad an-daor, is dócha!

Say: *Yes, but I don't care!*

Useful tips for learners

Each unit in this book contains many new words and phrases to learn, and it won't be possible for you to master all this language at the same time. You should, therefore, concentrate on learning what you regard as the most useful language. Say these words and phrases to yourself, and practise saying them aloud as you drive or do everyday tasks such as ironing.

Talking heads

Siobhán Patten (filmed in Temple Bar, Dublin)
Is breá liom éadaí agus faisean agus téim ag siopadóireacht d'éadaí aon seans a fhaighim.

Chuaigh mé ag siopadóireacht d'éadaí i gcomhair an tsamhraidh ansin le déanaí agus cheannaigh mé brístí géine, seaicéad agus cúpla gúna.

Páidí Ó Lionáird (filmed in An Spidéal, Galway)
Téim ag siopadóireacht i siopa Louis Copeland i nGaillimh de ghnáth. Taitníonn an siopa sin go mór liom mar tugann Mike agus John an-aire dom i gcónaí.

Is maith liom bheith ag siopadóireacht agus caithfidh mé a admháil go bhfuil laige na mbróg orm. Ceannaím péire bróg nua aon uair a bhím i dtír nó i gcathair nua. Is leor le rá go bhfuil i bhfad an iomarca péirí bróg agam dá bharr.

Caoimhe Ní Chonchoille (filmed in An Spidéal, Galway)
Ní chaithim an oiread sin airgid ar éadaí. Is breá liom na siopaí i Nua-Eabhrac siocair go bhfuil rogha i bhfad níos fearr iontu agus bíonn na héadaí ansin measartha saor de ghnáth. Is maith liom cuid mhór cineálacha éadaí ach déanaim iarracht cloí le stíleanna a oireann dom féin.

Téim ag siopadóireacht go measartha minic agus is maith liom é fhad is nach mbíonn na sluaite sna siopaí.

TRANSLATION

Siobhán Patten
I love clothes and fashion and I go shopping for clothes any chance I get.

I went shopping for clothes for the summer there recently and I bought jeans, a jacket and a few dresses.

Páidí Ó Lionáird
I usually go shopping in Louis Copeland's shop in Galway. I really like that shop because Mike and John always take great care of me.

I like shopping and I have to admit that I have a weakness for shoes. I buy a new pair of shoes any time I'm in a new country or city. Suffice to say that I have far too many pairs of shoes as a result of that.

Caoimhe Ní Chonchoille
I don't spend that much money on clothes. I love the shops in New York because there's a much better choice in them and the clothes there are usually quite inexpensive. I like many types of clothes but I try to stick to styles which suit me.

I go shopping reasonably often and I like it so long as there aren't crowds in the shops.

Exercise 11.9: Review of Unit 11

Have a go at this activity now to see if you know the most important phrases taught in Unit 11.

How would you say the following in Irish?

1. I like these red trousers.
2. I love these shoes.
3. That sweater is lovely.
4. Do you like this skirt? Yes.
5. Do you like that colour? No.
6. I think it's ugly.
7. This coat.
8. That shirt.
9. Do you like these shoes?
10. I love them.
11. How much is it?
12. How much are they?
13. How much is that shirt?
14. Which one?
15. This one.

Unit 12: Requests and Commands
Aonad 12: Garanna agus Orduithe

In this unit you will learn how to:
- give an order to one person
- give an order to more than one person
- warn someone
- give directions inside a building.

Grammar
- the imperative mood, singular and plural, affirmative and negative
- the possessive adjectives **do** and **bhur**
- the vocative case
- dependent forms

San aonad seo foghlaimeoidh tú conas:
- *ordú a thabhairt do dhuine amháin*
- *ordú a thabhairt do níos mó ná duine amháin*
- *foláireamh a thabhairt do dhuine*
- *treoracha a thabhairt taobh istigh d'fhoirgneamh.*

Gramadach
- *an modh ordaitheach, uatha agus iolra, dearfach agus diúltach*
- *na haidiachtaí sealbhacha* ***do*** *agus* ***bhur***
- *an tuiseal gairmeach*
- *foirmeacha spleácha*

Key sounds

CD 3 TR 69

do **bh**ricfeasta	(**b** with *séimhiú* followed by slender vowel, **i**)	*your breakfast*
cíor	(slender **c**)	*comb*
cuir ort	(broad **c**)	*put on*
do **ch**eann	(**c** with *séimhiú* followed by slender vowel, **e**)	*your head*
déan **d**eifir	(slender **d**)	*hurry up*
dún an **d**oras	(broad **d**)	*close the door*
éa**d**aí	(broad **d**)	*clothes*
grua**ig**	(broad **g** and slender **g**)	*hair*
nigh	(slender **n**)	*wash*
bhur **n**-aghaidh	(broad **n**)	*your faces*
suigh **s**íos	(broad **s** and slender **s**)	*sit down*
a **Sh**inéad	(**s** with *séimhiú*)	*Sinéad*

Come in

The imperative mood is the form of the verb used in the case of direct commands.

Below are two sentences containing the imperative mood which can be used when visitors come calling. The sentences in the column on the left are used when addressing one person and those in the column on the right are used when more than one person is being addressed.

Singular	Plural
Tar isteach. *Come in.*	**Tagaigí isteach.** *Come in.*
Suigh síos. *Sit down.*	**Suígí síos.** *Sit down.*

The instructions above are neutral and can be used when speaking to adults and to children, formally or informally.

Most of the phrases containing the imperative mood in the remaining part of the unit are usually only used when addressing children or a close friend. Be careful, then, not to use them when speaking to someone who's not a member of the family or a friend as you might cause offence!

Note: *The second person singular, imperative mood of the verb is the form used as the head word in Irish dictionaries.*

Get up!

The sentences below might prove useful first thing in the morning, when trying to get kids organised!

Singular	Plural
Éirigh! *Get up!*	**Éirígí!** *Get up!*
Cuir ort do chuid éadaí. *Put on your clothes.*	**Cuirigí oraibh bhur gcuid éadaí.** *Put on your clothes.*
Nigh d'aghaidh. *Wash your face.*	**Nígí bhur n-aghaidh.** *Wash your faces.*
Cíor do chuid gruaige. *Comb your hair.*	**Cíoraigí bhur gcuid gruaige.** *Comb your hair.*
Ith do bhricfeasta. *Eat your breakfast.*	**Ithigí bhur mbricfeasta.** *Eat your breakfast.*
Déan deifir. *Hurry up.*	**Déanaigí deifir.** *Hurry up.*

Do, d' and bhur

As we mentioned in Unit 3, **mo** (*my*) and **do** (*your*) are shortened when they precede a noun beginning with a vowel:

Nigh do lámha.
Wash your hands.
but
Nigh d'aghaidh.
Wash your face.

In the second person plural, the form **bhur** (*your*) is used. An *urú* is added to vowels and consonants which follow **bhur**:

Nígí bhur n-aghaidh.
Wash your faces.

Cuirigí oraibh bhur mbróga.
Put on your shoes.

Quiet!

The sentences below can be used with bold children or others who are misbehaving!

Singular	Plural
Ciúnas! *Quiet!*	**Ciúnas!** *Quiet!*
Bí ciúin! *Be quiet!*	**Bígí ciúin!** *Be quiet!*
Ná bí ag caint. *Stop talking* (literally, *don't be talking*).	**Ná bígí ag caint.** *Stop talking.*
Ná bí dána. *Don't be bold.*	**Ná bígí dána.** *Don't be bold.*

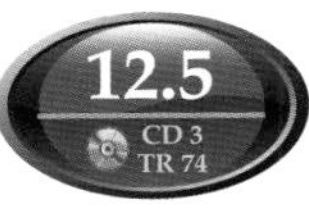

The negative

Ná, the negative verbal particle used in the imperative mood, does not change the beginning of verbs which have an initial consonant:

> **Ná bí dána!**
> *Don't be bold!*

An **h** is prefixed to verbs beginning with a vowel, however:

> **Ná hith na brioscaí go léir, a Ruth.**
> *Don't eat all the biscuits, Ruth.*

Insight

Various non-governmental organisations are engaged in the promotion of the Irish language throughout Ireland. Conradh na Gaeilge (The Gaelic League) (www.cnag.ie) is one of the best known and longest established of these. The organisation was founded in Dublin in July 1893 by a group of language activists, including Douglas Hyde, the son of a Church of Ireland rector from Roscommon who would later become the first president of Ireland.

Conradh na Gaeilge's headquarters are located in Harcourt Street, Dublin. Conradh's language classes are held there and the building also houses a bookshop and a social club.

Oireachtas na Gaeilge (www.antoireachtas.ie), the main Irish language festival, was established by Conradh in 1897, and still takes place annually in late October or early November. More than 10,000 people attend the event, which is held in a different location each year. Another Conradh na Gaeilge initiative, Seachtain na Gaeilge (Irish language week) (www.snag.ie), takes place in the days leading up to St Patrick's Day and has grown greatly in popularity in recent years, both in Ireland and abroad.

Exercise 12.1: The appropriate sentence

What sentence would be appropriate in each context?

1. You would like someone to sit down.
2. You'd like your children to get up.
3. You want someone to come in.
4. You want more than one person to come in.
5. You would like your son to wash his face.
6. You want your daughter to eat her breakfast.
7. You want someone to hurry.
8. You want your children to comb their hair.
9. You'd like your sons to stop being bold.
10. You don't want your daughter to eat all the biscuits.

Conversation 12A

Gearóid is having dinner in Angela's house with a few friends of theirs.

Angela: Á, Gearóid – tá fáilte romhat. Tar isteach.
Ah, Gearóid – you're welcome. Come in.

Gearóid: Go raibh maith agat, a Angela. Tá brón orm go bhfuil mé déanach.
Thank you, Angela. I'm sorry I'm late.

Angela: Ná bí buartha. Níl gach duine anseo fós.
Don't worry. Not everyone is here yet.

Gearóid: Sin faoiseamh!
That's a relief!

Angela: Suigh ansin in aice le Hilary agus lig do scíth. Cad ba mhaith leat a ól?
Sit there beside Hilary and rest yourself. What would you like to drink?

Conversation 12B

Áine is having a lot of difficulty getting her children organised for school. Listen to her giving them various orders.

Áine: Éirígí! Tá sé ceathrú tar éis a hocht.
Get up! It's a quarter past eight.

Ten minutes later

Áine: Nígí bhur n-aghaidh. A Shinéad, cíor do chuid gruaige.
Wash your faces. Sinéad, comb your hair.

Five minutes later

Áine: A Pheadair, ith do bhricfeasta. Déan deifir.
Peadar, eat your breakfast. Hurry up.

Just before they leave for school

Áine: A pháistí, nígí bhur lámha anois. Déanaigí deifir – tá sibh déanach.
Children, wash your hands now. Hurry up – you're late.

12.6 The vocative case

CD 3 TR 77

As we mentioned in earlier units, the vocative case is used when addressing someone directly. Changes occur to the beginning of many Irish language names, both male and female, in the vocative case and also to the end of some male names.

Here are two examples from Conversation 12B:

A Shinéad, cíor do chuid gruaige.
Sinéad, comb your hair.

A Pheadair, ith do bhricfeasta. Déan deifir.
Peadar, eat your breakfast. Hurry up.

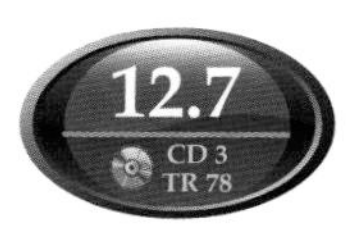

12.7 Dependent forms

CD 3 TR 78

In Unit 8, we looked at dependent forms of the verb. As we saw in that unit, the conjunction **go** (*that*) is followed by a dependent form of the verb. Here's an example from Conversation 12A:

Tá brón orm go bhfuil mé déanach.
I'm sorry (that) I'm late.

Exercise 12.2: Your turn!

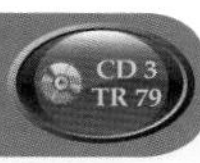

This is your chance to talk now. Pretend you're Angela and that you're talking to Gearóid.

Say: *Ah, Gearóid – you're welcome. Come in.*

Gearóid: Go raibh maith agat, a Angela. Tá brón orm go bhfuil mé déanach.

Say: *Don't worry. Not everyone is here yet.*

Gearóid: Sin faoiseamh!

Say: *Sit there beside Hilary and rest yourself. What would you like to drink?*

Exercise 12.3: Your turn!

This time, pretend you're Áine and that you're talking to your children.

Say: *Get up! It's a quarter past eight.*

Say: *Wash your faces. Sinéad, comb your hair.*

Say: *Peadar, eat your breakfast. Hurry up.*

Say: *Children, wash your hands now. Hurry up – you're late.*

Exercise 12.4: Translate the sentences

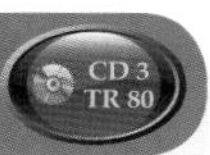

Give the Irish version of each of these sentences.
One person is being addressed in 1–5 and more than one person in 6–10.

1. Don't be bold.
2. Get up!

3. Comb your hair.
4. Put on your clothes.
5. Wash your hands.
6. Wash your faces.
7. Hurry up.
8. Stop talking.
9. Be quiet!
10. Wash your hands.

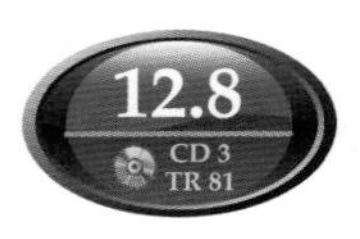

Wash the dishes

Here are some more sentences that would be appropriate to use with children:

Singular	Plural
Nigh na gréithe. *Wash the dishes.*	**Nígí na gréithe.** *Wash the dishes.*
Glan do sheomra. *Clean your room.*	**Glanaigí bhur seomraí.** *Clean your rooms.*
Déan d'obair bhaile. *Do your homework.*	**Déanaigí bhur n-obair bhaile.** *Do your homework.*
Oscail an fhuinneog sin. *Open that window.*	**Osclaígí na fuinneoga sin.** *Open those windows.*
Dún an doras. *Close the door.*	**Dúnaigí na doirse.** *Close the doors.*

Mind your head!

This is how you warn someone who's about to do harm to himself or someone/something else:

Seachain do cheann!
Mind your head!

Seachain an cat!
Mind the cat!

This is the plural form:

Seachnaígí na bláthanna.
Mind the flowers.

Get away from me!

If someone is annoying you, you can say:

Imigh leat!
Get away from me!

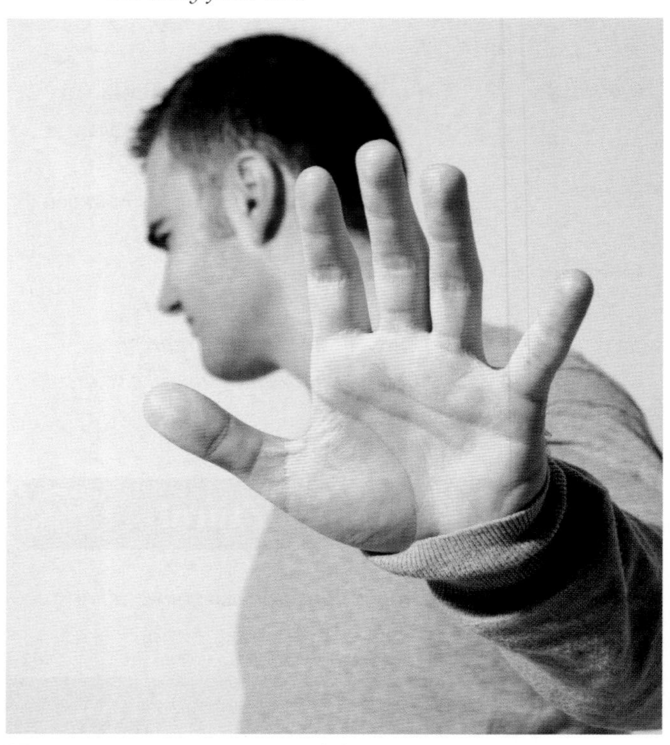

Here are some more useful sentences containing the imperative mood:

Singular	Plural
Fan liom. *Wait for me.*	**Fanaigí liom.** *Wait for me.*
Déan do dhícheall. *Do your best.*	**Déanaigí bhur ndícheall.** *Do your best.*
Ná habair sin leis. *Don't say that to him.*	**Ná habraigí sin leis.** *Don't say that to him.*
Tabhair cabhair dó. *Give him help.*	**Tugaigí cabhair dó.** *Give him help.*
Ná tabhair aon airgead dó. *Don't give him any money.*	**Ná tugaigí aon airgead dó.** *Don't give him any money.*

Conversation 12C

Eoin is in bed sick and feeling sorry for himself. His long-suffering wife is taking care of him.

Eoin: Tabhair dom an cupán sin.
Give me that cup.

Bairbre: Seo dhuit.
Here you are.

Eoin: Agus oscail an fhuinneog sin – tá sé an-te istigh anseo.
And open that window – it's very warm in here.

Bairbre: Ach bhí tú rófhuar cúpla nóiméad ó shin!
But you were too cold a few minutes ago!

Eoin: Tá mé te anois. Ó, agus múch an raidió sin – tá tinneas cinn ag teacht orm.
I'm warm now. Oh, and turn off that radio – I'm getting a headache.

Bairbre: Tá tinneas cinn ag teacht orm féin …
I'm getting a headache myself …

Eoin: Agus dún an doras i do dhiaidh. Tá mise chun codladh tamall.
*And close the door after you. **I**'m going to sleep for a while.*

Conversation 12D

Susan and Breandán are attending an Irish language conference in Trinity College Dublin. They ask one of the organisers where the toilets are.

Susan: Gabh mo leithscéal – cá bhfuil leithreas na mban?
Excuse me – where is the ladies' toilet?

Diarmuid: Téigh síos an halla agus cas ar dheis. Tá sé ansin ar thaobh na láimhe clé.
Go down the hall and turn right. It's there on the left-hand side.

Susan: Go raibh maith agat.
Thank you.

Breandán: Agus leithreas na bhfear?
And the men's toilet?

Diarmuid: Téigh suas ansin agus cas ar chlé. Tá sé ar thaobh na láimhe deise, in aice leis an siopa.
Go up there and turn left. It's on the right-hand side, beside the shop.

Go straight ahead

Here are some other useful phrases that can be used when giving directions:

Téigh díreach ar aghaidh.
Go straight ahead.

Téigh suas an staighre.
Go up the stairs.

Téigh síos an staighre.
Go down the stairs.

Tá sé ag barr an staighre.
It's at the top of the stairs.

These are the plural forms of **téigh** and **cas**:

Téigí suas an staighre agus casaigí ar dheis.
Go up the stairs and turn right.

Exercise 12.5: Translate the sentences

Give the Irish version of each of these sentences. One person is being addressed in 1–5 and more than one person in 6–10.

1. Mind your head!
2. Close that window.
3. Open the door.
4. Get away from me!
5. Don't wait for me.
6. Don't give him any money.
7. Close the doors.
8. Open those windows.
9. Wash the dishes.
10. Don't say that to him.

Exercise 12.6: Your turn!

This is your chance to talk now. Pretend you're Eoin and that you're talking to Bairbre.

Say: *Give me that cup.*

Bairbre: Seo dhuit.

Say: *And open that window – it's very warm in here.*

Bairbre: Ach bhí tú rófhuar cúpla nóiméad ó shin!

Say: *I'm warm now. Oh, and turn off that radio – I'm getting a headache.*

Bairbre: Tá tinneas cinn ag teacht orm féin …

Say: *And close the door after you. **I'm** going to sleep for a while.*

Exercise 12.7: Your turn!

This time, pretend you're Diarmuid and that you're talking to Susan and Breandán.

Susan: Gabh mo leithscéal – cá bhfuil leithreas na mban?

Say: *Go down the hall and turn right. It's there on the left-hand side.*

Susan: Go raibh maith agat.

Breandán: Agus leithreas na bhfear?

Say: *Go up there and turn left. It's on the right-hand side, beside the shop.*

Useful tips for learners

People learn languages in different ways. Something which works well for one person might not prove too useful for another. You should try various learning strategies and then stick to those which work best for you, rather than using the same approach being employed by someone else. Perhaps you're someone who needs to study grammar in detail or perhaps rules totally confuse you, and you prefer to listen to recordings or to read. You won't know until you've tried various strategies.

Exercise 12.8: Review of Unit 12

Have a go at this activity now to see if you know the most important phrases taught in Unit 12.

How would you say the following in Irish? You're addressing one person in numbers 1–9 and more than one person in numbers 10–15.

1. Come in.
2. Sit down.
3. Get up!
4. Clean your room.
5. Open that window.
6. Close the door.
7. Mind your head.
8. Go straight ahead.
9. Go up the stairs.
10. Come in.
11. Eat your breakfast.
12. Don't be bold.
13. Clean your rooms.
14. Wait for me.
15. Don't give him any money.

Unit 13: Last Weekend

Aonad 13: An Deireadh Seachtaine Seo Caite

In this unit you will learn how to:

- ask someone what he did at the weekend and answer that question
- ask someone what he did at a particular time and answer that question
- ask someone when he did a particular thing and answer that question
- ask someone if he did a particular thing and answer that question
- give an account of what you did at the weekend
- describe the weather.

Grammar

- statements in the past tense 1
- questions and answers in the past tense 1
- **chuig**, **go dtí** and **go**
- adverbs of time

San aonad seo foghlaimeoidh tú conas:

- *fiafraí de dhuine cad a rinne sé ag an deireadh seachtaine agus an cheist sin a fhreagairt*
- *fiafraí de dhuine cad a rinne sé ag am faoi leith agus an cheist sin a fhreagairt*
- *fiafraí de dhuine cathain a rinne sé rud faoi leith agus an cheist sin a fhreagairt*
- *fiafraí de dhuine an ndearna sé rud ar leith agus an cheist sin a fhreagairt*
- *cur síos a thabhairt ar nithe a rinne tú ag an deireadh seachtaine*
- *cur síos a dhéanamh ar an aimsir.*

Gramadach

- *ráitis san aimsir chaite 1*
- *ceisteanna agus freagraí san aimsir chaite 1*
- ***chuig, go dtí** agus **go***
- *dobhriathra ama*

Key sounds

CD 4 TR 1

cheannaigh mé	(**c** with *séimhiú* followed by slender vowel, **e**)	*I bought*
chonaic mé	(**c** with *séimhiú* followed by broad vowel, **o**)	*I saw*
chuig an **gc**lub	(**c** with *urú*)	*to the club*
an **nd**eachaigh tú?	(**d** with *urú*)	*did you go?*
ciúi**n**	(slender **n**)	*quiet*
mórá**n**	(broad **n**)	*much*
thug mé cuairt ar **Ph**ádraigín	(**p** with *séimhiú*)	*I visited Pádraigín*
Dé Sathai**r**n	(slender **r**)	*Saturday*
ag staidéa**r**	(broad **r**)	*studying*
thug mé	(**t** with *séimhiú*)	*I gave*

What did you do at the weekend?

To find out what someone did at the weekend, you can ask:

Cad a rinne tú ag an deireadh seachtaine?
What did you do at the weekend?

Here are some possible answers:

Chuaigh mé go Gaillimh.
I went to Galway.

Chuaigh mé abhaile go Maigh Eo.
I went home to Mayo.

Thug mé cuairt ar Phádraigín.
I visited Pádraigín.

Bhí mé ag staidéar.
I was studying.

Bhí mé ag obair Dé Sathairn agus Dé Domhnaigh.
I was working on Saturday and Sunday.

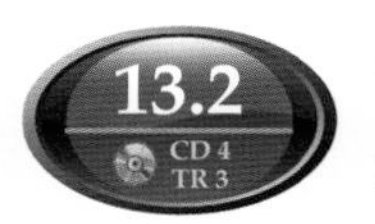

What did you do on Saturday night?

To find out what someone did at a particular time during the weekend, you can ask:

Cad a rinne tú oíche Dé Sathairn?
What did you do on Saturday night?
Chuaigh mé chuig scannán le Liz.
I went to a film with Liz.

Cad a rinne tú maidin Dé Domhnaigh?
What did you do on Sunday morning?
Chuaigh mé ar shiúlóid le Chris.
I went on a walk with Chris.

As we mentioned in Unit 6, there's no need to use the simple preposition **ar** (*on*) in cases like the above – it would be incorrect, in fact, to say or to write ***ar maidin Dé Domhnaigh**.

The past tense 1 (general)

The past tense is a verb tense that expresses actions or states in the past:

Chuaigh mé chuig dráma oíche Dé Domhnaigh.
I went to a play on Sunday night.

Bhí mé an-tuirseach.
I was very tired.

The past tense 2 (regular verbs)

Regular verbs beginning with a consonant
The past tense is formed by adding a *séimhiú* to the second person singular, imperative mood form of the verb:

ceannaigh	**Cheannaigh mé bróga nua.**
buy	*I bought new shoes.*

Regular verbs beginning with a vowel or f
The past tense is formed by placing **d'** before the verb:

ól	**D'ól mé trí phionta.**
drink	*I drank three pints.*
fan	**D'fhan mé ansin thar oíche.**
stay	*I stayed there overnight.*

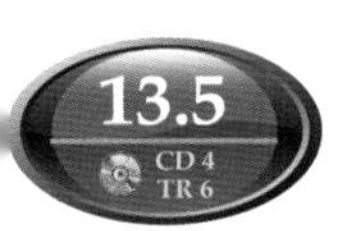

The past tense 3 (the negative)

Regular verbs
To form the negative in the past tense, **níor** is placed before regular verbs. The *séimhiú* remains in the case of verbs beginning with a consonant:

Cheannaigh sí bróga nua.
She bought new shoes.

Níor cheannaigh sí bróga nua.
She didn't buy new shoes.

In the case of verbs beginning with a vowel or **f**, the **d'** is lost:

D'fhan sé ansin thar oíche.
He stayed there overnight.

Níor fhan sé ansin thar oíche.
He didn't stay there overnight.

D'ól mé trí phionta.
I drank three pints.

Níor ól mé trí phionta.
I didn't drink three pints.

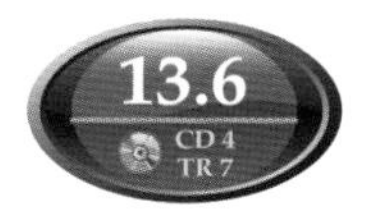

The past tense 4 (questions and answers)

Regular verbs
To form a question in the past tense, **ar** is placed before regular verbs. The *séimhiú* remains in the case of verbs beginning with a consonant:

Ar cheannaigh sí carr nua?
Did she buy a new car?
Cheannaigh./Níor cheannaigh.
Yes./No.

In the case of verbs beginning with a vowel or **f**, the **d'** is lost in the question:

Ar fhan siad sa bhaile?
Did they stay at home?
D'fhan./Níor fhan.
Yes./No.

Ar ól sí mórán?
Did she drink much?
D'ól./Níor ól.
Yes./No.

Note that a pronoun (e.g. **mé**, **tú**, **siad**) is not used when answering a question in the affirmative or in the negative in the past tense. A pronoun must be used, of course, when a statement is being made:

Cheannaigh sí carr nua.
She bought a new car.

The past tense 5 (irregular verbs)

Irregular verbs
There are only eleven irregular verbs in Irish. The past tense forms of those verbs are given below; it's important to learn these as they are the most frequently used verbs.

We're going to learn how to make statements in the past tense and return to questions and answers later in this unit.

Verb	1st person singular	2nd person singular	3rd person singular	1st person plural	2nd person plural	3rd person plural
abair (*say, sing*)	**dúirt mé** *I said*	**dúirt tú** *you said*	**dúirt sé/sí** *he/she said*	**dúramar** *we said*	**dúirt sibh** *you said*	**dúirt siad** *they said*
beir (*bring, take*)	**rug mé** *I brought*	**rug tú** *you brought*	**rug sé/sí** *he/she brought*	**rugamar** *we brought*	**rug sibh** *you brought*	**rug siad** *they brought*
bí (*be*)	**bhí mé** *I was*	**bhí tú** *you were*	**bhí sé/sí** *he/she was*	**bhíomar** *we were*	**bhí sibh** *you were*	**bhí siad** *they were*
clois (*hear*)	**chuala mé** *I heard*	**chuala tú** *you heard*	**chuala sé/sí** *he/she heard*	**chualamar** *we heard*	**chuala sibh** *you heard*	**chuala siad** *they heard*
déan (*do, make*)	**rinne mé** *I made*	**rinne tú** *you made*	**rinne sé/sí** *he/she made*	**rinneamar** *we made*	**rinne sibh** *you made*	**rinne siad** *they made*
faigh (*get*)	**fuair mé** *I got*	**fuair tú** *you got*	**fuair sé/sí** *he/she got*	**fuaireamar** *we got*	**fuair sibh** *you got*	**fuair siad** *they got*
feic (*see*)	**chonaic mé** *I saw*	**chonaic tú** *you saw*	**chonaic sé/sí** *he/she saw*	**chonaiceamar** *we saw*	**chonaic sibh** *you saw*	**chonaic siad** *they saw*
ith (*eat*)	**d'ith mé** *I ate*	**d'ith tú** *you ate*	**d'ith sé/sí** *he/she ate*	**d'itheamar** *we ate*	**d'ith sibh** *you ate*	**d'ith siad** *they ate*
tabhair (*give*)	**thug mé** *I gave*	**thug tú** *you gave*	**thug sé/sí** *he/she gave*	**thugamar** *we gave*	**thug sibh** *you gave*	**thug siad** *they gave*
tar (*come*)	**tháinig mé** *I came*	**tháinig tú** *you came*	**tháinig sé/sí** *he/she came*	**thángamar** *we came*	**tháinig sibh** *you came*	**tháinig siad** *they came*
téigh (*go*)	**chuaigh mé** *I went*	**chuaigh tú** *you went*	**chuaigh sé/sí** *he/she went*	**chuamar** *we went*	**chuaigh sibh** *you went*	**chuaigh siad** *they went*

Note that the pronouns **mé** and **sé** sound different when used with a verb, rather than on their own.

Exercise 13.1: Give the Irish version

Give the Irish version of each past tense form of the verb and the accompanying pronoun.

1. she bought
2. I didn't drink
3. he didn't stay
4. we said
5. they were
6. you (singular) ate

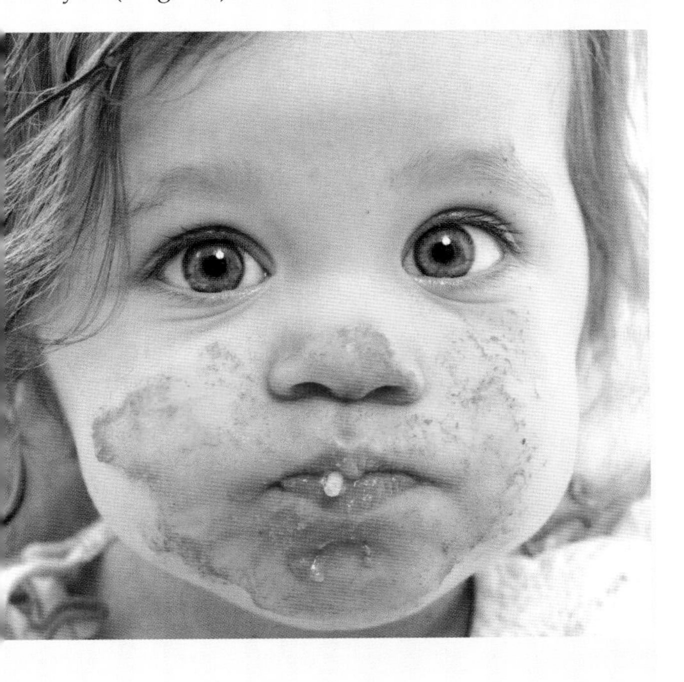

7. you (plural) went
8. we got
9. I did
10. she said
11. they gave
12. I came
13. I saw
14. they went
15. I heard

Insight

Daltaí na Gaeilge (www.daltai.com), a non-profit Irish language organisation based on the east coast of America, is dedicated to promoting and teaching the language. It was founded in 1981 by Ethel Brogan, an Armagh native who emigrated to the US in 1946. All of the organisation's work is done by a group of dedicated volunteers.

Daltaí runs immersion programmes throughout the year in New York State, New Jersey and Pennsylvania. These programmes offer classes which are suitable for every level of ability, from total beginners to native speakers, and attract learners of all ages. More than thirty people attended Daltaí's first programme in 1981; these days, the organisation's weekend courses attract well over a hundred learners.

Other organisations and individuals throughout Canada and the US also run Irish language courses and events throughout the year. Nikki Ragsdale's *Gaeltacht* Weekend in San Francisco, for example, has been held every September since 1999 and continues to attract learners from many West Coast states.

Conversation 13A

During coffee break on Monday morning, Tomás tells his colleague Karl about the weekend.

Karl: Cad a rinne tú ag an deireadh seachtaine?
What did you do at the weekend?

Tomás: Bhí deireadh seachtaine ciúin go leor agam. Bhí mé an-tuirseach.
I had a quiet enough weekend. I was very tired.

Karl: An ndeachaigh tú amach mórán?
Did you go out much?

Tomás: D'fhan mé sa bhaile oíche Dé hAoine ach chuaigh mé amach oíche Dé Sathairn.
I stayed at home on Friday night but I went out on Saturday night.

Karl: Cén áit a ndeachaigh tú?
Where did you go?

Tomás: Chuaigh mé féin agus Laura chuig an gclub nua sin ar Shráid an Chaisleáin. Bhí an-oíche againn.
Myself and Laura went to that new club on Castle Street. We had a great night.

Conversation 13B

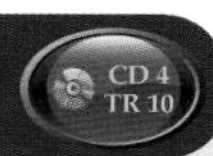

Tomás now finds out what Karl did.

Tomás: Cad a rinne tú féin ag an deireadh seachtaine?
What did you do yourself at the weekend?

Karl: Bhí am iontach agam! Chuaigh mé amach gach oíche.
I had a great time! I went out every night.

Tomás: Tá tú lán fuinnimh! Ar bhuail tú le Jenny agus Susan oíche Dé hAoine?
You're full of energy! Did you meet Jenny and Susan on Friday night?

Karl: Bhuail – bhí cúpla deoch agam leo. Agus chuamar chuig cóisir oíche Dé Sathairn.
Yes – I had a few drinks with them. And we went to a party on Saturday night.

Tomás: Ó, is ea, bhí lá breithe Gary ann, nach raibh?
Oh, yes, it was Gary's birthday, wasn't it?

Karl: Bhí. Bhí oíche go maidin againn!
Yes. We stayed up all night!

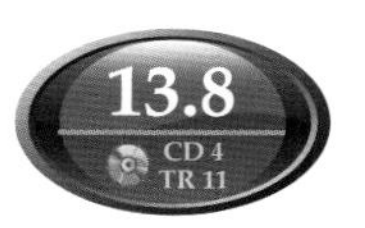

13.8 The past tense 6 (questions and answers: irregular verbs)

Earlier, we looked at how to form questions and answers in the case of regular verbs. We'll have a look now at how this is done in the case of irregular verbs.

Note that the interrogative particle **ar** is used before the irregular verbs **beir** (*bring, take*), **clois** (*hear*), **ith** (*eat*), **tar** (*come*) and **tabhair** (*give*), and that **an** is used in the case of all the other irregular verbs.

An ndúirt tú ...?
Did you say ...?
Dúirt./Ní dúirt.
Yes./No.

Ar rug tú ...?
Did you bring ...?
Rug./Níor rug.
Yes./No.

An raibh sé ...?
Was he ...?
Bhí./Ní raibh.
Yes./No.

Ar chuala sí ...?
Did she hear ...?
Chuala./Níor chuala.
Yes./No.

An ndearna sibh ...?
Did you do ...?
Rinne./Ní dhearna.
Yes./No.

An bhfuair siad ...?
Did they get ...?
Fuair./Ní bhfuair.
Yes./No.

An bhfaca tú ...?
Did you see ...?
Chonaic./Ní fhaca.
Yes./No.

Ar ith sé ...?
Did he eat ...?
D'ith./Níor ith.
Yes./No.

Ar thug sí ...?
Did she give ...?
Thug./Níor thug.
Yes./No.

Ar tháinig sibh ...?
Did you come ...?
Tháinig./Níor tháinig.
Yes./No.

An ndeachaigh siad ...?
Did they go ...?
Chuaigh./Ní dheachaigh.
Yes./No.

Notice that when the question contains **ar** the answer contains **níor**. And when **an** is used in the question, **ní** is used in the answer.

Exercise 13.2: Answer the questions

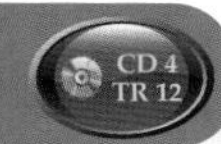

Answer each of these questions as indicated.

1. Cad a rinne tú ag an deireadh seachtaine? (*What did you do at the weekend?*)
   Say: I went home to Galway.
2. Cad a rinne tú ag an deireadh seachtaine? (*What did you do at the weekend?*)
   Say: I was studying.
3. Cad a rinne tú maidin Dé Sathairn? (*What did you do on Saturday morning?*)
   Say: I went on a walk with Liam.
4. Cad a rinne tú oíche Dé hAoine? (*What did you do on Friday night?*)
   Say: I went to a film with Barry.
5. An bhfaca tú Órla? (*Did you see Órla?*)
   Say: Yes.
6. Ar ith tú bia Síneach? (*Did you eat Chinese food?*)
   Say: No.
7. An ndeachaigh siad go Corcaigh? (*Did they go to Cork?*)
   Say: Yes.
8. Ar thug sí airgead do Lucy? (*Did she give Lucy money?*)
   Say: No.
9. An raibh sé fuar? (*Was it cold?*)
   Say: Yes.
10. An ndearna siad an obair? (*Did they do the work?*)
    Say: No.

Exercise 13.3: Your turn!

This is your chance to talk now. Pretend you're Tomás and that you're talking to Karl.

Karl: Cad a rinne tú ag an deireadh seachtaine?

Say: *I had a quiet enough weekend. I was very tired.*

Karl: An ndeachaigh tú amach mórán?

Say: *I stayed at home on Friday night but I went out on Saturday night.*

Karl: Cén áit a ndeachaigh tú?

Say: *Myself and Laura went to that new club on Castle Street. We had a great night.*

Exercise 13.4: Your turn!

This time, pretend you're Karl and that you're talking to Tomás.

Tomás: Cad a rinne tú féin ag an deireadh seachtaine?

Say: *I had a great time! I went out every night.*

Tomás: Tá tú lán fuinnimh! Ar bhuail tú le Jenny agus Susan oíche Dé hAoine?

Say: *Yes – I had a few drinks with them. And we went to a party on Saturday night.*

Tomás: Ó, is ea, bhí lá breithe Gary ann, nach raibh?

Say: *Yes. We stayed up all night!*

Exercise 13.5: Fill in the gaps

Write the correct form of the verb in each gap to complete the question.

1. *Did you go out on Saturday night? Yes.*
   An ______________ tú amach oíche Dé Sathairn? Chuaigh.
2. *Did you do all the work? No.*
   An ______________ sibh an obair go léir? Ní dhearna.
3. *Did you hear Dónall on the radio? No.*
   Ar ___________ tú Dónall ar an raidió? Níor chuala.
4. *Did Celine come home? Yes.*
   Ar ___________ Celine abhaile? Tháinig.
5. *Did they go there together? Yes.*
   An ________________ siad ansin le chéile? Chuaigh.
6. *Did she give money to the children? No.*
   Ar _________ sí airgead do na páistí? Níor thug.
7. *Did you say anything to him? No.*
   An _____________ tú aon rud leis? Ní dúirt.
8. *Was Martin there? No.*
   An ___________ Martin ansin? Ní raibh.
9. *Did you get a paper for me? Yes.*
   An __________ tú nuachtán dom? Fuair.
10. *Did you see that film yet? No.*
    An ___________ tú an scannán sin fós? Ní fhaca.

Chuig, go dtí and go

As we saw in Unit 5, the preposition **chuig** is usually used when talking about going to an event or an appointment:

Chuaigh mé chuig ceolchoirm le Dáithí.
I went to a concert with Dáithí.

Chuaigh mé chuig an dochtúir inné.
I went to the doctor yesterday.

Go dtí is used with nouns preceded by the article:

Chuaigh mé go dtí an phictiúrlann.
I went to the cinema.

Chuaigh mé do dtí an teach tábhairne.
I went to the pub.

Go is used before nouns *not* preceded by the article. An **h** is prefixed to nouns beginning with a vowel which follow **go**:

Corcaigh *Cork*	**go Corcaigh** *to Cork*
Baile Átha Cliath *Dublin*	**go Baile Átha Cliath** *to Dublin*
Aontroim *Antrim*	**go hAontroim** *to Antrim*

Note: Go dtí *also means* until. *An example of this usage can be found in Conversation 13D.*

Adverbs of time

To find out when someone did something, you can ask:

Cathain a chuaigh tú go Doire?
When did you go to Derry?
or
Cén lá a chuaigh tú go Maigh Eo?
What day did you go to Mayo?

Let's have a look now at various words which are used to refer to past time. We've seen some of them already.

inné
yesterday

arú inné
the day before yesterday

aréir
last night

arú aréir
the night before last

maidin inné
yesterday morning

tráthnóna inné
yesterday evening

dhá lá ó shin
two days ago

oíche Dé hAoine
(on) Friday night

maidin Dé Sathairn
(on) Saturday morning

tráthnóna Dé Sathairn
(on) Saturday evening

Exercise 13.6: Answer the questions

Answer each of these questions as indicated.

1. Cathain a chuaigh tú go Londain?
   Say: On Saturday night.
2. Cén lá a chuaigh tú go Páras?
   Say: On Friday.
3. Cén lá a d'imir tú galf le Séamas?
   Say: Yesterday.
4. Cathain a chuaigh tú chuig an dráma?
   Say: Yesterday evening.
5. Cathain a chuaigh tú chuig an scannán sin?
   Say: The day before yesterday.
6. Cathain a chonaic tú Síle?
   Say: Yesterday morning.
7. Cathain a bhí Derek sa bhaile?
   Say: Two days ago.
8. Cathain a bhí Bríd anseo?
   Say: The night before last.

Conversation 13C

Deirbhile tells her friend Martina about her weekend away.

Martina: An ndearna tú aon rud deas ag an deireadh seachtaine?
Did you do anything nice at the weekend?

Deirbhile: Rinne – chuaigh mé féin agus Colm go Gaillimh.
Yes – Colm and I went to Galway.

Martina: Ar fheabhas. Cén áit ar fhan sibh?
Great. Where did you stay?

Deirbhile: D'fhanamar in Óstán an Ard-Oileáin. Bhí an aimsir go hálainn.
We stayed in the Ardilaun Hotel. The weather was lovely.

Martina: Agus cad a rinne sibh agus sibh ansin?
And what did you do while you were there?

Deirbhile: Chuamar ar shiúlóidí cois farraige agus d'itheamar cúpla béile an-deas.
We went on walks by the sea and we ate a few very nice meals.

Martina: An ndearna sibh mórán siopadóireachta?
Did you do much shopping?

Deirbhile: Ní dhearna. Ní maith le Colm bheith ag siopadóireacht. Tá a fhios agat na fir …
No. Colm doesn't like to shop. You know men …

Conversation 13D

Órla tells her friend Ciarán about her weekend.

Ciarán: An ndeachaigh tú chuig an dráma sin ag an deireadh seachtaine?
Did you go to that play at the weekend?

Órla: Ní dheachaigh. Bhí mé an-ghnóthach Dé hAoine agus Dé Sathairn.
No. I was very busy on Friday and Saturday.

Ciarán: An raibh tú ag obair sa siopa?
Were you working in the shop?

Órla: Bhí – tá Michelle ar saoire. Ach bhí sos deas agam ón obair inné.
Yes – Michelle is on holidays. But I had a nice break from work yesterday.

Ciarán: Cad a rinne tú?
What did you do?

Órla: D'fhan mé sa leaba go dtí meán lae agus ansin chuaigh mé ar shiúlóid fhada le Denise.
I stayed in bed until midday and then I went on a long walk with Denise.

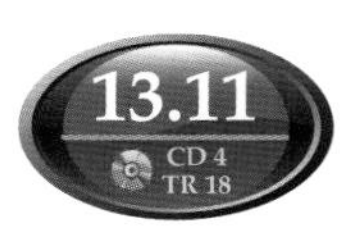

Mé féin

In Conversation 13C, Deirbhile said:

Chuaigh mé féin agus Colm go Gaillimh.
Colm and I went to Galway.

Learners often use **mise** instead of **mé féin** in sentences like the above but it's wrong to do so.

The weather

Deirbhile also mentioned the weather in Galway in Conversation 13C:

Bhí an aimsir go hálainn.
The weather was lovely.

Here are some more phrases you can use to talk about the weather:

Bhí aimsir mhaith ann.
The weather was good.

Bhí drochaimsir ann.
The weather was bad.

Bhí sé te.
It was warm/hot.

Bhí sé fuar.
It was cold.

Bhí sé fliuch.
It was wet.

Bhí sé ag stealladh báistí.
It was pouring rain.

You can use the present tense form of **bí** (*be*) when referring to the weather at the moment:

Tá aimsir mhaith ann.
The weather is good.

Exercise 13.7: Your turn!

This is your chance to talk now. Pretend you're Martina and that you're talking to Deirbhile.

Say:	*Did you do anything nice at the weekend?*
Deirbhile:	Rinne – chuaigh mé féin agus Colm go Gaillimh.
Say:	*Great. Where did you stay?*
Deirbhile:	D'fhanamar in Óstán an Ard-Oileáin. Bhí an aimsir go hálainn.
Say:	*And what did you do while you were there?*
Deirbhile:	Chuamar ar shiúlóidí cois farraige agus d'itheamar cúpla béile an-deas.
Say:	*Did you do much shopping?*
Deirbhile:	Ní dhearna. Ní maith le Colm bheith ag siopadóireacht. Tá a fhios agat na fir …

Exercise 13.8: Your turn!

This time, pretend you're Órla and that you're talking to Ciarán.

Ciarán:	An ndeachaigh tú chuig an dráma sin ag an deireadh seachtaine?
Say:	*No. I was very busy on Friday and Saturday.*
Ciarán:	An raibh tú ag obair sa siopa?
Say:	*Yes – Michelle is on holidays. But I had a nice break from work yesterday.*
Ciarán:	Cad a rinne tú?
Say:	*I stayed in bed until midday and then I went on a long walk with Denise.*

Useful tips for learners

One way of helping your progress as a learner is to attend a language course. Many people attend a course in their own area during the winter and do a course in the *Gaeltacht* during the summer.

There are courses aimed at adult learners of Irish held in the main *Gaeltacht* areas during the summer months and these are attended by learners, young and old, from many different parts of the world. People not only manage to learn Irish on these courses, but they also establish life-long friendships.

A list of organisations providing language courses can be found in the Irish Language Directory at the end of this book.

Talking heads

Colm Mac Séalaigh
(filmed at the Civic Offices, Dublin)
Dé Sathairn seo caite, chuaigh mé chuig cluiche iománaíochta le mo chairde. Bhain mé an-sult as. Bhí an cluiche go hiontach ar fad.

Ansin Dé Domhnaigh, bhí bricfeasta deas agam le mo chlann. Chuamar ar shiúlóid faoin tuath ina dhiaidh sin. Bhí an aimsir go hálainn.

Ní dhearna mé mórán tráthnóna; d'fhéach mé ar an teilifís agus lig mé mo scíth.

Siobhán Patten (filmed in Temple Bar, Dublin)
An deireadh seachtaine seo caite, tháinig mo chara Úna ar cuairt go Baile Átha Cliath.

Bhuail mé léi i lár na cathrach tráthnóna Dé hAoine. Bhí cúpla deoch againn i dteach tábhairne ar dtús agus ansin chuamar ar aghaidh chuig cóisir i dteach ár gcara Diarmuid.

Maidin Dé Sathairn, chuamar amach go Binn Éadair ag siúl. Chaitheamar an lá ar fad ansin. Bhí an aimsir go hálainn agus bhí sé go hiontach bheith amuigh faoin aer.

Cóilín Ó Floinn (filmed in Temple Bar, Dublin)
Ní raibh mé ag obair an deireadh seachtaine seo caite. Bhuail mé le cairde oíche Dé hAoine agus bhí cúpla deoch againn. Ghlan mé an t-árasán Dé Sathairn.

Lig mé mo scíth Dé Domhnaigh – léigh mé an páipéar nuachta agus chuaigh mé go dtí an phictiúrlann.

TRANSLATION

Colm Mac Séalaigh
Last Saturday, I went to a hurling match with my friends. I really enjoyed it. The match was really great.

Then on Sunday, I had a nice breakfast with my family. We went on a walk in the countryside after that. The weather was lovely.

I didn't do much in the evening; I watched television and I rested.

Siobhán Patten
Last weekend, my friend Úna came on a visit to Dublin.

I met her in the city centre on Friday evening. We had a few drinks in a pub first and then we went on to a party in our friend Diarmuid's house.

On Saturday morning, we went out to Howth to walk. We spent the whole day there. The weather was lovely and it was great to be out in the open air.

Cóilín Ó Floinn
I wasn't working last weekend. I met friends on Friday night and we had a few drinks. I cleaned the apartment on Saturday.

I rested on Sunday – I read the newspaper and I went to the cinema.

Exercise 13.9: Review of Unit 13

Have a go at this activity now to see if you know the most important phrases taught in Unit 13.

How would you say the following in Irish?

1. What did you do at the weekend?
2. What did you do yourself at the weekend?
3. I visited Pádraigín.
4. I was working on Saturday and Sunday.
5. What did you do on Sunday morning?
6. I went on a walk with Chris.
7. I went to a play on Sunday night.
8. Did they stay at home? Yes.
9. Did she drink much? No.
10. Did you go out much? No.
11. We went to a party on Saturday night.
12. Did you meet Jenny and Susan on Friday night?
13. When did you go to Derry? The day before yesterday.
14. Colm and I went to Galway.
15. We ate a few very nice meals.

Unit 14: Holidays and Travel
Aonad 14: Laethanta Saoire agus Taisteal

In this unit you will learn how to:

- ask someone where he went on holidays and answer that question
- name various countries
- ask someone if he was on holidays and answer that question
- ask someone who accompanied him and answer that question
- ask for and give information about accommodation
- refer to the weather
- ask someone if he enjoyed a holiday and answer that question
- seek and give opinions about a place.

Grammar

- **i(n)** and **sa(n)**
- statements in the past tense 2
- questions and answers in the past tense 2
- **go**, **go dtí** and **chun**
- **ar feadh** followed by the genitive case

San aonad seo foghlaimeoidh tú conas:

- *ceist a chur ar dhuine cén áit a ndeachaigh sé ar laethanta saoire agus an cheist sin a fhreagairt*
- *tíortha éagsúla a ainmniú*
- *fiafraí de dhuine an raibh sé ar laethanta saoire agus an cheist sin a fhreagairt*
- *fiafraí de dhuine cé a chuaigh leis agus an cheist sin a fhreagairt*
- *eolas a lorg agus a thabhairt faoi lóistín*
- *tagairt a dhéanamh don aimsir*
- *fiafraí de dhuine ar bhain sé sult as saoire agus an cheist sin a fhreagairt*
- *tuairimí a lorg agus a thabhairt faoi áit.*

Gramadach

- ***i(n)*** *agus* ***sa(n)***
- *ráitis san aimsir chaite 2*
- *ceisteanna agus freagraí san aimsir chaite 2*
- ***go**, **go dtí*** *agus* ***chun***
- ***ar feadh*** *agus an tuiseal ginideach*

Key sounds

CD 4 TR 23

i **mb**liana	(**b** with *urú*)	*this year*
an **Fh**rainc	(**f** with *séimhiú*)	*France*
an **Ghe**armáin	(**g** with *séimhiú* followed by slender vowel, **e**)	*Germany*
pubai**ll**	(slender **l**)	*tents*
puba**ll**	(broad **l**)	*(a) tent*
an **mhí**	(**m** with *séimhiú* followed by slender vowel, **i**)	*the month*
in Éiri**nn**, Albai**n**	(slender **n**)	*in Ireland, Scotland*
Cea**n**ada	(broad **n**)	*Canada*
an Rúi**s**	(slender **s**)	*Russia*
an A**s**tráil	(broad **s**)	*Australia*

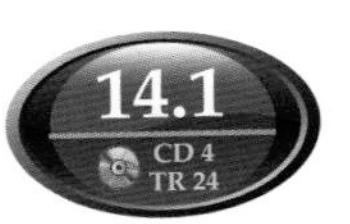

Where did you go on holidays?

To find out where someone was on holidays, you can ask:

Cén áit a ndeachaigh tú ar laethanta saoire i mbliana?
Where did you go on holidays this year?

You can omit the word **laethanta** and simply ask:

Cén áit a ndeachaigh tú ar saoire i mbliana?
Where did you go on holidays this year?

Here are two possible answers:

Chuaigh mé go Meiriceá.
I went to America.

Chaith mé coicís sa Spáinn.
I spent a fortnight in Spain.

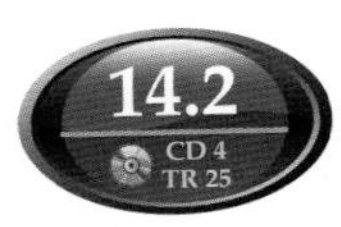

The names of countries

As you might remember from Unit 2, the article **an** is a part of the names of many countries in Irish:

An Ghearmáin
Germany

An Fhrainc
France

An Spáinn
Spain

An Bhreatain Bheag
Wales

There are quite a few countries, however, that don't contain the article in their names:

Éire
Ireland

Sasana
England

Albain
Scotland

Málta
Malta

Cúba
Cuba

If you can't remember what various countries are called in Irish, have a look again at the vocabulary section on page 16.

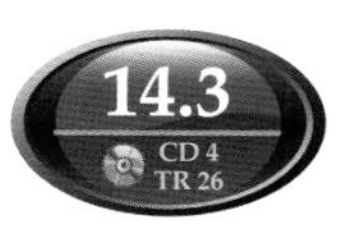

I(n) and sa(n)

When you're talking about being in a country, you use **i** or **in** before the countries which don't contain the article in their name:

Country names beginning with a consonant

Sasana *England*	**i Sasana** *in England*
Ceanada *Canada*	**i gCeanada** *in Canada*

Country names beginning with a vowel

Éire *Ireland*	**in Éirinn** *in Ireland*
Albain *Scotland*	**in Albain** *in Scotland*

You use **sa** or **san** before the countries which do contain the article in their name:

Country names beginning with a consonant

An Rúis *Russia*	**sa Rúis** *in Russia*
An Fhrainc *France*	**sa Fhrainc** *in France*

*Country names beginning with a vowel or **fh** + a vowel*

An Iodáil *Italy*	**san Iodáil** *in Italy*
An Astráil *Australia*	**san Astráil** *in Australia*
An Fhionlainn *Finland*	**san Fhionlainn** *in Finland*

***Note:** **Sa** and **san** are made up of the simple preposition **i** (in) and the article **an**.*

Were you on holidays?

To find out whether or not someone was on holidays, you can ask:

An raibh tú ar saoire fós?
Have you been on holidays yet?

Bhí. Bhí mé sa Spáinn.
Yes. I was in Spain.

Ní raibh. Tá mé ag dul go Ceanada an mhí seo chugainn.
No. I'm going to Canada next month.

Exercise 14.1: Fill in the gaps

*Write the correct preposition (**i**, **in**, **sa** or **san**) in the gap before each country name.*

1. an Ghearmáin (*Germany*)
   ____ Ghearmáin (*in Germany*)
2. Albain (*Scotland*)
   ____ Albain (*in Scotland*)
3. an Éigipt (*Egypt*)
   ____ Éigipt (*in Egypt*)
4. Cúba (*Cuba*)
   ____ gCúba (*in Cuba*)
5. an Ísiltír (*the Netherlands*)
   ____ Ísiltír (*in the Netherlands*)
6. Málta (*Malta*)
   ____ Málta (*in Malta*)
7. an Astráil (*Australia*)
   ____ Astráil (*in Australia*)
8. an Tuirc (*Turkey*)
   ____ Tuirc (*in Turkey*)

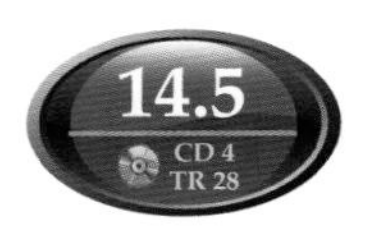

Who went with you?

This is how you say who went on holidays with you:

Bhí mo dheartháir liom.
My brother was with me.

Chuaigh mé ansin le mo chara Deirdre.
I went there with my friend Deirdre.

Chuaigh mé ansin i m'aonar.
I went there alone.

This is how you ask someone who accompanied him:

Cé a chuaigh leat?
Who went with you?

Here are two possible answers:

Mo dheartháir Breandán.
My brother Breandán.

Mo chairde Jill agus Mairéad.
My friends Jill and Mairéad.

Vocabulary: Holidays

lóistín	*accommodation*
lóistín leaba agus bricfeasta	*bed and breakfast accommodation*
lóistín iomlán	*full board*
lóistín féinfhreastail	*self-catering accommodation*
óstán / an t-óstán / óstáin	*(an) hotel / the hotel / hotels*
árasán / an t-árasán / árasáin	*(an) apartment / the apartment / apartments*
láithreán campála	*(a) camping site*
puball / an puball / pubaill	*(a) tent / the tent / tents*
carbhán / an carbhán / carbháin	*(a) caravan / the caravan / caravans*
brú óige / an brú óige / brúnna óige	*(a) youth hostel / the youth hostel / youth hostels*
seomra singil	*(a) single room*
seomra dúbailte	*(a) double room*
eitilt / an eitilt / eitiltí	*(a) flight / the flight / flights*
ar an eitleán	*by plane*
ar an traein	*by train*
ar an mbus	*by bus*
sa charr	*by car*
pas / an pas / pasanna	*(a) passport / the passport / passports*
réasúnta	*reasonable*
saor / an-saor	*cheap / very cheap*
daor / an-daor / ródhaor	*expensive / very expensive / too expensive*

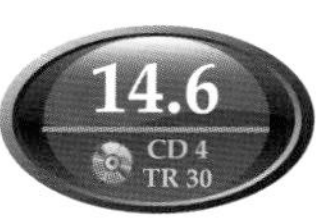

Where did you stay?

To find out where someone stayed, you can ask:

Cén áit ar fhan tú?
Where did you stay?

or

Cén cineál lóistín a bhí agat?
What kind of accommodation did you have?

You would, of course, use **sibh** in the first sentence above if you were referring to more than one person and **agaibh** in the second sentence.

Here are some possible answers to the above questions:

Fuair mé/Fuaireamar árasán ar cíos.
I/We rented an apartment.

D'fhan mé/D'fhanamar …
I/We stayed …

in óstán.
in an hotel.

i mbrú.
in a youth hostel.

i gcarbhán.
in a caravan.

Insight

Irish is proving a popular subject in American universities. Up to 4,000 students study the language annually, in prestigious institutions such as Harvard (pictured below) and Notre Dame, as well as smaller colleges throughout the country.

The Fulbright Commission – the official cultural exchange programme between the Irish and US governments – receives over €200,000 a year from the Irish government to partly finance the teaching of Irish in America. The Commission appoints Irish language assistants from Ireland to third-level institutions in the US.

Irish is offered as a subject in universities in other countries as well, including Karlova University in Prague, Adam Mickiewicz University in Poznan (Poland), University of Freiburg in Germany and Utrecht University in Holland.

Conversation 14A

Ciara tells her cousin Caitlín about her recent holidays.

Caitlín: Cén áit a ndeachaigh tú ar saoire i mbliana?
Where did you go on holidays this year?

Ciara: Chaith mé coicís sa Spáinn i mí na Bealtaine.
I spent a fortnight in Spain in May.

Caitlín: Go deas. Cé a chuaigh leat?
Very nice. Who went with you?

Ciara: Chuaigh mé ansin le mo chara Brídín. Chaitheamar seachtain in Santander agus seachtain eile in Bilbao.
I went there with my friend Brídín. We spent a week in Santander and another week in Bilbao.

Caitlín: Iontach. Cén cineál lóistín a bhí agaibh?
Great. What kind of accommodation did you have?

Ciara: D'fhanamar in dhá óstán an-deas nach raibh ródhaor.
We stayed in two very nice hotels that weren't too expensive.

Caitlín: Agus conas a bhí an aimsir? An raibh sé an-te?
And how was the weather? Was it very warm?

Ciara: Ní raibh. Bhí an aimsir go hálainn – timpeall fiche céim Celsius gach lá.
No. The weather was lovely – around twenty degrees Celsius every day.

Conversation 14B

Ciara now asks Caitlín about her holidays.

Ciara: Cén áit a ndeachaigh tú féin ar saoire?
Where did you go on holidays yourself?

Caitlín: Go hAlbain. Chaith mé féin agus Gary seachtain i nDún Éideann i mí Lúnasa.
To Scotland. Gary and I spent a week in Edinburgh in August.

Ciara: An raibh an fhéile ar siúl ag an am?
Was the festival taking place at the time?

Caitlín: Bhí – bhí an chathair plódaithe. Bhí am iontach againn.
Yes – the city was packed. We had a great time.

Ciara: Tá mé cinnte go raibh. Ar fhan sibh in óstán?
I'm sure you did. Did you stay in an hotel?

Caitlín: Níor fhan. D'fhanamar in árasán i lár na cathrach.
No. We stayed in an apartment in the city centre.

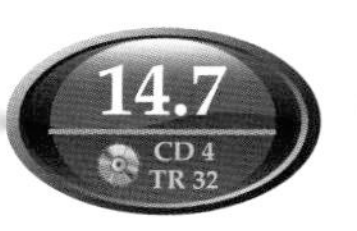

The months

In Conversation 14A, Ciara said:

Chaith mé coicís sa Spáinn i mí na Bealtaine.
I spent a fortnight in Spain in May.

In everyday speech, people tend to use the word **mí** (*month*) when referring to a particular month:

Bhí mé i gCeanada i mí Iúil.
I was in Canada in July.

We'll return to the months in Unit 15.

In

The preposition **in** (*in*) is used before foreign place names which don't have an Irish language version. We saw two examples of this in Conversation 14A:

Chaitheamar seachtain in Santander agus seachtain eile in Bilbao.
We spent a week in Santander and another week in Bilbao.

Where a place name has an Irish language version, the normal rule is followed, i.e. **i** (followed by an *urú*) is used before consonants:

Bostún *Boston*	**i mBostún** *in Boston*

In is used before all place names beginning with a vowel, regardless of language:

Amstardam *Amsterdam*	**in Amstardam** *in Amsterdam*
Ankara *Ankara*	**in Ankara** *in Ankara*

The weather

We looked at various sentences used to describe the weather in Unit 13. Here are two more useful sentences relating to the weather:

Bhí sé meirbh.
It was humid.

Bhí sneachta trom ann.
There was heavy snow.

Exercise 14.2: Your turn!

This is your chance to talk now. Pretend you're Caitlín and that you're talking to Ciara.

Say:	*Where did you go on holidays this year?*
Ciara:	Chaith mé coicís sa Spáinn i mí na Bealtaine.
Say:	*Very nice. Who went with you?*
Ciara:	Chuaigh mé ansin le mo chara Brídín. Chaitheamar seachtain in Santander agus seachtain eile in Bilbao.
Say:	*Great. What kind of accommodation did you have?*
Ciara:	D'fhanamar in dhá óstán an-deas nach raibh ródhaor.
Say:	*And how was the weather? Was it very warm?*
Ciara:	Ní raibh. Bhí an aimsir go hálainn – timpeall fiche céim Celsius gach lá.

Exercise 14.3: Your turn!

Again, pretend you're Caitlín and that you're talking to Ciara.

Ciara:	Cén áit a ndeachaigh tú féin ar saoire?
Say:	*To Scotland. Gary and I spent a week in Edinburgh in August.*
Ciara:	An raibh an fhéile ar siúl ag an am?
Say:	*Yes – the city was packed. We had a great time.*
Ciara:	Tá mé cinnte go raibh. Ar fhan sibh in óstán?
Say:	*No. We stayed in an apartment in the city centre.*

Exercise 14.4 Fill in the gaps

Fill in the gaps in these sentences.

1. *Where did you go on holidays this year?*
   Cén áit a ____________ tú ar saoire i mbliana?
2. *I spent a fortnight in Spain.*
   Chaith mé ____________ sa Spáinn.
3. *I'm going to Canada next month.*
   Tá mé ag _______ go Ceanada an mhí seo chugainn.
4. *Who went with you?*
   Cé a ____________ leat?

5. *My friend Deirdre.*
   Mo ________ Deirdre.
6. *My friends Jill and Mairéad.*
   Mo __________ Jill agus Mairéad.
7. *Where did you stay?*
   Cén áit ar _________ tú?
8. *We rented an apartment.*
   Fuaireamar árasán ar __________.
9. *What kind of accommodation did you have?*
   Cén cineál ____________ a bhí agaibh?
10. *Was the festival taking place at the time?*
    An raibh an _________ ar siúl ag an am?

Exercise 14.5: Answer the questions

Answer each of these questions as indicated.

1. An raibh tú ar saoire fós?
   Say: Yes. I was in Spain.
2. An raibh tú ar saoire fós?
   Say: Yes. I spent a fortnight in America.
3. An raibh tú ar saoire fós?
   Say: Yes. I was in Australia.
4. An raibh tú ar saoire fós?
   Say: Yes. I was in Cuba.
5. Cén áit a ndeachaigh tú ar saoire i mbliana?
   Say: I went to America.
6. Cé a chuaigh leat?
   Say: I went there alone.
7. Cé a chuaigh leat?
   Say: My friend Simon.
8. Cé a chuaigh leat?
   Say: I went there with my brother.
9. Cén áit ar fhan tú?
   Say: In an hotel in the city centre.
10. Cén áit ar fhan sibh?
    Say: We stayed in an apartment.

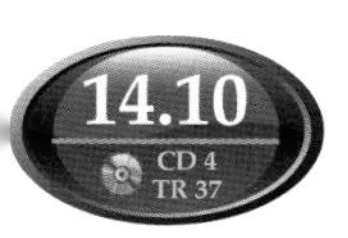

Go, go dtí and chun

You can use **go dtí** or **chun** when talking about going to a country which has the article **an** as part of its name. Nouns which follow **chun** are usually in the genitive case and undergo some changes. We'll focus on **go dtí** in this course, then, since it's easier to use.

An Ghearmáin *Germany*	**Chuaigh mé go dtí an Ghearmáin.** *I went to Germany.*
An Fhrainc *France*	**go dtí an Fhrainc** *to France*
An Spáinn *Spain*	**go dtí an Spáinn** *to Spain*
An Iodáil *Italy*	**go dtí an Iodáil** *to Italy*
An Astráil *Australia*	**go dtí an Astráil** *to Australia*

Go is used before those countries which don't have the article as part of their name:

Meiriceá
America
go Meiriceá
to America

Sasana
England
go Sasana
to England

As we mentioned in Unit 13, **h** is prefixed to nouns beginning with a vowel which follow **go**:

Albain
Scotland
go hAlbain
to Scotland

Éire
Ireland
go hÉirinn
to Ireland

Opinions

To find out if someone enjoyed something, you ask:

Ar bhain tú sult as?
Did you enjoy it?

Bhain./Níor bhain.
Yes./No.

Here are some sentences you could add to the above answers:

Bhí sé ar fheabhas.
or
Bhí sé go hiontach.
It was great.

Bhí sé róthe.
It was too hot.

Ní raibh an t-óstán ródheas.
The hotel wasn't very nice.

Conversation 14C

CD 4 TR 39

Cathal tells his friend Aodán about a recent family holiday.

Aodán: Bhí tú ar saoire leis an teaghlach le déanaí. Cén áit a ndeachaigh sibh?
You were on holidays with the family recently. Where did you go?

Cathal: Chuamar go Ciarraí. Fuaireamar teach ar cíos in aice leis an Daingean.
We went to Kerry. We rented a house beside An Daingean.

Aodán: Go deas. Cén fhad a bhí sibh ansin?
Very nice. How long were you there?

Cathal: Bhíomar ansin ar feadh coicíse. Thángamar ar ais Dé Domhnaigh seo caite.
We were there for a fortnight. We came back last Sunday.

Aodán: Ar bhain sibh sult as?
Did you enjoy it?

Cathal: Bhain – bhí sé ar fheabhas ar fad. Bhí an aimsir go hálainn an chuid is mó den am.
Yes – it was really great. The weather was lovely most of the time.

Aodán: Bhí an t-ádh libh.
You were lucky.

Conversation 14D

CD 4 TR 39

Ruth was in Bratislava recently but didn't enjoy her time there.

Stuart: Bhuel, conas a bhí an Bhratasláiv? Ar bhain tú sult as an tsaoire?
Well, how was Bratislava? Did you enjoy the holiday?

Ruth: Níor bhain, leis an bhfírinne a rá.
No, to be honest.

Stuart: Cén fáth? Cloisim go bhfuil an chathair go deas.
Why? I hear the city is nice.

Ruth: Tá, tá an chathair go hálainn. Ach ní raibh an t-óstán go ródheas.
Yes, the city is lovely. But the hotel wasn't very nice.

Stuart: Is mór an trua sin. An raibh na daoine ansin cairdiúil?
That's a pity. Were the people there friendly?

Ruth: Ní raibh siad róchairdiúil ar chor ar bith.
They weren't too friendly at all.

Periods of time

In Conversation 14C, when Cathal was asked how long the family spent in Kerry, he replied:

Bhíomar ansin ar feadh coicíse.
We were there for a fortnight.

Here are two other words used when periods of time are being referred to:

seachtain
(a) week

mí
(a) month

Nouns which directly follow **ar feadh** (*for*) are in the genitive case and undergo some changes. As we've mentioned before, you don't have to understand the rules of the genitive case at this level – just try learning examples of the genitive, such as those in the first three rows below:

seachtain *(a) week*	**ar feadh seachtaine** *for a week*
coicís *(a) fortnight*	**ar feadh coicíse** *for a fortnight*
mí *(a) month*	**ar feadh míosa** *for a month*
trí seachtaine *three weeks*	**ar feadh trí seachtaine** *for three weeks*
ceithre mhí *four months*	**ar feadh ceithre mhí** *for four months*

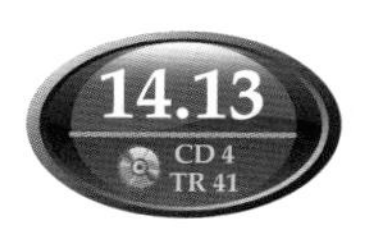

Did you like it?

This is how to ask someone if he liked something:

Ar thaitin an áit leat?
Did you like the place?
Thaitin. Bhí sé go deas.
Yes. It was nice.

Ar thaitin an t-óstán leat?
Did you like the hotel?
Níor thaitin. Ní raibh sé ródheas.
No. It wasn't very nice.

Exercise 14.6: Answer the questions

Answer each of these questions as indicated.

1. Cén áit a ndeachaigh tú ar saoire?

   Say: I went to Spain.

2. Cén áit a ndeachaigh tú ar saoire?

   Say: To Italy.

3. Cén áit a ndeachaigh sibh ar saoire?

   Say: We went to Australia.

4. Cén áit a ndeachaigh sibh ar saoire?

   Say: To England.

5. Cén áit a ndeachaigh tú ar saoire?

   Say: To Scotland.

6. Ar bhain tú sult as?

   Say: Yes. It was great.

7. Ar bhain tú sult as?

   Say: No. It was too hot.

8. Cén fhad a bhí tú ansin?

   Say: For a month.

9. Cén fhad a bhí sibh ansin?

   Say: For a fortnight.

10. Cén fhad a bhí tú ansin?

    Say: For a week.

Exercise 14.7: Your turn!

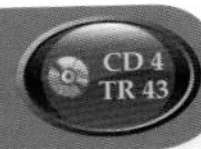

This is your chance to talk now. Pretend you're Cathal and that you're talking to Aodán.

Aodán:	Bhí tú ar saoire leis an teaghlach le déanaí. Cén áit a ndeachaigh sibh?
Say:	*We went to Kerry. We rented a house beside An Daingean.*
Aodán:	Go deas. Cén fhad a bhí sibh ansin?
Say:	*We were there for a fortnight. We came back last Sunday.*
Aodán:	Ar bhain sibh sult as?
Say:	*Yes – it was really great. The weather was lovely most of the time.*
Aodán:	Bhí an t-ádh libh.

Exercise 14.8: Your turn!

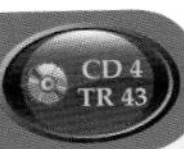

This time, pretend you're Ruth and that you're talking to Stuart.

Stuart:	Bhuel, conas a bhí an Bhratasláiv? Ar bhain tú sult as an tsaoire?
Say:	*No, to be honest.*
Stuart:	Cén fáth? Cloisim go bhfuil an chathair go deas.
Say:	*Yes, the city is lovely. But the hotel wasn't very nice.*
Stuart:	Is mór an trua sin. An raibh na daoine ansin cairdiúil?
Say:	*They weren't too friendly at all.*

Useful tips for learners

Consider doing one of the Teastas Eorpach na Gaeilge (The European Certificate in Irish) (www.teg.ie) examinations, which are available at six levels. These exams are held once a year (in April and May) in various towns and cities in Ireland, including Maynooth, Letterkenny, Belfast, Limerick and Cork. The exams are also run in centres outside Ireland, including New York, Paris, London and Prague.

Start by doing the beginners (A1) examination and, as you become more proficient, have a go at the higher-level examinations. Setting a goal like this will greatly increase your motivation as a learner.

Talking heads

Meadhbh Ní Eadhra (filmed in An Spidéal, Galway)
Chuaigh mé go hOrlando i Meiriceá an samhradh seo caite. Bhí mé ann ar feadh seachtaine le mo mháthair, mo dhearthár agus mo dheirfiúr. Breithlá mo dhearthár a bhí ann agus chuaigh muid chuig ionad siamsaíochta Universal. Bhí sé go hiontach.

Chonaiceamar domhan draíochtúil Harry Potter agus d'fhanamar in óstán galánta. Ní raibh sé róchostasach agus bhí trí linn snámha ann! Bhí an ghrian ag taitneamh gach lá agus níor theastaigh uaim Orlando a fhágáil le filleadh abhaile.

Colm Mac Séalaigh
(filmed at the Civic Offices, Dublin)
Bhí mé féin agus mo chlann ar laethanta saoire sa Phortaingéil ar feadh coicíse i mbliana. Bhí saoire iontach againn; bhí an aimsir go deas den chuid is mó ach bhí sé scamallach cúpla lá.

D'fhanamar in árasán deas in aice na farraige. Bhí sé go deas ciúin agus bhí linn snámha ann. Ba bhreá liom dul ar ais ann an bhliain seo chugainn.

Dairíne Ní Dhonnchú
(filmed in Temple Bar, Dublin)
Bhí mé ar saoire sa Fhrainc ar feadh seachtaine i mbliana. D'fhan mé in óstán deas in Nice. Bhí an aimsir go hálainn agus ní raibh sé róthe.

Chaith mé a lán ama ar an trá, ag léamh, ag snámh agus ag sú na gréine.

Thaitin Nice go mór liom; bhí na daoine an-chairdiúil agus bhí an bia an-bhlasta ar fad.

Notes
The first speaker, Meadhbh Ní Eadhra, used **chuaigh muid** (*we went*) instead of **chuamar**. **Chuaigh muid** is used by speakers of the Ulster and Connacht dialects.

Translation

Meadhbh Ní Eadhra
I went to Orlando in America last summer. I was there for a week with my mother, my brother and my sister. It was my brother's birthday and we went to the Universal entertainment centre. It was great.

We saw the magical world of Harry Potter and we stayed in an elegant hotel. It wasn't too expensive and there were three swimming pools! The sun was shining every day and I didn't want to leave Orlando to return home.

Colm Mac Séalaigh
My family and I were on holidays in Portugal for a fortnight this year. We had a great holiday; the weather was nice for the most part but it was cloudy a few days.

We stayed in a nice apartment beside the sea. It was nice and quiet and there was a swimming pool. I'd love to go back there next year.

Dairíne Ní Dhonnchú
I was on holidays in France for a week this year. I stayed in a nice hotel in Nice. The weather was lovely and it wasn't too hot.

I spent a lot of time on the beach, reading, swimming and sunbathing.

I really liked Nice; the people were very friendly and the food was really tasty.

The audio versions of these excerpts are available on the sound files accompanying this book. The video segments can be seen in the online version of *Gaeilge gan Stró! – Beginners Level*, available on Gaelchultúr's e-learning website, www.ranganna.com.

Exercise 14.9: Review of Unit 14

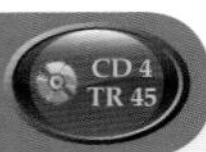

Have a go at this activity now to see if you know the most important phrases taught in Unit 14.

How would you say the following in Irish?

1. Where did you go on holidays this year?
2. I spent a fortnight in Spain.
3. Who went with you?
4. I went there with my friend Deirdre.
5. I went there alone.
6. Where did you stay (addressing one person)?
7. What kind of accommodation did you have (referring to more than one person)?
8. We rented an apartment.
9. I stayed in a youth hostel.
10. How was the weather?
11. We had a great time.
12. I was in Canada in July.
13. It was humid.
14. Did you like the place? Yes.
15. Did you like the hotel? No.

Unit 15: Making Arrangements

Aonad 15: Socruithe a Dhéanamh

In this unit you will learn how to:

- ask someone if he'll be free and answer that question
- refer to various events
- ask someone if he'll be attending a particular event and answer that question
- ask when something will be taking place and answer that question
- give someone an invitation
- accept and reject an invitation
- apologise
- name the months of the year
- arrange a time
- arrange a place.

Grammar

- pronouns and the gender of nouns
- the future tense
- adverbs of time
- simple prepositions + the article

San aonad seo foghlaimeoidh tú conas:

- *ceist a chur ar dhuine an mbeidh sé saor agus an cheist sin a fhreagairt*
- *tagairt a dhéanamh d'ócáidí éagsúla*
- *ceist a chur ar dhuine a mbeidh sé ag freastal ar ócáid ar leith agus an cheist sin a fhreagairt*
- *ceist a chur cathain a bheidh rud éigin ar siúl agus an cheist sin a fhreagairt*
- *cuireadh a thabhairt do dhuine*
- *glacadh le cuireadh agus diúltú do chuireadh*
- *leithscéal a ghabháil*
- *míonna na bliana a ainmniú*
- *am a shocrú*
- *áit a shocrú.*

Gramadach

- *forainmneacha agus inscne ainmfhocal*
- *an aimsir fháistineach*
- *dobhriathra ama*
- *réamhfhocail shimplí + an t-alt*

Key sounds

CD 4 TR 46

an **mb**eidh tú?	(**b** with *urú*)	*will you be?*
ceol**ch**oirm	(**c** with *séimhiú* followed by broad vowel, **o**)	*(a) concert*
gheobhaidh tú	(**g** with *séimhiú* followed by slender vowel, **e**)	*you'll get*
an-**gh**nóthach	(**g** with *séimhiú* followed by broad vowel, **o**)	*very busy*
mí an **Mh**árta	(**m** with *séimhiú* followed by broad vowel, **a**)	*March*
téacs	(slender **t**)	*text*
an **t**-eolas	(slender **t**)	*the information*
i **dt**igh Susan	(**t** with *urú*)	*in Susan's house*
ca**th**ain	(**t** with *séimhiú*)	*when*

Will you be free tomorrow night?

To find out if someone will be free at a particular time, you can ask:

An mbeidh tú saor san oíche amárach?
Will you be free tomorrow night?

Beidh. Cén fáth?
Yes. Why?

Ní bheidh. Beidh mé ag obair.
No. I'll be working.

As in English, speakers of Irish tend to use the present tense when referring to future events. You could therefore say the above sentences in the following way:

An bhfuil tú saor san oíche amárach?
Are you free tomorrow night?

Tá. Cén fáth?
Yes. Why?

Níl. Tá mé ag obair.
No. I'm working.

If you're asked one of the above questions, it's important to use the same tense in your answer as was used in the question.

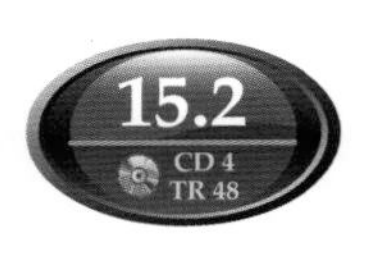

Various events

You can use these sentences to refer to events taking place in the future:

Tá breithlá Liam ann.
It's Liam's birthday.

Tá cóisir ag Bernie.
Bernie is having a party.

Tá dinnéar i dtigh Susan.
There's a dinner at Susan's house.

Tá ceolchoirm ar siúl san Odeon.
There's a concert on in the Odeon.

Will you be at Lucy's party?

To find out whether or not someone will be attending an event you can ask:

An mbeidh tú ag cóisir Lucy?
Will you be at Lucy's party?

Beidh. Tá mé ag súil go mór leis.
Yes. I'm really looking forward to it.

An mbeidh tú ag dinnéar Helen?
Will you be at Helen's dinner?

Ní bheidh.
No.

When is it taking place?

To find out when an event is taking place, you can ask:

Cathain atá sé ar siúl?
When is it taking place?
or
Cathain a bheidh sé ar siúl?
When will it be taking place?

Here are some possible answers:

san oíche amárach
tomorrow night

arú amárach
the day after tomorrow

Dé hAoine seo chugainn
next Friday

Dé Sathairn ag a hocht
Saturday at eight

an mhí seo chugainn
next month

i mí Lúnasa
in August

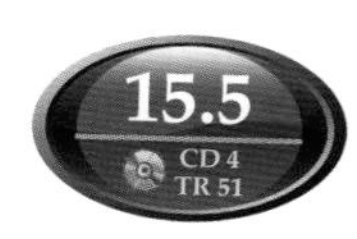

Would you like to go with me?

To invite someone to go to an event with you, you can ask:

Ar mhaith leat dul liom?
Would you like to go with me?

Ar mhaith leat dul chuig scannán liom san oíche amárach?
Would you like to go to a film with me tomorrow night?

In reply, you can say:

Ba bhreá liom.
I'd love to.

Tá brón orm ach níl mé saor.
I'm sorry but I'm not free.

Ba bhreá liom ach tá mé ag obair.
I'd love to but I'm working.

Here are other reasons why you might not be free:

Tá rang Fraincise agam.
I have a French class.

Beidh mé ag staidéar.
I'll be studying.

Tá mé an-ghnóthach faoi láthair.
I'm very busy at the moment.

Exercise 15.1: Answer the questions

Answer each of these questions as indicated.

1. An mbeidh tú saor san oíche amárach?
   Say: Yes. Why?
2. An mbeidh tú saor oíche Dé Máirt?
   Say: No. I'll be working.
3. An bhfuil tú saor san oíche amárach?
   Say: Yes. Why?
4. An mbeidh tú ag cóisir Lucy?
   Say: Yes. I'm really looking forward to it.
5. An mbeidh tú ag dinnéar Helen?
   Say: No. I have a French class.
6. Cathain atá sé ar siúl?
   Say: Friday at eight.
7. Cathain a bheidh sé ar siúl?
   Say: Next month.
8. Cathain a bheidh sé ar siúl?
   Say: Next Saturday.
9. Ar mhaith leat dul liom?
   Say: I'd love to.
10. Ar mhaith leat dul liom?
    Say: I'm sorry but I'm not free.

Insight

Technology, and the Internet in particular, has made minority languages such as Irish far more accessible than they were in the past. Learners of Irish now have access to a wide range of online resources and services in the language, including radio and television programmes, magazines and newspapers, bookshops, dictionaries and e-learning courses.

TG4 (www.tg4.ie), the national Irish language television service, has had a major impact since its establishment in 1996. It has exposed thousands of people in Ireland and abroad to Irish and has changed many people's view of the language.

Learners can instantly buy the latest books and resources in online shops such as litriocht.com and siopa.ie, and can add to their language skills by doing a course on Gaelchultúr's award-winning e-learning website, ranganna.com.

There is also a growing number of useful phone apps for learners and speakers of Irish, including the *Collins Pocket Irish Dictionary*.

A list of online resources can be found in the Irish Language Directory at the back of this book.

Conversation 15A

Tomás invites Gearóid to go to a concert with him.

Tomás: An bhfuil tú saor san oíche amárach?
Are you free tomorrow night?

Gearóid: Tá. Cén fáth?
Yes. Why?

Tomás: Tá an cheolchoirm sin ar siúl san Odeon. Ar mhaith leat dul liom?
That concert is on in the Odeon. Would you like to go with me?

Gearóid: Cinnte – ba bhreá liom. Cén t-am atá sé ag tosú?
Sure – I'd love to. What time is it starting?

Tomás: Níl mé cinnte. Gheobhaidh mé an t-eolas agus cuirfidh mé téacs chugat.
I'm not sure. I'll get the information and I'll send you a text.

Gearóid: Go raibh maith agat. Tá mé ag súil go mór leis.
Thank you. I'm really looking forward to it.

Conversation 15B

Deirdre invites Alan to go to a friend's birthday party with her.

Deirdre: An mbeidh tú ag cóisir Sarah?
Will you be at Sarah's party?

Alan: Cathain a bheidh sí ar siúl?
When will it be taking place?

Deirdre: Oíche Dé Sathairn sa Stag's Head. Ar mhaith leat dul liom?
On Saturday night in the Stag's Head. Would you like to go with me?

Alan: Tá brón orm ach beidh mé ag obair an oíche sin. Faraor!
I'm sorry but I'll be working that night. Alas!

Deirdre: Is mór an trua sin – beidh an-oíche ann. Tá mé féin ag súil go mór leis.
That's a pity – it'll be a great night. I'm really looking forward to it myself.

Pronouns

In Conversation 15A, Gearóid used the pronoun **sé** when he was referring to the concert in the Odeon, even though **ceolchoirm** (*concert*) is a feminine noun. There's a growing tendency to use the pronoun **sé** at all times when referring to inanimate objects, regardless of noun gender.

Many people still use the correct pronoun, however. In Conversation 15B, for example, Alan used **sí** when referring to **cóisir** (*party*), which is another feminine noun.

Exercise 15.2: Masculine & feminine

Write the correct version of each noun in the gap after the article, changing the noun if necessary. If you can't remember the rules, have a look again at the table in 4.4 on page 38.

1. am (masculine) (*time*)
   an ____________________
2. oíche (feminine) (*night*)
   an ____________________
3. breithlá (masculine) (*birthday*)
   an ____________________
4. dinnéar (masculine) (*dinner*)
   an ____________________
5. ceolchoirm (feminine) (*concert*)
   an ____________________
6. cóisir (feminine) (*party*)
   an ____________________
7. scannán (masculine) (*film*)
   an ____________________
8. bainis (feminine) (*wedding*)
   an ____________________
9. seisiún ceoil (masculine) (*music session*)
   an ____________________ ceoil
10. pictiúrlann (feminine) (*cinema*)
    an ____________________
11. amharclann (feminine) (*theatre*)
    an ____________________
12. caifé (masculine) (*café*)
    an ____________________

Exercise 15.3: Your turn!

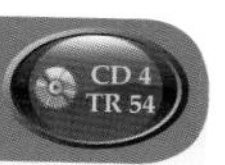

This is your chance to talk now. Pretend you're Tomás and that you're talking to Gearóid.

Say:	*Are you free tomorrow night?*
Gearóid:	Tá. Cén fáth?
Say:	*That concert is on in the Odeon. Would you like to go with me?*
Gearóid:	Cinnte – ba bhreá liom. Cén t-am atá sé ag tosú?
Say:	*I'm not sure. I'll get the information and I'll send you a text.*
Gearóid:	Go raibh maith agat. Tá mé ag súil go mór leis.

Exercise 15.4: Your turn!

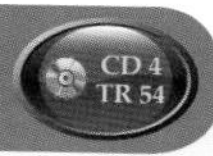

This time, pretend you're Alan and that you're talking to Deirdre.

Deirdre:	An mbeidh tú ag cóisir Sarah?
Say:	*When will it be taking place?*
Deirdre:	Oíche Dé Sathairn sa Stag's Head. Ar mhaith leat dul liom?
Say:	*I'm sorry but I'll be working that night. Alas!*
Deirdre:	Is mór an trua sin – beidh an-oíche ann. Tá mé féin ag súil go mór leis.

Exercise 15.5: Fill in the gaps

Fill in the gaps in these sentences.

1. *Will you be free tomorrow night?*

   An _________ tú saor san oíche amárach?
2. *Are you free tomorrow night?*

   An _________ tú saor san oíche amárach?
3. *Bernie is having a party.*

   Tá cóisir ____ Bernie.
4. *I'm really looking forward to it.*

   Tá mé ag _______ go mór leis.

5. *When is it taking place?*

   Cathain _______ sé ar siúl?
6. *When will it be taking place?*

   Cathain a __________ sé ar siúl?
7. *Next Friday.*

   Dé hAoine seo ______________.
8. *In August.*

   I mí ______________.
9. *Would you like to go with me?*

   Ar mhaith leat _______ liom?
10. *I'm sorry but I'm not free.*

    Tá brón orm ach níl mé _________.

The months of the year

In the first column below, you can see the months as they're written in Irish. In everyday speech, people tend to use the word **mí** (*month*) when referring to a particular month:

Beidh an bhainis ar siúl i mí Iúil.
The wedding will take place in July.

Beidh mé ar saoire i mí Feabhra.
I'll be on holidays in February.

Eanáir *January*	**mí Eanáir**
Feabhra *February*	**mí Feabhra**
Márta *March*	**mí an Mhárta**
Aibreán *April*	**mí Aibreáin**
Bealtaine *May*	**mí na Bealtaine**
Meitheamh *June*	**mí an Mheithimh**
Iúil *July*	**mí Iúil**
Lúnasa *August*	**mí Lúnasa**
Meán Fómhair *September*	**mí Mheán Fómhair**
Deireadh Fómhair *October*	**mí Dheireadh Fómhair**
Samhain *November*	**mí na Samhna**
Nollaig *December*	**mí na Nollag**

The future tense 1

In this course, we've given precedence to the most commonly used tenses in Irish: the present tense and the past tense. We're not going to focus on the future tense to the same extent as it's not used as much as the other two tenses. Here, however, are the main rules governing that particular tense:

Verbs beginning with a consonant
An and an *urú* in the question:

An mbeidh tú ag cóisir Laura?
Will you be at Laura's party?

Ní and a *séimhiú* in the negative:

Ní bheidh.
No.

Verbs beginning with a vowel
Verbs beginning with a vowel remain unchanged after **an**:

An imreoidh sibh an cluiche amárach?
Will you play the game tomorrow?

Verbs beginning with a vowel remain unchanged after **ní**:

Ní imreoidh.
No.

The future tense 2

As we've mentioned before, there is no equivalent in Irish to *yes* and *no* in English. When you're asked a question, you must use the same verb in your answer that was used in the question:

An mbeidh tú ag an gceolchoirm sin?
Will you be at that concert?
Beidh./Ní bheidh.
Yes./No.

An bhfeicfidh siad Susan ag an gcóisir?
Will they see Susan at the party?
Feicfidh./Ní fheicfidh.
Yes./No.

Note that a pronoun (e.g. **mé, tú, siad**) is not used when answering a question in the affirmative or in the negative in the future tense. A pronoun must be used, of course, when a statement is being made:

Beidh sé ag an gceolchoirm.
He'll be at the concert.

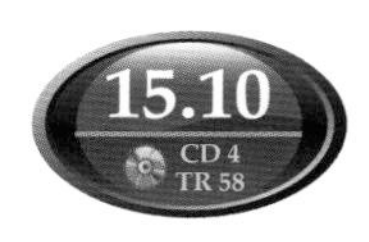

The future tense 3

Here are some useful questions and answers in the future tense for you to learn:

Question	Answer
An imeoidh sí anocht? *Will she leave tonight?*	**Imeoidh./** **Ní imeoidh.** *Yes./No.*
An dtiocfaidh sé ar ais amárach? *Will he come back tomorrow?*	**Tiocfaidh./** **Ní thiocfaidh.** *Yes./No.*
An rachaidh tú chuig scannán liom? *Will you go to a film with me?*	**Rachaidh./** **Ní rachaidh.** *Yes./No.*
An bhfeicfidh sibh Síle ansin? *Will you see Síle there?*	**Feicfidh./** **Ní fheicfidh.** *Yes./No.*
An gcloisfidh tú í ar an raidió? *Will you hear her on the radio?*	**Cloisfidh./** **Ní chloisfidh.** *Yes./No.*
An ndéanfaimid an obair sin anois? *Will we do that work now?*	**Déanfaidh./** **Ní dhéanfaidh.** *Yes./No.*
An ndéarfaidh siad leis imeacht? *Will they tell him to leave?*	**Déarfaidh./** **Ní déarfaidh.** *Yes./No.*
An bhfaighidh sí bronntanas duit? *Will she get a present for you?*	**Gheobhaidh./** **Ní bhfaighidh.** *Yes./No.*
An íosfaidh siad an bia go léir? *Will they eat all the food?*	**Íosfaidh./** **Ní íosfaidh.** *Yes./No.*
An dtabharfaidh sé airgead duit? *Will he give you money?*	**Tabharfaidh./** **Ní thabharfaidh.** *Yes./No.*

Exercise 15.6: Answer the questions

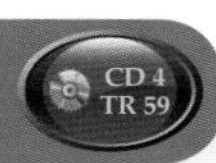

Answer each of these questions as indicated. In the case of questions 1–6, place the words ***i mí*** *before the names of the months in Irish.*

1. Cathain a bheidh an bhainis ar siúl?
   Say: In April.
2. Cathain a bheidh an chóisir ar siúl?
   Say: In June.
3. Cathain a bheidh an dinnéar ar siúl?
   Say: In May.
4. Cathain a bheidh an dráma ar siúl?
   Say: In December.
5. Cathain a bheidh an scannán ar siúl?
   Say: In February.
6. Cathain a bheidh sé ar siúl?
   Say: In March.
7. An bhfeicfidh siad Susan ag an gcóisir?
   Say: No.
8. An rachaidh tú chuig an gcóisir?
   Say: No.
9. An gcloisfidh tú é ar an raidió?
   Say: Yes.
10. An íosfaidh sí an bia go léir?
    Say: Yes.

Conversation 15C

It's the evening of the concert and Tomás rings Gearóid to arrange to meet him.

Tomás: Cén t-am a bhuailfimid le chéile?
What time will we meet?

Gearóid: Timpeall a hocht? Beidh mise ag obair go dtí a seacht.
*Around eight? **I**'ll be working until seven.*

Tomás: Ceart go leor. Agus cén áit a mbuailfimid le chéile?
Okay. And where will we meet?

Gearóid: Fan go bhfeice mé. Cad faoi Whelan's? Ní bheidh sé róphlódaithe anocht.
Let me see. What about Whelan's? It won't be too crowded tonight.

Tomás: Foirfe. Feicfidh mé ansin tú. Ní bheidh mé déanach!
Perfect. I'll see you there. I won't be late!

Gearóid: Mar athrú!
For a change!

Conversation 15D

Julie and her friend Denise are going to a film at the weekend. They arrange to meet beforehand.

Julie: Cén áit a mbuailfimid le chéile?
Where will we meet?

Denise: Cad faoin gcaifé nua sin in aice leis an bpictiúrlann?
What about that new café beside the cinema?

Julie: An ceann atá cúpla doras síos ón bpictiúrlann? Ar an gcúinne?
The one a few doors down from the cinema? On the corner?

Denise: Is ea – sin an ceann. Cén t-am a bhuailfidh mé leat?
Yes – that's the one. What time will I meet you?

Julie: Ceathrú chun a hocht?
A quarter to eight?

Denise: Maith go leor!
Okay!

15.11 Simple prepositions + the article

In Conversation 15D Denise said:

> **Cad faoin gcaifé nua sin in aice leis an bpictiúrlann?**
> *What about that new café beside the cinema?*

Faoin is the simple preposition **faoi** (*about/under*) combined with the article **an**:

> **faoi** + **an** = **faoin** (*about the/under the*)

The simple preposition **le** (*with*) becomes **leis** when it's used with the article **an**:

> **leis an** (*with the*)

When a noun follows a simple preposition + the article **an**, the beginning of the noun often changes. Here are two examples from Conversation 15D:

> **An ceann atá cúpla doras síos ón bpictiúrlann? Ar an gcúinne?**
> *The one a few doors down from the cinema? On the corner?*

Group 1
An *urú* is usually added to a noun beginning with **b**, **c**, **f**, **g** or **p** when it follows these simple prepositions + the definite article singular:

> **ag an** (*at the*), **ar an** (*on the*), **as an** (*from the*), **chuig an** (*to the*), **faoin** (*under/about the*), **leis an** (*with the*), **ón** (*from the*), **roimh an** (*before the*), **thar an** (*over/past the*), **tríd an** (*through the*)

Group 2
A *séimhiú* is usually added to a noun beginning with a consonant which follows these simple prepositions + the definite article singular:

> **den** (*of the*), **don** (*for the*), **sa** (*in the*)

Note: *In Ulster Irish, a* séimhiú *is added to nouns beginning with* ***b***, ***c***, ***f***, ***g***, ***p*** *which follow the prepositions in group 1 above.*

Exercise 15.7: Your turn!

This is your chance to talk now. Pretend you're Tomás and that you're talking to Gearóid.

Say:	*What time will we meet?*
Gearóid:	Timpeall a hocht? Beidh mise ag obair go dtí a seacht.
Say:	*Okay. And where will we meet?*
Gearóid:	Fan go bhfeice mé. Cad faoi Whelan's? Ní bheidh sé róphlódaithe anocht.
Say:	*Perfect. I'll see you there. I won't be late!*
Gearóid:	Mar athrú!

Exercise 15.8: Your turn!

This time, pretend you're Denise and that you're talking to Julie.

Julie:	Cén áit a mbuailfimid le chéile?
Say:	*What about that new café beside the cinema?*
Julie:	An ceann atá cúpla doras síos ón bpictiúrlann? Ar an gcúinne?
Say:	*Yes – that's the one. What time will I meet you?*
Julie:	Ceathrú chun a hocht?
Say:	*Okay!*

Useful tips for learners

In the past, learners who lived a long way from the *Gaeltacht* found it difficult to find opportunities to use their Irish. The Web has helped alleviate this problem. Get to know some of the thousands of Irish speakers who take part regularly in discussions on email lists such as Gaelic-B or on the various discussion forums, such as that of Daltaí na Gaeilge (www.daltai.com).

Find people who are willing to be your email friends, and write to them on a regular basis.

It's worth subscribing to free newsletters such as those of Gaelchultúr (www.gaelchultur.com) and Gaelport (www.gaelport.com) in order to find out about new resources for learners, Irish language events, etc.

Talking heads

Siobhán Patten (filmed in Temple Bar, Dublin)
Tá mé chun bualadh le mo chara Linda tráthnóna Dé Céadaoin an tseachtain seo. Is cara de mo chuid ón meánscoil í. Tá cónaí uirthi i mBaile Átha Cliath, ach ní fheicim go rómhinic í toisc go mbíonn an bheirt againn an-ghnóthach i gcónaí.

Tá sé socraithe agam bualadh léi i lár na cathrach ag a sé a chlog. Táimid chun dul go dtí an phictiúrlann ar dtús agus ansin rachaimid chuig Ukiyo – bialann Sheapánach ar Shráid an Chiste a thaitníonn go mór leis an mbeirt againn.

Ní fhaca mé le fada í agus tá mé ag súil go mór leis na scéalta ar fad a chloisteáil uaithi.

Fionnuala Croker
(filmed in Dún Laoghaire, County Dublin)
Tá sé i gceist agam bualadh le cara de mo chuid an tseachtain seo chugainn. Tá cónaí uirthi san Astráil, ach tá sí féin agus a fear céile ar ais anseo ar saoire faoi láthair.

Tá mé ag dul chuig rang Spáinnise oíche Dé Máirt. Tá mé ag foghlaim Spáinnise le ceithre bliana anois agus bainim an-taitneamh as.

Ansin, Dé Domhnaigh, má bhíonn an aimsir go deas rachaidh mé go dtí an trá.

Dairíne Ní Dhonnchú
(filmed in Temple Bar, Dublin)
Tá mé ag dul chuig bainis Dé Sathairn seo chugainn – tá mo chara Audrey ag pósadh. Tá mé ag súil go mór leis an lá, caithfidh mé a rá.

Ansin, Dé Domhnaigh, tá mé ag bualadh le mo chara Síle ar a haon a chlog. Beidh lón againn le chéile agus ina dhiaidh sin rachaimid ag siopadóireacht i lár na cathrach.

Translation

Siobhán Patten
I'm going to meet my friend Linda on Wednesday evening this week. She's a friend of mine from secondary school. She lives in Dublin, but I don't see her too often because both of us are always very busy.

I've arranged to meet her in the city centre at six o'clock. We're going to go to the cinema first and then we'll go to Ukiyo – a Japanese restaurant on Exchequer Street which both of us really like.

I haven't seen her in a long time and I'm really looking forward to hearing all the stories from her.

Fionnuala Croker
I intend to meet a friend of mine next week. She lives in Australia, but herself and her husband are back here on holidays at the moment.

I'm going to a Spanish class on Tuesday night. I've been learning Spanish for four years now and I really enjoy it.

Then, on Sunday, if the weather is nice I'll go to the beach.

Dairíne Ní Dhonnchú
I'm going to a wedding next Saturday – my friend Audrey is getting married. I'm really looking forward to the day, I have to say.

Then, on Sunday, I'm meeting my friend Síle at one o'clock. We'll have lunch together and after that we'll go shopping in the city centre.

Exercise 15.9: Review of Unit 15

Have a go at this activity now to see if you know the most important phrases taught in Unit 15.

How would you say the following in Irish?

1. Will you be free tomorrow night? Yes.
2. Are you free tomorrow night? No.
3. It's Liam's birthday.
4. There's a dinner at Susan's house.
5. I'm really looking forward to it.
6. When is it taking place?
7. Tomorrow night.
8. Next Friday.
9. Would you like to go to a film with me?
10. I'd love to but I'm working.
11. I'm very busy at the moment.
12. What time is it starting?
13. That's a pity – it'll be a great night.
14. Where will we meet?
15. What time will I meet you?

ANSWERS, DIRECTORY AND INDEXES / *FREAGRAÍ, EOLAIRE AGUS INNÉACSANNA*

- Answers to the Activities / Freagraí na gCleachtaí
- Irish Language Directory / Eolaire na Gaeilge
- Indexes / Innéacsanna

Answers to the Activities / Freagraí na gCleachtaí

Unit 1: Meeting People

Exercise 1.1: Your turn!

Michelle: *How are you? **I'm** Michelle – what's **your** name?*
Cén chaoi a bhfuil tú? Is mise Michelle – cén t-ainm atá ortsa?
Eoin: Mise Eoin.
Michelle: *It's nice to meet you, Eoin.*
Tá sé go deas bualadh leat, a Eoin.

Exercise 1.2: Your turn!

Áine: *Hello, Liam.*
Dia duit, a Liam.
Liam: Dia is Muire duit, a Áine. Cén chaoi a bhfuil tú na laethanta seo?
Áine: *I'm well, thank you. And yourself?*
Tá mé go maith, go raibh maith agat. Agus tú féin?
Liam: Tá mé go breá. Tá sé go deas tú a fheiceáil arís!

Exercise 1.3: Fill in the gaps

1. *How are you?*
Cén chaoi a bhfuil tú?
2. *I'm well.*
Tá mé go maith.
3. *I'm fine.*
Tá mé go breá.
4. ***I'm** Alan.*
Is mise Alan.
5. *My name is Jennifer.*
Jennifer is ainm dom.
6. ***My** name is Dónall.*
Dónall is ainm domsa.
7. *What's your name?*
Cén t-ainm atá ort?
8. *What's **your** name?*
Cén t-ainm atá ortsa?
9. *It's nice to meet you, Eoin.*
Tá sé go deas bualadh leat, a Eoin.
10. *It's nice to see you again!*
Tá sé go deas tú a fheiceáil arís!

Exercise 1.4: Your turn!

Caitlín: *This is Barry.*
Seo é Barry.
Barry: Tá sé go deas bualadh leat, a Nóra.
Caitlín: *This is Laura.*
Seo í Laura.
Nóra: Cén chaoi a bhfuil tú?
Caitlín: *And this is Stiofán and Peadar.*
Agus seo iad Stiofán agus Peadar.
Nóra: Cén chaoi a bhfuil sibh?

Exercise 1.5: Your turn!

Séamas: *Goodbye, Siobhán. I'll be talking to you tomorrow.*
Slán leat, a Shiobhán. Beidh mé ag caint leat amárach.
Siobhán: Slán agat, a Shéamais, agus go raibh maith agat arís.
Séamas: *Goodbye, Máire. Safe home.*
Slán leat, a Mháire. Slán abhaile.
Máire: Slán agat, a Shéamais. Feicfidh mé amárach tú.

Exercise 1.7: Review of Unit 1

1. *Hello (formal).*
Dia duit.
2. *How are you (Connacht dialect)?*
Cén chaoi a bhfuil tú?
3. *I'm well.*
Tá mé go maith.
4. ***I'm** Sharon.*
Is mise Sharon.
5. *My name is Máirtín.*
Máirtín is ainm dom.
6. ***My** name is Bríd.*
Bríd is ainm domsa.
7. *What's your name?*
Cén t-ainm atá ort?
8. *It's nice to meet you, Eoin.*
Tá sé go deas bualadh leat, a Eoin.
9. *It's nice to meet **you** as well.*
Tá sé go deas bualadh leatsa freisin.
10. *Goodbye (said to the person leaving).*
Slán leat.
11. *Goodbye (said to the person staying).*
Slán agat.
12. *Goodbye for now.*
Slán go fóill.
13. *This is Nóra.*
Seo í Nóra.
14. *This is Seán.*
Seo é Seán.
15. *This is Stiofán and Peadar.*
Seo iad Stiofán agus Peadar.

Unit 2: Your Background and Where You Live

Exercise 2.1: Your turn!

Helen: *How are you? **I'm** Helen – what's **your** name?*
Cén chaoi a bhfuil tú? Is mise Helen – cén t-ainm atá ortsa?
Brian: Brian. Tá sé go deas bualadh leat, a Helen.
Helen: *Where are you from, Brian?*
Cé as thú, a Bhriain?
Brian: Is as Glaschú mé. Cé as thú féin?
Helen: *From New York but I live in Cork now.*
As Nua-Eabhrac ach tá mé i mo chónaí i gCorcaigh anois.

Exercise 2.2: Your turn!

Alan: ***I'm** Alan and I'm Australian. What's **your** name?*
Is mise Alan agus is Astrálach mé. Cén t-ainm atá ortsa?
Francesca: Francesca. Francesca Saltini.
Alan: *Are you Italian, Francesca?*
An Iodálach tú, a Francesca?
Francesca: Is ea. Is as an Róimh mé ach tá mé i mo chónaí i mBaile Átha Cliath anois.
Alan: *Rome is lovely. I was there last year.*
Tá an Róimh go hálainn. Bhí mé ansin anuraidh.
Francesca: Cá bhfuil tusa i do chónaí, a Alan?
Alan: *I'm from Sydney but I live in London now.*
As Sydney mé ach tá mé i mo chónaí i Londain anois.

Exercise 2.3: Fill in the gaps

1. *Where are you from?*
Cé as thú?
2. *Where are you from yourself?*
Cé as thú féin?
3. *I'm from Derry.*
Is as Doire mé.
4. ***I'm** from Madrid.*
Is as Maidrid mise.
5. *Where do you live?*
Cá bhfuil tú i do chónaí?
6. *Where do **you** live?*
Cá bhfuil tusa i do chónaí?
7. *I live in Paris.*
Tá mé i mo chónaí i bPáras.
8. *Are you American? No.*
An Meiriceánach tú? Ní hea.

9. *I'm German.*
   Is Gearmánach mé.
10. *It's nice to meet you, Brian.*
   Tá sé go deas bualadh leat, a Bhriain.

Exercise 2.4: Answer the questions
1. Cé as thú?
   Say: I'm from Paris.
   Is as Páras mé.
2. Cé as thú?
   Say: I'm from Spain.
   Is as an Spáinn mé.
3. Cé as thú?
   Say: I'm from America.
   Is as Meiriceá mé.
4. Cá bhfuil tú i do chónaí?
   Say: In Dublin.
   I mBaile Átha Cliath.
5. Cá bhfuil tú i do chónaí?
   Say: In Belfast.
   I mBéal Feirste.
6. Cá bhfuil tú i do chónaí?
   Say: In Derry.
   I nDoire.
7. An Sasanach tú?
   Say: Yes. I'm from Birmingham.
   Is ea. Is as Birmingham mé.
8. An Francach tú?
   Say: No. I'm Spanish.
   Ní hea. Is Spáinneach mé.

Exercise 2.5: Addresses
1. 15 Páirc na Coille
2. 9 Ascaill na Mainistreach
3. 12 Bóthar an tSléibhe
4. 6 Sráid na Siopaí
5. 18 Páirc Bhríde
6. 10 Ascaill an Lagáin
7. 19 Bóthar na Trá
8. 13 Sráid na hEaglaise

Exercise 2.6: Your turn!
Caitríona: *Where are you living now, Stuart?*
Cá bhfuil tú i do chónaí anois, a Stuart?
Stuart: Tá mé i mo chónaí i mbaile beag i gContae Chill Dara na laethanta seo.
Caitríona: *Do you like the town?*
An maith leat an baile?
Stuart: Is breá liom é. Tá áiseanna maithe ann: ionad siopadóireachta, cúpla teach tábhairne, bialann álainn, óstán agus linn snámha.
Caitríona: *There are good facilities there, then.*
Tá áiseanna maithe ann, mar sin.
Stuart: Tá. Tá mé an-sásta ansin.

Exercise 2.7: Your turn!
Stuart: *Where are **you** living now, Caitríona?*
Cá bhfuil tusa i do chónaí anois, a Chaitríona?
Caitríona: Tá mé i mo chónaí in Órán Mór i gContae na Gaillimhe.
Stuart: *That town is beside Galway city, isn't it?*
Tá an baile sin in aice le cathair na Gaillimhe, nach bhfuil?
Caitríona: Tá. Níl sé ach cúpla míle ó Ghaillimh.

Exercise 2.8: Review of Unit 2
1. *Where are you from?*
   Cé as thú?
2. *Where are **you** from?*
   Cé as thusa?
3. *I'm from London.*
   Is as Londain mé.
4. *Where do you live?*
   Cá bhfuil tú i do chónaí?
5. *Where do **you** live?*
   Cá bhfuil tusa i do chónaí?
6. *I live in Dublin.*
   Tá mé i mo chónaí i mBaile Átha Cliath.
7. *I'm American.*
   Is Meiriceánach mé.
8. *I'm Australian.*
   Is Astrálach mé.
9. *Are you Canadian? Yes.*
   An Ceanadach tú? Is ea.
10. *Are you German? No.*
   An Gearmánach tú? Ní hea.
11. *What's your address?*
   Cén seoladh atá agat?
12. *I live in a small town.*
   Tá mé i mo chónaí i mbaile beag.
13. *I live beside the sea.*
   Tá mé i mo chónaí cois farraige.
14. *I live in the country.*
   Tá mé i mo chónaí faoin tuath.
15. *Do you like the town? I love it.*
   An maith leat an baile? Is breá liom é.

Unit 3: The Family

Exercise 3.1: Your turn!
Siobhán: *You're not married yourself?*
Níl tú féin pósta?
Bernie: Níl. Bhí mé pósta ach tá mé colscartha anois.
Siobhán: *I'm sorry to hear that.*
Tá brón orm é sin a chloisteáil.
Bernie: Tá tú féin geallta.
Siobhán: *Yes, I'm engaged to Caoimhín. We're very happy together.*
Tá, tá mé geallta le Caoimhín. Táimid an-sona le chéile.
Bernie: Tá sé sin go hiontach!

Exercise 3.2: Your turn!
Siobhán: An bhfuil páistí agat?
Bernie: *Yes, I have two – a son and a daughter.*
Tá, tá beirt agam – mac agus iníon.
Siobhán: Agus cén aois atá siad?
Bernie: *Eimear is seven years (old) and Dara is ten years (old). Do you have children yourself?*
Tá Eimear seacht mbliana agus tá Dara deich mbliana. An bhfuil páistí agat féin?
Siobhán: Tá mac amháin agam, Stiofán – tá sé cúig bliana d'aois.

Exercise 3.3: Fill in the gaps
1. *Are you married?*
   An bhfuil tú pósta?
2. *Are **you** married?*
   An bhfuil tusa pósta?
3. *Are you married yourself?*
   An bhfuil tú féin pósta?
4. *I'm divorced.*
   Tá mé colscartha.
5. *I'm a widow.*
   Is baintreach mé.
6. *Do you have children (addressing one person)?*
   An bhfuil páistí agat?
7. *Do you have children (addressing more than one person)?*
   An bhfuil páistí agaibh?
8. *How many children do you have?*
   Cé mhéad páiste atá agat?
9. *I have no children.*
   Níl páistí ar bith agam.
10. *Two – a son and a daughter.*
   Beirt – mac agus iníon.

Exercise 3.4: Answer the questions

1. An bhfuil tú pósta?
   Say: No.
   Níl.
2. An bhfuil tú pósta?
   Say: Yes. Are you married yourself?
   Tá. An bhfuil tú féin pósta?
3. An bhfuil páistí agat?
   Say: Yes, two.
   Tá, beirt.
4. An bhfuil páistí agat?
   *Say: No. Do **you** have children (speaking to one person)?*
   Níl. An bhfuil páistí agatsa?
5. An bhfuil páistí agaibh?
   *Say: No. Do **you** have children (speaking to more than one person)?*
   Níl. An bhfuil páistí agaibhse?
6. An bhfuil páistí agat?
   Say: I have no children.
   Níl páistí ar bith agam.
7. An bhfuil páistí agaibh?
   Say: We have no children.
   Níl páistí ar bith againn.
8. Cé mhéad páiste atá agat?
   Say: Four.
   Ceathrar.
9. Cé mhéad páiste atá agat?
   Say: Three.
   Triúr.
10. Cén aois atá siad?
    Say: Three years (old) and seven years (old).
    Trí bliana agus seacht mbliana.

Exercise 3.5: Fill in the gaps

1. Seo <u>í</u> <u>m'aintín</u> Síle.
2. Seo <u>é</u> <u>m'uncail</u> Seosamh.
3. Seo <u>iad</u> mo <u>dheirfiúracha</u> Michelle agus Bríd.
4. Seo <u>iad</u> mo <u>dheartháireacha</u> Liam agus Aodán.
5. Seo <u>iad</u> mo <u>thuismitheoirí</u> Cóilín agus Sorcha.
6. Seo <u>é</u> mo <u>dheartháir</u> Tomás.
7. Seo <u>é</u> <u>m'athair</u> Ciarán.
8. Seo <u>í</u> mo <u>dheirfiúr</u> Órla.

Exercise 3.6: Your turn!

Deirdre: *These are my parents Séamas and Regina.*
Seo iad mo thuismitheoirí Séamas agus Regina.
Cathal: Dia daoibh.
Deirdre: *And this is my sister Laoise.*
Agus seo í mo dheirfiúr Laoise.
Laoise: Tá sé go deas bualadh leat.
Deirdre: *And these are my brothers Cormac and Eoin.*
Agus seo iad mo dheartháireacha Cormac agus Eoin.
Cathal: Cén chaoi a bhfuil sibh?
Regina: An mbeidh cupán tae agat, a Chathail?

Exercise 3.7: Your turn!

Cáit: *How many brothers do you have?*
Cé mhéad deartháir atá agat?
Gearóid: Beirt – Máirtín agus Ruairí.
Cáit: *And how many sisters do you have?*
Agus cé mhéad deirfiúr atá agat?
Gearóid: Deirfiúr amháin – Sinéad. Cé mhéad deartháir agus deirfiúr atá agatsa?
Cáit: *I have no brothers or sisters – I'm an only child.*
Níl deartháir ná deirfiúr ar bith agam – is páiste aonair mé.

Exercise 3.8: Review of Unit 3

1. *I'm married.*
   Tá mé pósta.
2. *I'm separated.*
   Tá mé scartha.
3. *Are you married?*
   An bhfuil tú pósta?
4. *Are **you** married?*
   An bhfuil tusa pósta?
5. *Do you have children (speaking to one person)?*
   An bhfuil páistí agat?
   or
   An bhfuil clann agat?
6. *Do **you** have children (speaking to one person)?*
   An bhfuil páistí agatsa?
   or
   An bhfuil clann agatsa?
7. *I have no children.*
   Níl páistí ar bith agam.
8. *We have no children.*
   Níl páistí ar bith againn.
9. *How many children do you have?*
   Cé mhéad páiste atá agat?
10. *What age is she?*
    Cén aois atá sí?
11. *What ages are they?*
    Cén aois atá siad?
12. *How many brothers and sisters do you have?*
    Cé mhéad deartháir agus deirfiúr atá agat?
13. *This is my sister.*
    Seo í mo dheirfiúr.
14. *This is my brother.*
    Seo é mo dheartháir.
15. *These are my parents.*
    Seo iad mo thuismitheoirí.

Unit 4: The House and Accommodation

Exercise 4.1: Answer the questions

1. Cén cineál lóistín atá agat?
   Say: I'm living alone.
   Tá mé i mo chónaí i m'aonar.
2. Cén cineál lóistín atá agat?
   Say: I'm sharing an apartment with three others.
   Tá mé ag roinnt árasáin le triúr eile.
3. Cén cineál lóistín atá agat?
   Say: I'm sharing a house with two others.
   Tá mé ag roinnt tí le beirt eile.
4. Cá bhfuil tú i do chónaí faoi láthair?
   Say: I live in a detached house.
   Tá mé i mo chónaí i dteach scoite.
5. Cá bhfuil tú i do chónaí faoi láthair?
   Say: I live in a semi-detached house.
   Tá mé i mo chónaí i dteach leathscoite.
6. Cá bhfuil an t-árasán suite?
   Say: It's on the edge of town.
   Tá sé ar imeall an bhaile.
7. Cá bhfuil an t-árasán suite?
   Say: It's in the city centre.
   Tá sé i lár na cathrach.
8. Cá bhfuil an teach suite?
   Say: It's in that new estate.
   Tá sé san eastát nua sin.

Exercise 4.2: Fill in the gaps

1. eastát (masculine) (*estate*)
   an <u>t-eastát</u>
2. íoslach (masculine) (*basement*)
   an <u>t-íoslach</u>
3. cathaoir (feminine) (*chair*)
   an <u>chathaoir</u>
4. cuisneoir (masculine) (*fridge*)
   an <u>cuisneoir</u>
5. bord (masculine) (*table*)
   an <u>bord</u>
6. sorn (masculine) (*cooker*)
   an <u>sorn</u>

7. cathair (feminine) (*city*)
   an <u>chathair</u>
8. fuinneog (feminine) (*window*)
   an <u>fhuinneog</u>

Exercise 4.3: Your turn!

Simon: An bhfuil an t-árasán mór?
Jim: *Yes. There are two bedrooms, a very nice kitchen and a very big sitting room.*
Tá. Tá dhá sheomra codlata ann, cistin an-deas agus seomra suí an-mhór.
Simon: An bhfuil tú i do chónaí i d'aonar?
Jim: *No. I'm sharing the apartment with a friend of mine, Judy. She's very nice.*
Níl. Tá mé ag roinnt an árasáin le cara liom, Judy. Tá sí an-deas.

Exercise 4.4: Your turn!

Jim: Cá bhfuil tú féin i do chónaí faoi láthair?
Simon: *I'm living alone in the city centre.*
Tá mé i mo chónaí i m'aonar i lár na cathrach.
Jim: In árasán nó i dteach?
Simon: *In a terraced house. It's very nice.*
I dteach sraithe. Tá sé an-deas.
Jim: Cá bhfuil an teach suite?
Simon: *It's near the river.*
Tá sé gar don abhainn.

Exercise 4.5: Fill in the gaps

1. *What kind of accommodation do you have?*
   Cén cineál <u>lóistín</u> atá agat?
2. *I live in a detached house.*
   Tá mé i mo chónaí i <u>dteach</u> <u>scoite</u>.
3. *I'm living alone.*
   Tá mé i mo chónaí i <u>m'aonar</u>.
4. *I live in an apartment.*
   Tá mé i mo chónaí <u>in</u> <u>árasán</u>.
5. *Where is the apartment situated?*
   Cá bhfuil an <u>t-árasán</u> suite?
6. *It's on the edge of the city.*
   Tá sé ar <u>imeall</u> na cathrach.
7. *It's in the centre of town.*
   Tá sé i <u>lár</u> an bhaile.
8. *It's in the country.*
   Tá sé <u>faoin</u> <u>tuath</u>.
9. *Are you living alone?*
   An bhfuil tú i do chónaí i <u>d'aonar</u>?
10. *Where's the house located?*
    Cá bhfuil an teach <u>suite</u>?

Exercise 4.6: Give the Irish version

1. *two rooms*
   dhá sheomra
2. *three hotels*
   trí óstán
3. *eight nights*
   ocht n-oíche
4. *seven hotels*
   seacht n-óstán
5. *ten chairs*
   deich gcathaoir
6. *two of something*
   dhá cheann
7. *three of something*
   trí cinn
8. *seven of something*
   seacht gcinn
9. *three hundred euro per week*
   trí chéad euro sa tseachtain
10. *five hundred and fifty euro per month*
    cúig chéad caoga euro sa mhí

Exercise 4.7: Your turn!

Jill: Cá bhfuil an teach suite?
Seosamh: *It's in that new estate on the edge of town: Riverside.*
Tá sé san eastát nua sin ar imeall an bhaile: Cois Abhann.
Jill: Go deas. Cé mhéad seomra codlata atá ann?
Seosamh: *Three. Two of them are very big but the other one is very small.*
Trí cinn. Tá dhá cheann acu an-mhór ach tá an ceann eile an-bheag.
Jill: An bhfuil an cíos daor?
Seosamh: *It's okay: three hundred euro each per month.*
Tá sé ceart go leor: trí chéad euro an duine sa mhí.

Exercise 4.8: Your turn!

Seosamh: An bhfuil tusa fós ag roinnt árasáin le Laura?
Jill: *Yes. We've been there for two years now.*
Tá. Táimid ansin le dhá bhliain anois.
Seosamh: Cá bhfuil an t-árasán?
Jill: *It's near the centre of town, beside the shopping centre.*
Tá sé gar do lár an bhaile, in aice leis an ionad siopadóireachta.
Seosamh: Agus an maith leat é?
Jill: *Yes. It's nice and quiet.*
Is maith. Tá sé breá ciúin.

Exercise 4.9: Review of Unit 4

1. *What kind of accommodation do you have?*
   Cén cineál lóistín atá agat?
2. *Where are you living at the moment?*
   Cá bhfuil tú i do chónaí faoi láthair?
3. *I'm living alone.*
   Tá mé i mo chónaí i m'aonar.
4. *I'm sharing a house with a friend of mine.*
   Tá mé ag roinnt tí le cara liom.
5. *I'm sharing an apartment with two others.*
   Tá mé ag roinnt árasáin le beirt eile.
6. *Where is the house situated?*
   Cá bhfuil an teach suite?
7. *It's on the edge of town.*
   Tá sé ar imeall an bhaile.
8. *It's in the city centre.*
   Tá sé i lár na cathrach.
9. *It's in that new estate.*
   Tá sé san eastát nua sin.
10. *Is the rent expensive?*
    An bhfuil an cíos daor?
11. *It's okay.*
    Tá sé ceart go leor.
12. *It's very expensive.*
    Tá sé an-daor.
13. *I like the house.*
    Is maith liom an teach.
14. *I don't like the apartment.*
    Ní maith liom an t-árasán.
15. *Do you like it? Yes.*
    An maith leat é? Is maith.

Unit 5: Pastimes

Exercise 5.1: Answer the questions

1. Céard a dhéanann tú nuair a bhíonn am saor agat?
   Say: I go to the pub.
   Téim go dtí an teach tábhairne.
2. Céard a dhéanann tú nuair a bhíonn am saor agat?
   Say: I watch television.
   Féachaim ar an teilifís.
3. An imríonn tú leadóg?
   Say: Yes.
   Imrím.
4. An dtéann tú go dtí an phictiúrlann?
   Say: No.
   Ní théim.

5. An bhféachann tú ar an teilifís?
   Say: No.
   Ní fhéachaim.
6. An éisteann tú le ceol?
   Say: Yes.
   Éistim.
7. An maith leat ceol traidisiúnta?
   Say: No.
   Ní maith.
8. An maith leat ceol traidisiúnta?
   Say: No. I hate it.
   Ní maith. Is fuath liom é.

Exercise 5.2: Your turn!

Susan: Céard a dhéanann tú nuair a bhíonn am saor agat?
David: *I'm very fit. I go running and swimming every day.*
Tá mé an-aclaí. Téim ag rith agus ag snámh gach lá.
Susan: Gach lá! Maith thú!
David: *What do you do yourself when you have free time?*
Céard a dhéanann tú féin nuair a bhíonn am saor agat?
Susan: Is maith liom bheith ag léamh agus is breá liom bheith ag seinm ceoil.

Exercise 5.3: Your turn!

Breandán: An éisteann tú le ceol?
Caroline: *Yes. I love traditional music.*
Éistim. Is breá liom ceol traidisiúnta.
Breandán: An bhfuil ceol agat féin?
Caroline: *Yes. I play the fiddle. Are* ***you*** *musical?*
Tá. Seinnim an fhidil. An bhfuil ceol agatsa?
Breandán: Níl. Níl ceol ar bith agam – faraor!
Caroline: *Do you play sport?*
An imríonn tú spórt?
Breandán: Imrím. Imrím peil agus leadóg.

Exercise 5.4: Fill in the gaps

1. *What do you do when you have free time?*
   Céard a <u>dhéanann</u> tú nuair a bhíonn am saor agat?
2. *I go running.*
   Téim ag <u>rith</u>.
3. *I watch television.*
   <u>Féachaim</u> ar an teilifís.
4. *I listen to music.*
   <u>Éistim</u> le ceol.
5. *I go to the cinema.*
   <u>Téim</u> go dtí an phictiúrlann.
6. *Do you play tennis?*
   An <u>imríonn</u> tú leadóg?
7. *Do you go to the pub?*
   An <u>dtéann</u> tú go dtí an teach tábhairne?
8. *Do you like traditional music?*
   An <u>maith</u> leat ceol traidisiúnta?
9. *It's okay.*
   Tá sé <u>ceart</u> go leor.
10. *I like to read.*
    Is maith liom <u>bheith</u> ag léamh.

Exercise 5.5: Compose questions

1. An dtéann tú ag rith?
2. An imríonn tú peil?
3. An éisteann tú leis an raidió?
4. An bhféachann tú ar an teilifís?
5. An dtéann tú chuig ceolchoirmeacha?
6. An éisteann tú le ceol?
7. An maith leat ceol clasaiceach?
8. An bhfuil ceol agat?

Exercise 5.6: Your turn!

Áine: *I go to the pub nearly every night!*
Téim go dtí an teach tábhairne beagnach gach oíche!
Lucy: Tá sé sin an-dána! An dtéann tú chuig ceolchoirmeacha?
Áine: *Yes, usually on Friday night or on Saturday night.*
Téim, oíche Dé hAoine nó oíche Dé Sathairn de ghnáth.
Lucy: Go hiontach.
Áine: *And I often go to a play or a film as well.*
Agus téim chuig dráma nó chuig scannán go minic freisin.
Lucy: Tá saol iontach agat!

Exercise 5.7: Your turn!

Interviewer: Céard a dhéanann tú nuair a bhíonn am saor agat?
Mark: *I watch television.*
Féachaim ar an teilifís.
Interviewer: An imríonn tú spórt?
Mark: *No. I haven't the slightest interest in it.*
Ní imrím. Níl suim dá laghad agam ann.
Interviewer: Em. Cé chomh minic is a théann tú chuig drámaí?
Mark: *Very seldom.*
Go fíorannamh.

Exercise 5.8: Review of Unit 5

1. *I go swimming.*
   Téim ag snámh.
2. *I play tennis.*
   Imrím leadóg.
3. *I listen to the radio.*
   Éistim leis an raidió.
4. *I go to the cinema.*
   Téim go dtí an phictiúrlann.
5. *Do you play tennis? No.*
   An imríonn tú leadóg? Ní imrím.
6. *Do you go to the pub? Yes.*
   An dtéann tú go dtí an teach tábhairne? Téim.
7. *Do you watch television? No.*
   An bhféachann tú ar an teilifís? Ní fhéachaim.
8. *Do you like classical music? Yes.*
   An maith leat ceol clasaiceach? Is maith.
9. *Do you like rugby? I love it.*
   An maith leat rugbaí? Is breá liom é.
10. *I like to read.*
    Is maith liom bheith ag léamh.
11. *I love to sing.*
    Is breá liom bheith ag canadh.
12. *I often go to concerts.*
    Téim chuig ceolchoirmeacha go minic.
13. *I like to play soccer.*
    Is maith liom sacar a imirt.
14. *I haven't the slightest interest in tennis.*
    Níl suim dá laghad agam i leadóg.
15. *I go to a play once a week.*
    Téim chuig dráma uair sa tseachtain.

Unit 6: Daily Life

Exercise 6.1: It's three o'clock

1. Person 1: Clock C, Tá sé a cúig a chlog.
2. Person 2: Clock A, Tá sé a trí a chlog.
3. Person 3: Clock F, Tá sé ceathrú tar éis a seacht.
4. Person 4: Clock B, Tá sé leathuair tar éis a dó dhéag.
5. Person 5: Clock E, Tá sé ceathrú chun a haon déag.
6. Person 6: Clock D, Tá sé leathuair tar éis a dó.

Exercise 6.2: Answer the questions

1. Cén t-am a éiríonn tú ar maidin?
   Say: Around seven o'clock.
   Timpeall a seacht a chlog.
2. Cén t-am a éiríonn tú ar maidin?
   Say: At half past seven.
   Ag leathuair tar éis a seacht.
3. Cén t-am a théann tú ag obair?
   Say: At a quarter past eight.
   Ag ceathrú tar éis a hocht.

4. Cén t-am a théann tú ag obair de ghnáth?
   Say: At five o'clock.
   Ag a cúig a chlog.
5. Cén t-am a bhíonn do lón agat?
   Say: Between one and two.
   Idir a haon agus a dó.
6. Cén t-am a bhíonn do lón agat?
   Say: Around two o'clock.
   Timpeall a dó a chlog.
7. Cén t-am a bhíonn tú sa bhaile?
   Say: At six o'clock.
   Ag a sé a chlog.
8. Cén t-am a bhíonn tú sa bhaile?
   Say: At a quarter to eight.
   Ag ceathrú chun a hocht.
9. Cén t-am a itheann tú do dhinnéar?
   Say: At half past eight.
   Ag leathuair tar éis a hocht.
10. Cén t-am a théann tú a chodladh?
    Say: Between ten and eleven.
    Idir a deich agus a haon déag.

Exercise 6.3: Translate the sentences

1. *Excuse me. What time is it?*
   Gabh mo leithscéal. Cén t-am atá sé?
2. *Half past three.*
   Leathuair tar éis a trí.
3. *A quarter to eleven.*
   Ceathrú chun a haon déag.
4. *What time do you get up in the morning?*
   Cén t-am a éiríonn tú ar maidin?
5. *What time do you usually go to work?*
   Cén t-am a théann tú ag obair de ghnáth?
6. *What time do **you** go to work?*
   Cén t-am a théann tusa ag obair?
7. *I start working at eight o'clock.*
   Tosaím ag obair ag a hocht a chlog.
8. *I'm home around seven o'clock.*
   Bím sa bhaile timpeall a seacht a chlog.
9. *I eat my dinner between seven and eight.*
   Ithim mo dhinnéar idir a seacht agus a hocht.
10. *I go to bed at eleven.*
    Téim a chodladh ag a haon déag.

Exercise 6.4: Your turn!

Jenny: Cén t-am a éiríonn tú de ghnáth?
Pádraig: *I get up around eight and I have breakfast at home.*
Éirím timpeall a hocht agus bíonn bricfeasta agam sa bhaile.
Jenny: Níl sé sin róluath.
Pádraig: *No, it's not too bad. I'm at work around nine.*
Níl, níl sé ró-olc. Bím san obair timpeall a naoi.
Jenny: Agus cén t-am a fhágann tú an obair?
Pádraig: *Between five and half past five.*
Idir a cúig agus leathuair tar éis a cúig.

Exercise 6.5: Your turn!

Jenny: An mbíonn dinnéar agat sa bhaile?
Pádraig: *Yes, usually. Sometimes I have dinner in a restaurant with my friends.*
Bíonn, de ghnáth. Uaireanta bíonn dinnéar agam i mbialann le mo chairde.
Jenny: An dtéann tú amach mórán san oíche?
Pádraig: *I'm very tired after work but I go out one or two nights.*
Bím an-tuirseach tar éis na hoibre ach téim amach oíche nó dhó.
Jenny: Céard a dhéanann tú?
Pádraig: *I usually go to a concert or a music session.*
Téim chuig ceolchoirm nó chuig seisiún ceoil de ghnáth.

Exercise 6.6: Fill in the gaps

1. *What time is it, please?*
   Cén t-am atá sé, le <u>do</u> <u>thoil</u>?
2. *It's half past ten.*
   Tá sé <u>leathuair</u> tar éis a deich.
3. *What time do you go to work?*
   Cén t-am a <u>théann</u> tú ag obair?
4. *I start working at nine o'clock.*
   <u>Tosaím</u> ag obair ag a naoi a chlog.
5. *I leave work around five.*
   <u>Fágaim</u> an obair timpeall a cúig.
6. *I go to bed at eleven at the latest.*
   Téim a chodladh ag a haon déag ar <u>a</u> <u>dhéanaí</u>.
7. *What time do you have a break?*
   Cén t-am a <u>bhíonn</u> sos agat?
8. *Do you go out sometimes?*
   An <u>dtéann</u> tú amach uaireanta?
9. *I'm very tired after work.*
   <u>Bím</u> an-tuirseach tar éis na hoibre.
10. *I'm very tired today.*
    <u>Tá</u> mé an-tuirseach inniu.

Exercise 6.7: Answer the questions

1. An mbíonn dinnéar agat sa bhaile?
   Bíonn./Ní bhíonn.
2. An éiríonn tú go luath?
   Éirím./Ní éirím.
3. An itheann tú do dhinnéar sa bhaile?
   Ithim./Ní ithim.
4. An dtéann tú chuig drámaí?
   Téim./Ní théim.
5. An bhfaigheann tú traein abhaile?
   Faighim./Ní fhaighim.
6. An bhfágann tú an obair ag a sé a chlog?
   Fágaim./Ní fhágaim.
7. An bhfuil tú tuirseach inniu?
   Tá./Níl.
8. An mbíonn tú tuirseach gach tráthnóna?
   Bím./Ní bhím.

Exercise 6.8: Your turn!

Peter: An maith leat an post nua?
Cathy: *I love it. It's very interesting.*
Is breá liom é. Tá sé an-suimiúil.
Peter: An mbíonn tú ag obair gach deireadh seachtaine?
Cathy: *Yes. The bar is very busy on Friday and Saturday.*
Bím. Bíonn an beár an-ghnóthach Dé hAoine agus Dé Sathairn.
Peter: An mbíonn tú ag obair déanach?
Cathy: *Yes. I usually get a taxi home around three o'clock.*
Bím. Faighim tacsaí abhaile timpeall a trí a chlog de ghnáth.

Exercise 6.9: Your turn!

Peter: An mbíonn tú i gcónaí an-tuirseach tar éis an deireadh seachtaine?
Cathy: *Yes. I'm exhausted.*
Bím. Bím traochta.
Peter: Tá tú an-tuirseach faoi láthair, nach bhfuil?
Cathy: *Sorry – I'm very tired. The weekend was tough.*
Tá brón orm – tá mé an-tuirseach. Bhí an deireadh seachtaine dian.
Peter: An bhfuil tú ag obair gan stop?
Cathy: *No. I have a very good social life as well.*
Níl. Tá saol sóisialta an-mhaith agam freisin.

Exercise 6.10: Review of Unit 6

1. *What time is it, please?*
   Cén t-am atá sé, le do thoil?
2. *It's a quarter to twelve.*
   Tá sé ceathrú chun a dó dhéag.
3. *It's half past six.*
   Tá sé leathuair tar éis a sé.
4. *What time do you have a break?*
   Cén t-am a bhíonn sos agat?

5. *At a quarter past ten.*
Ag ceathrú tar éis a deich.
6. *What time are you home?*
Cén t-am a bhíonn tú sa bhaile?
7. *Do you get the train home?*
An bhfaigheann tú an traein abhaile?
8. *Do you have dinner at home? Yes.*
An mbíonn dinnéar agat sa bhaile? Bíonn.
9. *Do you eat your dinner around seven?*
An itheann tú do dhinnéar timpeall a seacht?
10. *What time do you go to bed/to sleep?*
Cén t-am a théann tú a chodladh?
11. *At midnight at the latest.*
Ag meán oíche ar a dhéanaí.
12. *I get a taxi home around three o'clock.*
Faighim tacsaí abhaile timpeall a trí a chlog.
13. *Are you tired every Saturday?*
An mbíonn tú tuirseach gach Satharn?
14. *You're very tired at the moment, aren't you?*
Tá tú an-tuirseach faoi láthair, nach bhfuil?
15. *The weekend was tough.*
Bhí an deireadh seachtaine dian.

Unit 7: Talents and Skills

Exercise 7.1: Answer the questions

1. An bhfuil Fraincis agat?
Say: Yes.
Tá.
2. Cé chomh maith is atá tú?
Say: I'm okay.
Tá mé maith go leor.
3. Cé chomh maith is atá tú?
Say: I'm not too good.
Níl mé rómhaith.
4. Cé chomh maith is atá tú?
Say: I'm very good.
Tá mé an-mhaith.
5. An bhfuil sé furasta?
Say: It's easy enough.
Tá sé furasta go leor.
6. An bhfuil sé furasta?
Say: It's very easy.
Tá sé an-fhurasta.
7. An bhfuil sé deacair?
Say: It's very difficult.
Tá sé an-deacair.
8. An bhfuil sé deacair?
Say: It's not too difficult.
Níl sé ródheacair.

Exercise 7.2: Give the Irish version

1. *very good*
an-mhaith
2. *very hot*
an-te
3. *too difficult*
ródheacair
4. *very difficult*
an-deacair
5. *too easy* (use *éasca*)
ró-éasca
6. *very easy* (use *éasca*)
an-éasca
7. *too old*
róshean
8. *very easy* (use *furasta*)
an-fhurasta

Exercise 7.3: Your turn!

Interviewer: Cé chomh maith is atá tú ag clóscríobh?
Sinéad: *I'm reasonably good – I can type fifty words per minute.*
Tá mé réasúnta maith – tá mé ábalta caoga focal sa nóiméad a chlóscríobh.
Interviewer: Go breá. Tá Fraincis agat, feicim. Cé chomh maith is atá tú?
Sinéad: *I'm very good. I did French in university. And I'm learning Spanish.*
Tá mé an-mhaith. Rinne mé Fraincis san ollscoil. Agus tá mé ag foghlaim Spáinnise.
Interviewer: An bhfuil an Spáinnis deacair?
Sinéad: *It's difficult enough.*
Tá sí deacair go leor.

Exercise 7.4: Your turn!

Interviewer: Céard a dhéanann tú nuair a bhíonn am saor agat?
Sinéad: *I like to read and I have a lot of interest in music.*
Is maith liom bheith ag léamh agus tá suim mhór agam sa cheol.
Interviewer: An bhfuil ceol agat féin?
Sinéad: *Yes. I play the fiddle and the tin whistle.*
Tá. Seinnim an fhidil agus an fheadóg stáin.
Interviewer: Cé chomh maith is atá tú ar an bhfidil?
Sinéad: *I'm okay. I'm learning for three years now.*
Tá mé maith go leor. Tá mé ag foghlaim le trí bliana anois.

Exercise 7.5: Fill in the gaps

1. *Can you type?*
An bhfuil <u>clóscríobh</u> agat?
2. *Can you use a computer?*
An bhfuil tú <u>ábalta</u> ríomhaire a <u>úsáid</u>?
3. *How good are you?*
Cé chomh maith is <u>atá</u> tú?
4. *I'm reasonably good.*
Tá mé <u>réasúnta</u> maith.
5. *It's not too easy.*
Níl sé <u>rófhurasta</u>.
6. *It's too difficult.*
Tá sé <u>ródheacair</u>.
7. *It's very difficult.*
Tá sé <u>an-deacair</u>.
8. *And I'm learning Spanish.*
Agus tá mé ag foghlaim <u>Spáinnise</u>.
9. *Are you musical yourself?*
An bhfuil ceol <u>agat</u> <u>féin</u>?
10. *How good are you on the fiddle?*
Cé chomh maith is <u>atá</u> tú ar an <u>bhfidil</u>?

Exercise 7.6: Answer the questions

1. Cén fhad atá tú ag foghlaim Gaeilge?
Say: For a month now.
Le mí anois.
2. Cén fhad atá tú ag foghlaim Iodáilise?
Say: For the past three years.
Le trí bliana anuas.
3. Cén fhad atá tú ag foghlaim Gearmáinise?
Say: For a few years.
Le cúpla bliain.
4. An bhfuil an Rúisis deacair?
Say: It's very difficult.
Tá sí an-deacair.
5. An bhfuil Gearmáinis agat?
Say: Yes. I'm fluent.
Tá. Tá mé líofa.
6. Cad iad na teangacha atá agat?
Say: Irish, English and Japanese.
Gaeilge, Béarla agus Seapáinis.
7. An bhfuil Iodáilis agat?
Say: Yes. I speak some Italian.
Tá. Tá beagán Iodáilise agam.

8. An bhfuil Fraincis agat?
   Say: I speak fluent French.
   Tá Fraincis líofa agam.

Exercise 7.7: Your turn!

Colm: *What languages do you speak?*
Cad iad na teangacha atá agat?
Clíona: Tá Gearmáinis líofa agam agus beagán Fraincise.
Colm: *And you speak fluent English, of course!*
Agus tá Béarla líofa agat, gan amhras!
Clíona: Tá!
Colm: *Do you speak any other language?*
An bhfuil teanga ar bith eile agat?
Clíona: Bhuel, tá cúpla focal Iodáilise agam.

Exercise 7.8: Your turn!

Clíona: Cad iad na teangacha atá agat féin?
Colm: *Well, I'm a native speaker of Irish. I was brought up through English and Irish.*
Bhuel, is cainteoir dúchais Gaeilge mé. Tógadh le Béarla agus Gaeilge mé.
Clíona: An-suimiúil. An bhfuil teangacha iasachta ar bith agat?
Colm: *I'm learning French at the moment. I'm attending a course.*
Tá mé ag foghlaim Fraincise faoi láthair. Tá mé ag freastal ar chúrsa.
Clíona: Conas atá ag éirí leat?
Colm: *Okay.*
Maith go leor.

Exercise 7.9: Review of Unit 7

1. *How good are you?*
   Cé chomh maith is atá tú?
2. *I'm reasonably good.*
   Tá mé réasúnta maith.
3. *It's not too easy* (use *furasta*).
   Níl sé rófhurasta.
4. *It's easy enough.*
   Tá sé furasta go leor.
5. *It's too difficult.*
   Tá sé ródheacair.
6. *You speak French, I see.*
   Tá Fraincis agat, feicim.
7. *Is Spanish difficult?*
   An bhfuil an Spáinnis deacair?
8. *Are you musical yourself?*
   An bhfuil ceol agat féin?
9. *I've been learning for three years now.*
   Tá mé ag foghlaim le trí bliana anois.
10. *How long have you been learning Irish?*
    Cén fhad atá tú ag foghlaim Gaeilge?
11. *For the past fortnight.*
    Le coicís anuas.
12. *For a few years.*
    Le cúpla bliain.
13. *Japanese is very difficult.*
    Tá an tSeapáinis an-deacair.
14. *I speak some French.*
    Tá beagán Fraincise agam.
15. *I have a few words of Italian.*
    Tá cúpla focal Iodáilise agam.

Unit 8: Work

Exercise 8.1: Match the words

1. ospidéal and (g) hospital
2. gruagaire and (a) hairdresser
3. monarcha and (k) factory
4. comhlacht and (i) company
5. bainisteoir and (h) manager
6. tiománaí and (j) driver
7. ollmhargadh and (e) supermarket
8. bialann and (f) restaurant
9. óstán and (c) hotel
10. altra and (b) nurse

Exercise 8.2: Answer the questions

1. Cén post atá agat?
   Say: I'm a manager.
   Is bainisteoir mé.
2. Cén obair a dhéanann tú?
   Say: I'm a teacher.
   Is múinteoir mé.
3. Cén post atá agat?
   Say: I'm a secretary.
   Is rúnaí mé.
4. Cén obair a dhéanann tú?
   Say: I'm a waiter.
   Is freastalaí mé.
5. Cén post atá agat?
   Say: I'm a mechanic.
   Is meicneoir mé.
6. Cén obair a dhéanann tú?
   Say: I'm a doctor.
   Is dochtúir mé.
7. Cén áit a bhfuil tú ag obair?
   Say: I'm working in an office.
   Tá mé ag obair in oifig.
8. Cén áit a bhfuil tú ag obair?
   Say: I'm working in a company.
   Tá mé ag obair i gcomhlacht.
9. Cén áit a bhfuil tú ag obair?
   Say: In a supermarket.
   In ollmhargadh.
10. Cén áit a bhfuil tú ag obair?
    Say: In a restaurant.
    I mbialann.

Exercise 8.3: Your turn!

Alan: Cén post atá agat na laethanta seo?
Diarmuid: *I'm a waiter. I'm working in an Italian restaurant in the city centre.*
Is freastalaí mé. Tá mé ag obair i mbialann Iodálach i lár na cathrach.
Alan: An maith leat an post?
Diarmuid: *It's okay. The other people who are working with me are nice.*
Tá sé ceart go leor. Tá na daoine eile atá ag obair liom go deas.
Alan: An bhfuil an pá go maith?
Diarmuid: *No. It's terrible!*
Níl. Tá sé go dona!

Exercise 8.4: Your turn!

Diarmuid: Cén áit a bhfuil tú féin ag obair anois?
Alan: *I'm unemployed at the moment. I'm looking for work.*
Tá mé dífhostaithe faoi láthair. Tá mé ag lorg oibre.
Diarmuid: Tá brón orm é sin a chloisteáil. Cén fhad atá tú dífhostaithe?
Alan: *For the past six months. I lost my job in January.*
Le sé mhí anuas. Chaill mé mo phost i mí Eanáir.
Diarmuid: Sin tamall fada. Tá mé cinnte go bhfuil tú bréan de bheith as obair.
Alan: *Yes. I hate it.*
Tá. Is fuath liom é.

Exercise 8.5: Fill in the gaps

1. *What do you work at?*
   Cén obair a dhéanann tú?
2. *What job do **you** have?*
   Cén post atá agatsa?
3. *I'm working in an office in the city centre.*
   Tá mé ag obair in oifig i lár na cathrach.

4. *I'm working in a pub on the edge of town.*
   Tá mé ag obair i dteach tábhairne ar imeall an bhaile.
5. *Where are you working?*
   Cén áit a bhfuil tú ag obair?
6. *I'm self-employed.*
   Tá mé féinfhostaithe.
7. *I'm looking for work at the moment.*
   Tá mé ag lorg oibre faoi láthair.
8. *I don't like the job at all.*
   Ní maith liom an post ar chor ar bith.
9. *I hate it.*
   Is fuath liom é.
10. *How long have you been unemployed?*
   Cén fhad atá tú dífhostaithe?

Exercise 8.6: Answer the questions

1. An bhfuil tú ag obair i mbialann?
   Say: No. I'm working in a pub.
   Níl. Tá mé ag obair i dteach tábhairne.
2. An freastalaí tú?
   Say: Yes.
   Is ea.
3. An dochtúir tú?
   Say: No. I'm a nurse.
   Ní hea. Is altra mé.
4. An bainisteoir tú?
   Say: No. I'm a secretary.
   Ní hea. Is rúnaí mé.
5. An freastalaí tú?
   Say: Yes. I'm working in a restaurant.
   Is ea. Tá mé ag obair i mbialann.
6. An meicneoir tú?
   Say: No. I'm a driver.
   Ní hea. Is tiománaí mé.
7. An maith leat do phost?
   Say: I don't like it at all.
   Ní maith liom ar chor ar bith é.
8. An post lánaimseartha é?
   Say: No. It's a part-time job.
   Ní hea. Is post páirtaimseartha é.
9. An post sealadach é?
   Say: Yes.
   Is ea.
10. An post sealadach é?
   Say: No. It's a permanent job.
   Ní hea. Is post buan é.

Exercise 8.7: Your turn!

Caoimhe: Cén obair a dhéanann tú?
Martin: *I'm a nurse. I work in Saint James' Hospital.*
Is altra mé. Tá mé ag obair in Ospidéal San Séamas.
Caoimhe: An-suimiúil. An post deacair é?
Martin: *Yes, it's difficult enough. I work long hours.*
Is ea, tá sé deacair go leor. Oibrím uaireanta fada.
Caoimhe: An maith leat an post, mar sin féin?
Martin: *Yes – I love it.*
Is maith – is breá liom é.

Exercise 8.8: Your turn!

Martin: Cén obair a dhéanann tú féin?
Caoimhe: *I'm a secretary. I'm working in a small company.*
Is rúnaí mé. Tá mé ag obair i gcomhlacht beag.
Martin: An post lánaimseartha é?
Caoimhe: *Yes. I work the usual hours.*
Is ea. Oibrím na gnáthuaireanta.
Martin: An maith leat é?
Caoimhe: *No. It's very boring.*
Ní maith. Tá sé an-leadránach.

Exercise 8.9: Review of Unit 8

1. *What do you work at?*
   Cén obair a dhéanann tú?
2. *What do you work at yourself?*
   Cén obair a dhéanann tú féin?
3. *I'm a butcher.*
   Is búistéir mé.
4. *I'm a builder.*
   Is tógálaí mé.
5. *Where are you working?*
   Cén áit a bhfuil tú ag obair?
6. *I work in a factory.*
   Tá mé ag obair i monarcha.
7. *I work in an hotel.*
   Tá mé ag obair in óstán.
8. *I'm self-employed.*
   Tá mé féinfhostaithe.
9. *I'm unemployed at the moment.*
   Tá mé dífhostaithe faoi láthair.
10. *Do you like your job? No.*
   An maith leat do phost? Ní maith.
11. *Are you a secretary? Yes.*
   An rúnaí tú? Is ea.
12. *What hours do you work?*
   Cad iad na huaireanta a oibríonn tú?
13. *I work long hours.*
   Oibrím uaireanta fada.
14. *Is it a permanent job? No.*
   An post buan é? Ní hea.
15. *It's a temporary job.*
   Is post sealadach é.

Unit 9: Food and Drink

Exercise 9.1: Match the words

1. siúcra and (f) sugar
2. gloine bainne and (j) glass of milk
3. arán donn and (a) brown bread
4. arán bán and (m) white bread
5. torthaí and (k) fruit
6. im and (l) butter
7. iasc and (i) fish
8. bia mara and (g) seafood
9. feoil and (e) meat
10. milseog and (c) dessert
11. briosca and (h) biscuit
12. anraith and (b) soup

Exercise 9.2: Give the Irish version

1. *orange juice*
   sú oráiste
2. *white bread*
   arán bán
3. *a cup of tea*
   cupán tae
4. *sugar*
   siúcra
5. *cornflakes*
   calóga arbhair
6. *fish*
   iasc
7. *dessert*
   milseog
8. *biscuits*
   brioscaí
9. *fruit salad*
   sailéad torthaí
10. *a glass of milk*
   gloine bainne

Exercise 9.3: Your turn!

Fiona: An itheann tú feoil?
Aoife: *Yes, indeed. I eat all kinds of food.*
Ithim, cinnte. Ithim gach cineál bia.

Fiona: Ithimse feoil freisin ach ní ithim bia mara.
Aoife: *Do you like Indian food? There's an Indian restaurant near the centre of town.*
An maith leat bia Indiach? Tá bialann Indiach gar do lár an bhaile.
Fiona: An bhfuil sé daor?
Aoife: *No, and the food is very tasty.*
Níl, agus tá an bia an-bhlasta.

Exercise 9.4: Your turn!
Fiona: Conas atá an sicín?
Aoife: *It's very spicy but very nice. How is your own meal?*
Tá sé an-spíosrach ach an-deas. Conas atá do bhéile féin?
Fiona: Tá sé an-bhlasta ach rud beag fuar.
Aoife: *That's a pity. Is the naan bread nice?*
Is mór an trua sin. An bhfuil an t-arán naan go deas?
Fiona: Tá, tá sé deas úr. Ar mhaith leat píosa?
Aoife: *No, thanks. I'm full!*
Níor mhaith, go raibh maith agat. Tá mé lán!

Exercise 9.5: Fill in the gaps
1. *I'm hungry.*
Tá ocras orm.
2. *Are you thirsty?*
An bhfuil tart ort?
3. *I don't eat meat. I'm a vegetarian.*
Ní ithim feoil. Is veigeatóir mé.
4. *I don't drink red wine.*
Ní ólaim fíon dearg.
5. *Do you eat meat?*
An itheann tú feoil?
6. *I love Italian food.*
Is breá liom bia Iodálach.
7. *I think Japanese food is nice.*
Ceapaim go bhfuil bia Seapánach go deas.
8. *It's very spicy but very nice.*
Tá sé an-spíosrach ach an-deas.
9. *It's nice and fresh.*
Tá sé deas úr.
10. *Would you like a piece?*
Ar mhaith leat píosa?

Exercise 9.6: Answer the questions
1. An maith leat bia Meicsiceach?
Say: I love it.
Is breá liom é.
2. An maith leat bia Seapánach?
Say: Yes. I think it's nice.
Is maith. Ceapaim go bhfuil sé go deas.
3. Conas atá an sicín?
Say: It's very spicy but very nice.
Tá sé an-spíosrach ach an-deas.
4. An mbeidh deoch agat?
Say: I'll have a black coffee, please.
Beidh caife dubh agam, le do thoil.
5. Cad ba mhaith leat?
Say: Red wine, please.
Fíon dearg, le do thoil.
6. Cé mhéad sin?
Say: Four euro seventy cent.
Ceithre euro seachtó cent.
7. Cé mhéad sin?
Say: Eight euro thirty cent.
Ocht euro tríocha cent.
8. Cé mhéad sin?
Say: Ten euro twenty cent.
Deich euro fiche cent.

Exercise 9.7: Your turn!
Gearóidín: Ar mhaith leat tae nó caife? Nó arbh fhearr leat gloine uisce?
Cormac: *I'll have a cup of coffee, please.*
Beidh cupán caife agam, le do thoil.
Gearóidín: An dtógann tú siúcra?
Cormac: *Yes. Two spoons, please.*
Tógaim. Dhá spúnóg, le do thoil.
Gearóidín: Agus bainne?
Cormac: *I don't take milk. Thank you.*
Ní thógaim bainne. Go raibh maith agat.
Gearóidín: Go ndéana a mhaith duit.

Exercise 9.8: Your turn!
Seosamh: *What would you like?*
Cad ba mhaith leat?
Peadar: Pionta Guinness, le do thoil. Cad a bheidh agatsa?
Seosamh: *I'll have a pint as well.*
Beidh pionta agamsa freisin.
Peadar: Ar mhaith leat rud éigin a ithe?
Seosamh: *Yes. I'm really hungry.*
Ba mhaith. Tá an-ocras orm.

Exercise 9.9: Masculine and feminine
1. putóg (feminine) (*pudding*)
an phutóg
2. arán (masculine) (*bread*)
an t-arán
3. siúcra (masculine) (*sugar*)
an siúcra
4. milseog (feminine) (*dessert*)
an mhilseog
5. anraith (masculine) (*soup*)
an t-anraith
6. beoir (feminine) (*beer*)
an bheoir
7. ubh (feminine) (*egg*)
an ubh
8. fíon (masculine) (*wine*)
an fíon
9. bia (masculine) (*food*)
an bia
10. bialann (feminine) (*restaurant*)
an bhialann

Exercise 9.10: Review of Unit 9
1. *I'm hungry.*
Tá ocras orm.
2. *Are you thirsty?*
An bhfuil tart ort?
3. *I don't eat meat. I'm a vegetarian.*
Ní ithim feoil. Is veigeatóir mé.
4. *I don't drink red wine.*
Ní ólaim fíon dearg.
5. *Do you drink white wine? Yes.*
An ólann tú fíon geal? Ólaim.
6. *I love Japanese food.*
Is breá liom bia Seapánach.
7. *I think Chinese food is nice.*
Ceapaim go bhfuil bia Síneach go deas.
8. *Do you like Italian food? Yes.*
An maith leat bia Iodálach? Is maith.
9. *Do you like French food? No.*
An maith leat bia Francach? Ní maith.
10. *It's very tasty.*
Tá sé an-bhlasta.
11. *It's very spicy but very nice.*
Tá sé an-spíosrach ach an-deas.
12. *Will you have a drink? No, thanks.*
An mbeidh deoch agat? Ní bheidh, go raibh maith agat.
13. *I'll have a glass of wine, please.*
Beidh gloine fíona agam, le do thoil.
14. *What would you like?*
Cad ba mhaith leat?

15. *How much is that? Three euro fifty cent.*
Cé mhéad sin? Trí euro caoga cent.

Unit 10: Health Matters

Exercise 10.1: Answer the questions

1. An bhfuil tú tinn?
Say: Yes. I have the flu.
Tá. Tá fliú orm.
2. An bhfuil tú tinn?
Say: Yes. I have a pain in my stomach.
Tá. Tá pian i mo bholg.
3. An bhfuil tú tinn?
Say: Yes. I'm very sick.
Tá. Tá mé an-tinn.
4. Cad atá ort?
Say: I have a headache.
Tá tinneas cinn orm.
5. Cad atá ort?
Say: I have a cold.
Tá slaghdán orm.
6. Cad atá ort?
Say: I have a toothache.
Tá tinneas fiacaile orm.
7. Cad atá ort?
Say: I have a cough.
Tá casachtach orm.
8. Cad atá ort?
Say: I have a sore throat.
Tá scornach thinn orm.

Exercise 10.2: Your turn!

Méabh: *I don't feel well at all.*
Níl mé ag mothú go maith ar chor ar bith.
Siobhán: Cad atá ort?
Méabh: *I have a sore throat and a bad cough.*
Tá scornach thinn orm agus droch-chasachtach.
Siobhán: A chréatúir! Seans go bhfuil fliú ag teacht ort.
Méabh: *I'd say so. I feel terrible.*
Déarfainn é. Tá mé ag mothú go dona.
Siobhán: Téigh go dtí do leaba agus beidh tú níos fearr amárach.

Exercise 10.3: Your turn!

Máirín: *Are you okay, Séamas? You look sick.*
An bhfuil tú ceart go leor, a Shéamais? Tá cuma thinn ort.
Séamas: Níl mé ag mothú go maith ar chor ar bith.
Máirín: *What's wrong with you?*
Cad atá ort?
Séamas: Tá pian uafásach i mo bholg.
Máirín: *How long have you had that?*
Cén fhad atá sé sin ort?
Séamas: Tá sé orm ó mhaidin. Agus tá sé ag éirí níos measa.
Máirín: *Go on home. You'll have recovered by the morning, I'm sure.*
Imigh leat abhaile. Beidh biseach ort ar maidin, tá mé cinnte.

Exercise 10.4: Fill in the gaps

1. *I don't feel well.*
Níl mé ag <u>mothú</u> go maith.
2. *I have a sore throat.*
Tá scornach <u>thinn</u> orm.
3. *I have a toothache.*
Tá <u>tinneas</u> <u>fiacaile</u> orm.
4. *That's a pity.*
Is mór an <u>trua</u> sin.
5. *How long have you had that?*
Cén <u>fhad</u> atá sé sin ort?
6. *For the past few days.*
Le cúpla lá <u>anuas</u>.
7. *For a week now.*
Le <u>seachtain</u> anois.
8. *Are you recovering?*
An bhfuil <u>biseach</u> ag teacht ort?
9. *Are you better?*
An bhfuil tú níos <u>fearr</u>?
10. *No, I'm worse.*
Níl, tá mé níos <u>measa</u>.

Exercise 10.5: Give the Irish version

1. *breast*
brollach
2. *face*
aghaidh
3. *hands*
lámha
4. *eyes*
súile
5. *hair*
gruaig
6. *backside*
tóin
7. *nose*
srón
8. *neck*
muineál
9. *fingers*
méara
10. *leg*
cos
11. *legs*
cosa
12. *stomach*
bolg

Exercise 10.6: Your turn!

Nollaig: Cén chuma atá ar an mbainisteoir nua?
Niamh: *She's very good-looking. She has long brown hair …*
Tá sí an-dathúil. Tá gruaig fhada dhonn uirthi …
Nollaig: Go deas!
Niamh: *… and she has blue eyes.*
… agus tá súile gorma aici.
Nollaig: An bhfuil sí cairdiúil?
Niamh: *Yes. She's very friendly. Oh, and too young for **you**.*
Tá. Tá sí an-chairdiúil. Ó, agus ró-óg duitse.

Exercise 10.7: Your turn!

Rebecca: *Are you okay? What happened?*
An bhfuil tú ceart go leor? Cad a tharla?
Deirbhile: Thit mé de mo rothar inné agus ghortaigh mé mo chos.
Rebecca: *It's not broken?*
Níl sí briste?
Deirbhile: Níl, buíochas le Dia.
Rebecca: *You were lucky. Is it sore?*
Bhí an t-ádh leat. An bhfuil sí tinn?
Deirbhile: Níl sí ró-olc. Chuaigh mé chuig an dochtúir agus thug sé táibléid dom don phian.
Rebecca: *That's good. **I** fell while skiing last year and I broke my arm.*
Is maith sin. Thit mise agus mé ag sciáil anuraidh agus bhris mé mo lámh.

Exercise 10.8: Give the Irish version

1. *my breast*
mo bhrollach
2. *your face*
d'aghaidh
3. *your hands*
do lámha
4. *my eyes*
mo shúile
5. *your hair*
do ghruaig
6. *my backside*
mo thóin

7. *my nose*
mo shrón
8. *your neck*
do mhuineál
9. *your fingers*
do mhéara
10. *my leg*
mo chos
11. *your legs*
do chosa
12. *my stomach*
mo bholg

Exercise 10.9: Review of Unit 10

1. *I don't feel well.*
Níl mé ag mothú go maith.
2. *I'm very sick.*
Tá mé an-tinn.
3. *What's wrong with you?*
Cad atá ort?
4. *I have a cold.*
Tá slaghdán orm.
5. *I have a sore throat.*
Tá scornach thinn orm.
6. *How long have you been sick?*
Cén fhad atá tú tinn?
7. *Are you better?*
An bhfuil tú níos fearr?
8. *Are you recovering?*
An bhfuil biseach ag teacht ort?
9. *I'm much better.*
Tá mé i bhfad níos fearr.
10. *She has a cough.*
Tá casachtach uirthi.
11. *He has long hair.*
Tá gruaig fhada air.
12. *What does he look like?*
Cén chuma atá air?
13. *He has blue eyes.*
Tá súile gorma aige.
14. *She has nice teeth.*
Tá fiacla deasa aici.
15. *I hurt my leg.*
Ghortaigh mé mo chos.

Unit 11: Clothes and Shopping

Exercise 11.1: Answer the questions

1. An maith leat an geansaí sin?
Say: Yes.
Is maith.
2. An maith leat an léine seo?
Say: No.
Ní maith.
3. An maith leat an cóta seo?
Say: I love it.
Is breá liom é.
4. An maith leat an chulaith sin?
Say: I don't like it at all.
Ní maith liom ar chor ar bith í.
5. An maith leat na bróga sin?
Say: I don't like them at all.
Ní maith liom ar chor ar bith iad.
6. An maith leat an carbhat seo?
Say: Yes. I love it.
Is maith. Is breá liom é.
7. An maith leat na riteoga sin?
Say: I love them.
Is breá liom iad.
8. An maith leat na stocaí seo?
Say: I don't like them at all.
Ní maith liom ar chor ar bith iad.
9. An maith leat na buataisí seo?
Say: No.
Ní maith.
10. An maith leat an gúna seo?
Say: I love it.
Is breá liom é.

Exercise 11.2: Match the words

1. bróga and (i) shoes
2. crios and (k) belt
3. gúnaí and (m) dresses
4. culaith and (h) suit/dress
5. cóta báistí and (j) raincoat
6. geansaí and (c) sweater
7. bróg and (e) shoe
8. fo-éadaí and (b) underwear
9. riteoga and (f) tights
10. carbhat and (g) tie
11. geansaithe and (l) sweaters
12. cíochbheart and (a) bra

Exercise 11.3: Your turn!

Helen: An maith leat an T-léine seo?
Martina: *No. I think it's ugly.*
Ní maith. Ceapaim go bhfuil sí gránna.
Helen: Dáiríre! Ceapaimse go bhfuil sí go deas.
Martina: *That red one is nicer.*
Tá an ceann dearg sin níos deise.
Helen: Tá sí an-daor: tríocha a cúig euro.
Martina: *That's far too expensive.*
Tá sin i bhfad ródhaor.

Exercise 11.4: Your turn!

Derek: An maith leat na bróga seo?
Eithne: *I don't like them at all. They're ugly.*
Ní maith liom ar chor ar bith iad. Tá siad gránna.
Derek: Tá an seaicéad seo go deas, nach bhfuil?
Eithne: *No. I don't like the colour – it's too light.*
Níl. Ní maith liom an dath – tá sé ró-éadrom.
Derek: An maith leat an cóta seo?
Eithne: *No – it's too dark. And too expensive: two hundred euro!*
Ní maith – tá sé ródhorcha. Agus ródhaor: dhá chéad euro!
Derek: Tá mise ag dul abhaile …

Exercise 11.5: Fill in the gaps

1. *I love these shoes.*
Is breá liom na <u>bróga</u> seo.
2. *That sweater is lovely.*
Tá an geansaí sin go <u>hálainn</u>.
3. *This skirt is too big for me.*
Tá an sciorta seo <u>rómhór</u> agam.
4. *This coat is too tight.*
Tá an cóta seo <u>rótheann.</u>
5. *I think it's ugly.*
Ceapaim go <u>bhfuil</u> sé gránna.
6. *Do you like them?*
An maith leat <u>iad</u>?
7. *Do you like this shirt? I love it.*
An maith leat an léine seo? Is breá liom <u>í</u>.
8. *I don't like it at all.*
Ní maith liom ar <u>chor</u> ar bith é.
9. *This jacket is nice, isn't it?*
Tá an seaicéad seo go deas, nach <u>bhfuil</u>?
10. *It's too dark.*
Tá sé <u>ródhorcha</u>.

Exercise 11.6: Answer the questions

1. Tá an sciorta seo go deas, nach bhfuil?
   Say: No. It's too short.
   Níl. Tá sé róghearr.
2. An maith leat an gúna seo?
   Say: No. It's very long.
   Ní maith. Tá sé an-fhada.
3. An maith leat na stocaí seo?
   Say: No. They're very dark.
   Ní maith. Tá siad an-dorcha.
4. An maith leat na bróga seo?
   Say: Yes. They're lovely.
   Is maith. Tá siad go hálainn.
5. Cé mhéad atá sé?
   Say: Fifty euro.
   Caoga euro.
6. Cé mhéad atá an cóta sin?
   Say: Two hundred and twenty euro.
   Dhá chéad fiche euro.
7. Cé mhéad atá an léine sin?
   Say: Sixty euro.
   Seasca euro.
8. Cé mhéad atá siad?
   Say: Twenty-five euro.
   Fiche a cúig euro.

Exercise 11.7: Your turn!

Martina: *Do you like that hat?*
An maith leat an hata sin?
Helen: Cé acu ceann?
Martina: *That black and red one.*
An ceann dubh agus dearg sin.
Helen: Tá sé an-mhór. Agus an-daor, déarfainn.
Martina: *It's expensive enough: eighty euro.*
Tá sé daor go leor: ochtó euro.

Exercise 11.8: Your turn!

Caitríona: Cheannaigh mé sciorta nua inné.
Janice: *Oh? Is it nice?*
Ó? An bhfuil sé go deas?
Caitríona: Tá sé go hálainn. Tá dath deas gorm air agus tá sé an-ghearr.
Janice: *I bought black boots myself at the weekend.*
Cheannaigh mé féin buataisí dubha ag an deireadh seachtaine.
Caitríona: Bhí siad an-daor, is dócha!
Janice: *Yes, but I don't care!*
Bhí, ach is cuma liom!

Exercise 11.9: Review of Unit 11

1. *I like these red trousers.*
   Is maith liom an bríste dearg seo.
2. *I love these shoes.*
   Is breá liom na bróga seo.
3. *That sweater is lovely.*
   Tá an geansaí sin go hálainn.
4. *Do you like this skirt? Yes.*
   An maith leat an sciorta seo? Is maith.
5. *Do you like that colour? No.*
   An maith leat an dath sin? Ní maith.
6. *I think it's ugly.*
   Ceapaim go bhfuil sé gránna.
7. *This coat.*
   An cóta seo.
8. *That shirt.*
   An léine sin.
9. *Do you like these shoes?*
   An maith leat na bróga seo?
10. *I love them.*
    Is breá liom iad.
11. *How much is it?*
    Cé mhéad atá sé?
12. *How much are they?*
    Cé mhéad atá siad?
13. *How much is that shirt?*
    Cé mhéad atá an léine sin?
14. *Which one?*
    Cé acu ceann?
15. *This one.*
    An ceann seo.

Unit 12: Requests and Commands

Exercise 12.1: The appropriate sentence

1. *You would like someone to sit down.*
   Suigh síos.
2. *You'd like your children to get up.*
   Éirígí!
3. *You want someone to come in.*
   Tar isteach.
4. *You want more than one person to come in.*
   Tagaigí isteach.
5. *You would like your son to wash his face.*
   Nigh d'aghaidh.
6. *You want your daughter to eat her breakfast.*
   Ith do bhricfeasta.
7. *You want someone to hurry.*
   Déan deifir.
8. *You want your children to comb their hair.*
   Cíoraigí bhur gcuid gruaige.
9. *You'd like your sons to stop being bold.*
   Ná bígí dána.
10. *You don't want your daughter to eat all the biscuits.*
    Ná hith na brioscaí go léir.

Exercise 12.2: Your turn!

Angela: *Ah, Gearóid – you're welcome. Come in.*
Á, Gearóid – tá fáilte romhat. Tar isteach.
Gearóid: Go raibh maith agat, a Angela. Tá brón orm go bhfuil mé déanach.
Angela: *Don't worry. Not everyone is here yet.*
Ná bí buartha. Níl gach duine anseo fós.
Gearóid: Sin faoiseamh!
Angela: *Sit there beside Hilary and rest yourself. What would you like to drink?*
Suigh ansin in aice le Hilary agus lig do scíth. Cad ba mhaith leat a ól?

Exercise 12.3: Your turn!

Áine: *Get up! It's a quarter past eight.*
Éirígí! Tá sé ceathrú tar éis a hocht.
Áine: *Wash your faces. Sinéad, comb your hair.*
Nígí bhur n-aghaidh. A Shinéad, cíor do chuid gruaige.
Áine: *Peadar, eat your breakfast. Hurry up.*
A Pheadair, ith do bhricfeasta. Déan deifir.
Áine: *Children, wash your hands now. Hurry up – you're late.*
A pháistí, nígí bhur lámha anois. Déanaigí deifir – tá sibh déanach.

Exercise 12.4: Translate the sentences

1. *Don't be bold.*
   Ná bí dána.
2. *Get up!*
   Éirigh!
3. *Comb your hair.*
   Cíor do chuid gruaige.
4. *Put on your clothes.*
   Cuir ort do chuid éadaí.
5. *Wash your hands.*
   Nigh do lámha.
6. *Wash your faces.*
   Nígí bhur n-aghaidh.

7. *Hurry up.*
   Déanaigí deifir.
8. *Stop talking.*
   Ná bígí ag caint.
9. *Be quiet!*
   Bígí ciúin!
   or
   Ciúnas!
10. *Wash your hands.*
    Nígí bhur lámha.

Exercise 12.5: Translate the sentences

1. *Mind your head!*
   Seachain do cheann!
2. *Close that window.*
   Dún an fhuinneog sin.
3. *Open the door.*
   Oscail an doras.
4. *Get away from me!*
   Imigh leat!
5. *Don't wait for me.*
   Ná fan liom.
6. *Don't give him any money.*
   Ná tugaigí aon airgead dó.
7. *Close the doors.*
   Dúnaigí na doirse.
8. *Open those windows.*
   Osclaígí na fuinneoga sin.
9. *Wash the dishes.*
   Nígí na gréithe.
10. *Don't say that to him.*
    Ná habraigí sin leis.

Exercise 12.6: Your turn!

Eoin: *Give me that cup.*
Tabhair dom an cupán sin.
Bairbre: Seo dhuit.
Eoin: *And open that window – it's very warm in here.*
Agus oscail an fhuinneog sin – tá sé an-te istigh anseo.
Bairbre: Ach bhí tú rófhuar cúpla nóiméad ó shin!
Eoin: *I'm warm now. Oh, and turn off that radio – I'm getting a headache.*
Tá mé te anois. Ó, agus múch an raidió sin – tá tinneas cinn ag teacht orm.
Bairbre: Tá tinneas cinn ag teacht orm féin …
Eoin: *And close the door after you. I'm going to sleep for a while.*
Agus dún an doras i do dhiaidh. Tá mise chun codladh tamall.

Exercise 12.7: Your turn!

Susan: Gabh mo leithscéal – cá bhfuil leithreas na mban?
Diarmuid: *Go down the hall and turn right. It's there on the left-hand side.*
Téigh síos an halla agus cas ar dheis. Tá sé ansin ar thaobh na láimhe clé.
Susan: Go raibh maith agat.
Breandán: Agus leithreas na bhfear?
Diarmuid: *Go up there and turn left. It's on the right-hand side, beside the shop.*
Téigh suas ansin agus cas ar chlé. Tá sé ar thaobh na láimhe deise, in aice leis an siopa.

Exercise 12.8: Review of Unit 12

1. *Come in.*
   Tar isteach.
2. *Sit down.*
   Suigh síos.
3. *Get up!*
   Éirigh!
4. *Clean your room.*
   Glan do sheomra.
5. *Open that window.*
   Oscail an fhuinneog sin.
6. *Close the door.*
   Dún an doras.
7. *Mind your head.*
   Seachain do cheann.
8. *Go straight ahead.*
   Téigh díreach ar aghaidh.
9. *Go up the stairs.*
   Téigh suas an staighre.
10. *Come in.*
    Tagaigí isteach.
11. *Eat your breakfast.*
    Ithigí bhur mbricfeasta.
12. *Don't be bold.*
    Ná bígí dána.
13. *Clean your rooms.*
    Glanaigí bhur seomraí.
14. *Wait for me.*
    Fanaigí liom.
15. *Don't give him any money.*
    Ná tugaigí aon airgead dó.

Aonad 13: Last Weekend

Exercise 13.1: Give the Irish version

1. *she bought*
   cheannaigh sí
2. *I didn't drink*
   níor ól mé
3. *he didn't stay*
   níor fhan sé
4. *we said*
   dúramar
5. *they were*
   bhí siad
6. *you (singular) ate*
   d'ith tú
7. *you (plural) went*
   chuaigh sibh
8. *we got*
   fuaireamar
9. *I did*
   rinne mé
10. *she said*
    dúirt sí
11. *they gave*
    thug siad
12. *I came*
    tháinig mé
13. *I saw*
    chonaic mé
14. *they went*
    chuaigh siad
15. *I heard*
    chuala mé

Exercise 13.2: Answer the questions

1. Cad a rinne tú ag an deireadh seachtaine?
   Say: I went home to Galway.
   Chuaigh mé abhaile go Gaillimh.
2. Cad a rinne tú ag an deireadh seachtaine?
   Say: I was studying.
   Bhí mé ag staidéar.
3. Cad a rinne tú maidin Dé Sathairn?
   Say: I went on a walk with Liam.
   Chuaigh mé ar shiúlóid le Liam.
4. Cad a rinne tú oíche Dé hAoine?
   Say: I went to a film with Barry.
   Chuaigh mé chuig scannán le Barry.

5. An bhfaca tú Órla?
   Say: Yes.
   Chonaic.
6. Ar ith tú bia Síneach?
   Say: No.
   Níor ith.
7. An ndeachaigh siad go Corcaigh?
   Say: Yes.
   Chuaigh.
8. Ar thug sí airgead do Lucy?
   Say: No.
   Níor thug.
9. An raibh sé fuar?
   Say: Yes.
   Bhí.
10. An ndearna siad an obair?
   Say: No.
   Ní dhearna.

Exercise 13.3: Your turn!

Karl: Cad a rinne tú ag an deireadh seachtaine?
Tomás: *I had a quiet enough weekend. I was very tired.*
Bhí deireadh seachtaine ciúin go leor agam.
Bhí mé an-tuirseach.
Karl: An ndeachaigh tú amach mórán?
Tomás: *I stayed at home on Friday night but I went out on Saturday night.*
D'fhan mé sa bhaile oíche Dé hAoine ach chuaigh mé amach oíche Dé Sathairn.
Karl: Cén áit a ndeachaigh tú?
Tomás: *Myself and Laura went to that new club on Castle Street. We had a great night.*
Chuaigh mé féin agus Laura chuig an gclub nua sin ar Shráid an Chaisleáin. Bhí an-oíche againn.

Exercise 13.4: Your turn!

Tomás: Cad a rinne tú féin ag an deireadh seachtaine?
Karl: *I had a great time! I went out every night.*
Bhí am iontach agam! Chuaigh mé amach gach oíche.
Tomás: Tá tú lán fuinnimh! Ar bhuail tú le Jenny agus Susan oíche Dé hAoine?
Karl: *Yes – I had a few drinks with them. And we went to a party on Saturday night.*
Bhuail – bhí cúpla deoch agam leo. Agus chuamar chuig cóisir oíche Dé Sathairn.
Tomás: Ó, is ea, bhí lá breithe Gary ann, nach raibh?
Karl: *Yes. We stayed up all night!*
Bhí. Bhí oíche go maidin againn!

Exercise 13.5: Fill in the gaps

1. *Did you go out on Saturday night? Yes.*
   An <u>ndeachaigh</u> tú amach oíche Dé Sathairn? Chuaigh.
2. *Did you do all the work? No.*
   An <u>ndearna</u> sibh an obair go léir? Ní dhearna.
3. *Did you hear Dónall on the radio? No.*
   Ar <u>chuala</u> tú Dónall ar an raidió? Níor chuala.
4. *Did Celine come home? Yes.*
   Ar <u>tháinig</u> Celine abhaile? Tháinig.
5. *Did they go there together? Yes.*
   An <u>ndeachaigh</u> siad ansin le chéile? Chuaigh.
6. *Did she give money to the children? No.*
   Ar <u>thug</u> sí airgead do na páistí? Níor thug.
7. *Did you say anything to him? No.*
   An <u>ndúirt</u> tú aon rud leis? Ní dúirt.
8. *Was Martin there? No.*
   An <u>raibh</u> Martin ansin? Ní raibh.
9. *Did you get a paper for me? Yes.*
   An <u>bhfuair</u> tú nuachtán dom? Fuair.
10. *Did you see that film yet? No.*
   An <u>bhfaca</u> tú an scannán sin fós? Ní fhaca.

Exercise 13.6: Answer the questions

1. Cathain a chuaigh tú go Londain?
   Say: On Saturday night.
   Oíche Dé Sathairn.
2. Cén lá a chuaigh tú go Páras?
   Say: On Friday.
   Dé hAoine.
3. Cén lá a d'imir tú galf le Séamas?
   Say: Yesterday.
   Inné.
4. Cathain a chuaigh tú chuig an dráma?
   Say: Yesterday evening.
   Tráthnóna inné.
5. Cathain a chuaigh tú chuig an scannán sin?
   Say: The day before yesterday.
   Arú inné.
6. Cathain a chonaic tú Síle?
   Say: Yesterday morning.
   Maidin inné.
7. Cathain a bhí Derek sa bhaile?
   Say: Two days ago.
   Dhá lá ó shin.
8. Cathain a bhí Bríd anseo?
   Say: The night before last.
   Arú aréir.

Exercise 13.7: Your turn!

Martina: *Did you do anything nice at the weekend?*
An ndearna tú aon rud deas ag an deireadh seachtaine?
Deirbhile: Rinne – chuaigh mé féin agus Colm go Gaillimh.
Martina: *Great. Where did you stay?*
Ar fheabhas. Cén áit ar fhan sibh?
Deirbhile: D'fhanamar in Óstán an Ard-Oileáin. Bhí an aimsir go hálainn.
Martina: *And what did you do while you were there?*
Agus cad a rinne sibh agus sibh ansin?
Deirbhile: Chuamar ar shiúlóidí cois farraige agus d'itheamar cúpla béile an-deas.
Martina: *Did you do much shopping?*
An ndearna sibh mórán siopadóireachta?
Deirbhile: Ní dhearna. Ní maith le Colm bheith ag siopadóireacht. Tá a fhios agat na fir …

Exercise 13.8: Your turn!

Ciarán: An ndeachaigh tú chuig an dráma sin ag an deireadh seachtaine?
Órla: *No. I was very busy on Friday and Saturday.*
Ní dheachaigh. Bhí mé an-ghnóthach Dé hAoine agus Dé Sathairn.
Ciarán: An raibh tú ag obair sa siopa?
Órla: *Yes – Michelle is on holidays. But I had a nice break from work yesterday.*
Bhí – tá Michelle ar saoire. Ach bhí sos deas agam ón obair inné.
Ciarán: Cad a rinne tú?
Órla: *I stayed in bed until midday and then I went on a long walk with Denise.*
D'fhan mé sa leaba go dtí meán lae agus ansin chuaigh mé ar shiúlóid fhada le Denise.

Exercise 13.9: Review of Unit 13

1. *What did you do at the weekend?*
   Cad a rinne tú ag an deireadh seachtaine?
2. *What did you do yourself at the weekend?*
   Cad a rinne tú féin ag an deireadh seachtaine?
3. *I visited Pádraigín.*
   Thug mé cuairt ar Phádraigín.
4. *I was working on Saturday and Sunday.*
   Bhí mé ag obair Dé Sathairn agus Dé Domhnaigh.
5. *What did you do on Sunday morning?*
   Cad a rinne tú maidin Dé Domhnaigh?

6. *I went on a walk with Chris.*
Chuaigh mé ar shiúlóid le Chris.
7. *I went to a play on Sunday night.*
Chuaigh mé chuig dráma oíche Dé Domhnaigh.
8. *Did they stay at home? Yes.*
Ar fhan siad sa bhaile? D'fhan.
9. *Did she drink much? No.*
Ar ól sí mórán? Níor ól.
10. *Did you go out much? No.*
An ndeachaigh tú amach mórán? Ní dheachaigh.
11. *We went to a party on Saturday night.*
Chuamar chuig cóisir oíche Dé Sathairn.
12. *Did you meet Jenny and Susan on Friday night?*
Ar bhuail tú le Jenny agus Susan oíche Dé hAoine?
13. *When did you go to Derry? The day before yesterday.*
Cathain a chuaigh tú go Doire? Arú inné.
14. *Colm and I went to Galway.*
Chuaigh mé féin agus Colm go Gaillimh.
15. *We ate a few very nice meals.*
D'itheamar cúpla béile an-deas.

Unit 14: Holidays and Travel

Exercise 14.1: Fill in the gaps
1. an Ghearmáin (*Germany*)
<u>sa</u> Ghearmáin (*in Germany*)
2. Albain (*Scotland*)
<u>in</u> Albain (*in Scotland*)
3. an Éigipt (*Egypt*)
<u>san</u> Éigipt (*in Egypt*)
4. Cúba (*Cuba*)
<u>i</u> gCúba (*in Cuba*)
5. an Ísiltír (*the Netherlands*)
<u>san</u> Ísiltír (*in the Netherlands*)
6. Málta (*Malta*)
<u>i</u> Málta (*in Malta*)
7. an Astráil (*Australia*)
<u>san</u> Astráil (*in Australia*)
8. an Tuirc (*Turkey*)
<u>sa</u> Tuirc (*in Turkey*)

Exercise 14.2: Your turn!
Caitlín: *Where did you go on holidays this year?*
Cén áit a ndeachaigh tú ar saoire i mbliana?
Ciara: Chaith mé coicís sa Spáinn i mí na Bealtaine.
Caitlín: *Very nice. Who went with you?*
Go deas. Cé a chuaigh leat?
Ciara: Chuaigh mé ansin le mo chara Brídín. Chaitheamar seachtain in Santander agus seachtain eile in Bilbao.
Caitlín: *Great. What kind of accommodation did you have?*
Iontach. Cén cineál lóistín a bhí agaibh?
Ciara: D'fhanamar in dhá óstán an-deas nach raibh ródhaor.
Caitlín: *And how was the weather? Was it very warm?*
Agus conas a bhí an aimsir? An raibh sé an-te?
Ciara: Ní raibh. Bhí an aimsir go hálainn – timpeall fiche céim Celsius gach lá.

Exercise 14.3: Your turn!
Ciara: Cén áit a ndeachaigh tú féin ar saoire?
Caitlín: *To Scotland. Gary and I spent a week in Edinburgh in August.*
Go hAlbain. Chaith mé féin agus Gary seachtain i nDún Éideann i mí Lúnasa.
Ciara: An raibh an fhéile ar siúl ag an am?
Caitlín: *Yes – the city was packed. We had a great time.*
Bhí – bhí an chathair plódaithe. Bhí am iontach againn.
Ciara: Tá mé cinnte go raibh. Ar fhan sibh in óstán?
Caitlín: *No. We stayed in an apartment in the city centre.*
Níor fhan. D'fhanamar in árasán i lár na cathrach.

Exercise 14.4: Fill in the gaps
1. *Where did you go on holidays this year?*
Cén áit a <u>ndeachaigh</u> tú ar saoire i mbliana?
2. *I spent a fortnight in Spain.*
Chaith mé <u>coicís</u> sa Spáinn.
3. *I'm going to Canada next month.*
Tá mé ag <u>dul</u> go Ceanada an mhí seo chugainn.
4. *Who went with you?*
Cé a <u>chuaigh</u> leat?
5. *My friend Deirdre.*
Mo <u>chara</u> Deirdre.
6. *My friends Jill and Mairéad.*
Mo <u>chairde</u> Jill agus Mairéad.
7. *Where did you stay?*
Cén áit ar <u>fhan</u> tú?
8. *We rented an apartment.*
Fuaireamar árasán ar <u>cíos</u>.
9. *What kind of accommodation did you have?*
Cén cineál <u>lóistín</u> a bhí agaibh?
10. *Was the festival taking place at the time?*
An raibh an <u>fhéile</u> ar siúl ag an am?

Exercise 14.5: Answer the questions
1. An raibh tú ar saoire fós?
Say: Yes. I was in Spain.
Bhí. Bhí mé sa Spáinn.
2. An raibh tú ar saoire fós?
Say: Yes. I spent a fortnight in America.
Bhí. Chaith mé coicís i Meiriceá.
3. An raibh tú ar saoire fós?
Say: Yes. I was in Australia.
Bhí. Bhí mé san Astráil.
4. An raibh tú ar saoire fós?
Say: Yes. I was in Cuba.
Bhí. Bhí mé i gCúba.
5. Cén áit a ndeachaigh tú ar saoire i mbliana?
Say: I went to America.
Chuaigh mé go Meiriceá.
6. Cé a chuaigh leat?
Say: I went there alone.
Chuaigh mé ansin i m'aonar.
7. Cé a chuaigh leat?
Say: My friend Simon.
Mo chara Simon.
8. Cé a chuaigh leat?
Say: I went there with my brother.
Chuaigh mé ansin le mo dheartháir.
9. Cén áit ar fhan tú?
Say: In an hotel in the city centre.
In óstán i lár na cathrach.
10. Cén áit ar fhan sibh?
Say: We stayed in an apartment.
D'fhanamar in árasán.

Exercise 14.6: Answer the questions
1. Cén áit a ndeachaigh tú ar saoire?
Say: I went to Spain.
Chuaigh mé go dtí an Spáinn.
2. Cén áit a ndeachaigh tú ar saoire?
Say: To Italy.
Go dtí an Iodáil.
3. Cén áit a ndeachaigh sibh ar saoire?
Say: We went to Australia.
Chuamar go dtí an Astráil.
4. Cén áit a ndeachaigh sibh ar saoire?
Say: To England.
Go Sasana.
5. Cén áit a ndeachaigh tú ar saoire?
Say: To Scotland.
Go hAlbain.

6. Ar bhain tú sult as?
   Say: Yes. It was great.
   Bhain. Bhí sé ar feabhas/go hiontach.
7. Ar bhain tú sult as?
   Say: No. It was too hot.
   Níor bhain. Bhí sé róthe.
8. Cén fhad a bhí tú ansin?
   Say: For a month.
   Ar feadh míosa.
9. Cén fhad a bhí sibh ansin?
   Say: For a fortnight.
   Ar feadh coicíse.
10. Cén fhad a bhí tú ansin?
    Say: For a week.
    Ar feadh seachtaine.

Exercise 14.7: Your turn!

Aodán: Bhí tú ar saoire leis an teaghlach le déanaí. Cén áit a ndeachaigh sibh?
Cathal: *We went to Kerry. We rented a house beside An Daingean.*
Chuamar go Ciarraí. Fuaireamar teach ar cíos in aice leis an Daingean.
Aodán: Go deas. Cén fhad a bhí sibh ansin?
Cathal: *We were there for a fortnight. We came back last Sunday.*
Bhíomar ansin ar feadh coicíse. Thángamar ar ais Dé Domhnaigh seo caite.
Aodán: Ar bhain sibh sult as?
Cathal: *Yes – it was really great. The weather was lovely most of the time.*
Bhain – bhí sé ar fheabhas ar fad. Bhí an aimsir go hálainn an chuid is mó den am.
Aodán: Bhí an t-ádh libh.

Exercise 14.8: Your turn!

Stuart: Bhuel, conas a bhí an Bhratasláiv? Ar bhain tú sult as an tsaoire?
Ruth: *No, to be honest.*
Níor bhain, leis an bhfírinne a rá.
Stuart: Cén fáth? Cloisim go bhfuil an chathair go deas.
Ruth: *Yes, the city is lovely. But the hotel wasn't very nice.*
Tá, tá an chathair go hálainn. Ach ní raibh an t-óstán go ródheas.
Stuart: Is mór an trua sin. An raibh na daoine ansin cairdiúil?
Ruth: *They weren't too friendly at all.*
Ní raibh siad róchairdiúil ar chor ar bith.

Exercise 14.9: Review of Unit 14

1. *Where did you go on holidays this year?*
   Cén áit a ndeachaigh tú ar saoire i mbliana?
2. *I spent a fortnight in Spain.*
   Chaith mé coicís sa Spáinn.
3. *Who went with you?*
   Cé a chuaigh leat?
4. *I went there with my friend Deirdre.*
   Chuaigh mé ansin le mo chara Deirdre.
5. *I went there alone.*
   Chuaigh mé ansin i m'aonar.
6. *Where did you stay (addressing one person)?*
   Cén áit ar fhan tú?
7. *What kind of accommodation did you have (referring to more than one person)?*
   Cén cineál lóistín a bhí agaibh?
8. *We rented an apartment.*
   Fuaireamar árasán ar cíos.
9. *I stayed in a youth hostel.*
   D'fhan mé i mbrú óige.
10. *How was the weather?*
    Conas a bhí an aimsir?
11. *We had a great time.*
    Bhí am iontach againn.
12. *I was in Canada in July.*
    Bhí mé i gCeanada i mí Iúil.
13. *It was humid.*
    Bhí sé meirbh.
14. *Did you like the place? Yes.*
    Ar thaitin an áit leat? Thaitin.
15. *Did you like the hotel? No.*
    Ar thaitin an t-óstán leat? Níor thaitin.

Unit 15: Making Arrangements

Exercise 15.1: Answer the questions

1. An mbeidh tú saor san oíche amárach?
   Say: Yes. Why?
   Beidh. Cén fáth?
2. An mbeidh tú saor oíche Dé Máirt?
   Say: No. I'll be working.
   Ní bheidh. Beidh mé ag obair.
3. An bhfuil tú saor san oíche amárach?
   Say: Yes. Why?
   Tá. Cén fáth?
4. An mbeidh tú ag cóisir Lucy?
   Say: Yes. I'm really looking forward to it.
   Beidh. Tá mé ag súil go mór leis.
5. An mbeidh tú ag dinnéar Helen?
   Say: No. I have a French class.
   Ní bheidh. Tá rang Fraincise agam.
6. Cathain atá sé ar siúl?
   Say: Friday at eight.
   Dé hAoine ag a hocht.
7. Cathain a bheidh sé ar siúl?
   Say: Next month.
   An mhí seo chugainn.
8. Cathain a bheidh sé ar siúl?
   Say: Next Saturday.
   Dé Sathairn seo chugainn.
9. Ar mhaith leat dul liom?
   Say: I'd love to.
   Ba bhreá liom.
10. Ar mhaith leat dul liom?
    Say: I'm sorry but I'm not free.
    Tá brón orm ach níl mé saor.

Exercise 15.2: Masculine and feminine

1. am (masculine) (*time*)
   an <u>t-am</u>
2. oíche (feminine) (*night*)
   an <u>oíche</u>
3. breithlá (masculine) (*birthday*)
   an <u>breithlá</u>
4. dinnéar (masculine) (*dinner*)
   an <u>dinnéar</u>
5. ceolchoirm (feminine) (*concert*)
   an <u>cheolchoirm</u>
6. cóisir (feminine) (*party*)
   an <u>chóisir</u>
7. scannán (masculine) (*film*)
   an <u>scannán</u>
8. bainis (feminine) (*wedding*)
   an <u>bhainis</u>
9. seisiún ceoil (masculine) (*music session*)
   an <u>seisiún</u> ceoil
10. pictiúrlann (feminine) (*cinema*)
    an <u>phictiúrlann</u>
11. amharclann (feminine) (*theatre*)
    an <u>amharclann</u>
12. caifé (masculine) (*café*)
    an <u>caifé</u>

Exercise 15.3: Your turn!

Tomás: *Are you free tomorrow night?*
An bhfuil tú saor san oíche amárach?
Gearóid: Tá. Cén fáth?
Tomás: *That concert is on in the Odeon. Would you like to go with me?*
Tá an cheolchoirm sin ar siúl san Odeon. Ar mhaith leat dul liom?
Gearóid: Cinnte – ba bhreá liom. Cén t-am atá sé ag tosú?
Tomás: *I'm not sure. I'll get the information and I'll send you a text.*
Níl mé cinnte. Gheobhaidh mé an t-eolas agus cuirfidh mé téacs chugat.
Gearóid: Go raibh maith agat. Tá mé ag súil go mór leis.

Exercise 15.4: Your turn!

Deirdre: An mbeidh tú ag cóisir Sarah?
Alan: *When will it be taking place?*
Cathain a bheidh sí ar siúl?
Deirdre: Oíche Dé Sathairn sa Stag's Head. Ar mhaith leat dul liom?
Alan: *I'm sorry but I'll be working that night. Alas!*
Tá brón orm ach beidh mé ag obair an oíche sin. Faraor!
Deirdre: Is mór an trua sin – beidh an-oíche ann. Tá mé féin ag súil go mór leis.

Exercise 15.5: Fill in the gaps

1. *Will you be free tomorrow night?*
An <u>mbeidh</u> tú saor san oíche amárach?
2. *Are you free tomorrow night?*
An <u>bhfuil</u> tú saor san oíche amárach?
3. *Bernie is having a party.*
Tá cóisir <u>ag</u> Bernie.
4. *I'm really looking forward to it.*
Tá mé ag <u>súil</u> go mór leis.
5. *When is it taking place?*
Cathain <u>atá</u> sé ar siúl?
6. *When will it be taking place?*
Cathain a <u>bheidh</u> sé ar siúl?
7. *Next Friday.*
Dé hAoine seo <u>chugainn</u>.
8. *In August.*
I mí <u>Lúnasa</u>.
9. *Would you like to go with me?*
Ar mhaith leat <u>dul</u> liom?
10. *I'm sorry but I'm not free.*
Tá brón orm ach níl mé <u>saor</u>.

Exercise 15.6: Answer the questions

1. Cathain a bheidh an bhainis ar siúl?
Say: In April.
I mí Aibreáin.
2. Cathain a bheidh an chóisir ar siúl?
Say: In June.
I mí an Mheithimh.
3. Cathain a bheidh an dinnéar ar siúl?
Say: In May.
I mí na Bealtaine.
4. Cathain a bheidh an dráma ar siúl?
Say: In December.
I mí na Nollag.
5. Cathain a bheidh an scannán ar siúl?
Say: In February.
I mí Feabhra.
6. Cathain a bheidh sé ar siúl?
Say: In March.
I mí an Mhárta.
7. An bhfeicfidh siad Susan ag an gcóisir?
Say: No.
Ní fheicfidh.
8. An rachaidh tú chuig an gcóisir?
Say: No.
Ní rachaidh.
9. An gcloisfidh tú é ar an raidió?
Say: Yes.
Cloisfidh.
10. An íosfaidh sí an bia go léir?
Say: Yes.
Íosfaidh.

Exercise 15.7: Your turn!

Tomás: *What time will we meet?*
Cén t-am a bhuailfimid le chéile?
Gearóid: Timpeall a hocht? Beidh mise ag obair go dtí a seacht.
Tomás: *Okay. And where will we meet?*
Ceart go leor. Agus cén áit a mbuailfimid le chéile?
Gearóid: Fan go bhfeice mé. Cad faoi Whelan's? Ní bheidh sé róphlódaithe anocht.
Tomás: *Perfect. I'll see you there. I won't be late!*
Foirfe. Feicfidh mé ansin tú. Ní bheidh mé déanach!
Gearóid: Mar athrú!

Exercise 15.8: Your turn!

Julie: Cén áit a mbuailfimid le chéile?
Denise: *What about that new café beside the cinema?*
Cad faoin gcaifé nua sin in aice leis an bpictiúrlann?
Julie: An ceann atá cúpla doras síos ón bpictiúrlann? Ar an gcúinne?
Denise: *Yes – that's the one. What time will I meet you?*
Is ea – sin an ceann. Cén t-am a bhuailfidh mé leat?
Julie: Ceathrú chun a hocht?
Denise: *Okay!*
Maith go leor!

Exercise 15.9: Review of Unit 15

1. *Will you be free tomorrow night? Yes.*
An mbeidh tú saor san oíche amárach? Beidh.
2. *Are you free tomorrow night? No.*
An bhfuil tú saor san oíche amárach? Níl.
3. *It's Liam's birthday.*
Tá breithlá Liam ann.
4. *There's a dinner at Susan's house.*
Tá dinnéar i dtigh Susan.
5. *I'm really looking forward to it.*
Tá mé ag súil go mór leis.
6. *When is it taking place?*
Cathain atá sé ar siúl?
7. *Tomorrow night.*
San oíche amárach.
8. *Next Friday.*
Dé hAoine seo chugainn.
9. *Would you like to go to a film with me?*
Ar mhaith leat dul chuig scannán liom?
10. *I'd love to but I'm working.*
Ba bhreá liom ach tá mé ag obair.
11. *I'm very busy at the moment.*
Tá mé an-ghnóthach faoi láthair.
12. *What time is it starting?*
Cén t-am atá sé ag tosú?
13. *That's a pity – it'll be a great night.*
Is mór an trua sin – beidh an-oíche ann.
14. *Where will we meet?*
Cén áit a mbuailfimid le chéile?
15. *What time will I meet you?*
Cén t-am a bhuailfidh mé leat?

Irish Language Directory / *Eolaire na Gaeilge*

This directory contains information about Irish language organisations, publications, materials for learners and online resources.

Abair.ie
Abair.ie is a text-to-speech system for Irish being developed by the Phonetics and Speech Laboratory, part of the Centre for Language and Communication Studies, Trinity College, Dublin. Words and sentences typed into the text box on the website's home page are converted to a sound file. Available in the main dialects of Irish.
Address: Phonetics and Speech Laboratory, Room 4091, Arts Building, Trinity College, Dublin 2
Phone: (01) 896 1348
Fax: (01) 896 2941
Email: abair@tcd.ie
Website: www.abair.ie

Acmhainn.ie
Links to online dictionaries and terminology in Irish.
Email: doc@acmhainn.ie
Website: www.acmhainn.ie

Áras Chrónáin
Cultural centre where Irish language classes, music classes and other activities are held.
Address: Watery Lane, Orchard Road, Clondalkin, Dublin 22
Phone: (01) 457 4847
Fax: (01) 457 4117
Email: eolas@araschronain.ie
Website: www.araschronain.ie

BBC Gaeilge
This website is a gateway to the BBC's Irish language material. You can browse articles containing text, video and audio, or choose to watch video clips or listen to audio clips, all of which can be browsed by category.
Website: www.bbc.co.uk/irish/gaeilge

Beo!
This monthly online magazine was published by Oideas Gael between 2001 and 2014 and contained a wide range of articles, each accompanied by an extensive glossary. All the articles published in the magazine can still be accessed by clicking on the 'Cartlann' (archive) link on the left-hand side of the home page.
Email: eagar@beo.ie
Website: www.beo.ie

Ceart
Irish language grammar checker from technology services company Cruinneog.
Email: eolas@cruinneog.com
Website: www.cruinneog.com

Cló Iar-Chonnacht
Conamara-based book publisher which also releases music and song CDs.
Address: Indreabhán, Conamara, Contae na Gaillimhe
Phone: (091) 593 307
Fax: (091) 593 362
Email: eolas@cic.ie
Website: www.cic.ie

Cló Mhaigh Eo
Publisher of books in Irish for children and young people as well as a series of acclaimed Irish graphic novels.
Address: Colmán & Mairéad Ó Raghallaigh, Droimnín, Clár Chlainne Mhuiris, Contae Mhaigh Eo
Phone: (094) 937 1744
Email: eolas@leabhar.com
Website: www.leabhar.com

Club Chonradh na Gaeilge
Irish language social club, situated in the basement of Conradh na Gaeilge's building in the centre of Dublin.
Address: 6 Harcourt Street, Dublin 2
Phone: (01) 475 1480
Email: runai@anclub.ie
Website: www.anclub.ie

ClubLeabhar.com
The ClubLeabhar.com project, which is managed by Gaelchultúr, aims to encourage people in Ireland and abroad to read Irish language books. A new book is discussed each month and club members have an opportunity to discuss this book in the website's forum. Members have access to English translations of the most difficult words and phrases in the books being discussed, which makes reading them a lot easier. There is no membership fee.
Address: 11 Clare Street, Dublin 2
Phone: (01) 484 5220
Email: eolas@clubleabhar.com
Website: www.clubleabhar.com

Na Cnocadóirí
Dublin-based Irish language hillwalking club, established in 2003.
Email: cnocadoiri@yahoo.com
Website: www.cnocadoiri.com

COGG
An Chomhairle um Oideachas Gaeltachta agus Gaelscolaíochta was founded under the provisions of Article 31 of the Education Act of 1998 and caters for the educational needs of *Gaeltacht* schools and of *Gaelscoileanna* (Irish language schools). Its role relates to both primary and post-primary education and the three main areas of work are:

- the provision of teaching resources
- the provision of support services
- research.

Address: 23 Windsor Pl, Dublin 2
Phone: (01) 634 0831
Email: eolas@cogg.ie
Website: www.cogg.ie

Cois Life Teo
Publisher of works of literature and research in the Irish language. Also publishes books for learners of the language, books for young people, scripts, fiction, poetry and academic monographs.
Address: 62 Páirc na Rós, Ascaill na Cille, Dún Laoghaire, Contae Bhaile Átha Cliath
Phone: (01) 280 7951
Email: eolas@coislife.ie
Website: www.coislife.ie

Coiscéim
Irish language publisher of novels, short story collections, poetry, folklore, plays, history books and books for teenagers.
Address: Tig Bhríde, 91 Bóthar Bhinn Éadair, Páirc na bhFianna, Binn Éadair, Baile Átha Cliath 13
Phone: (01) 832 2509
Fax: (01) 832 0131
Email: nuachtchoisceim@yahoo.ie
Website: www.coisceim.ie

Coláiste na bhFiann
Coláiste na bhFiann, founded in the early Seventies, is Ireland's longest established Irish language courses organiser. It aims to teach young people to speak Irish in a welcoming environment that encourages a positive attitude towards the language.
Address: Coláiste na bhFiann, Droim Rí, Contae na Mí
Phone: (01) 825 9342
Email: eolas@colaistenabhfiann.ie
Website: www.colaistenabhfiann.ie

Colmcille
Colmcille is a partnership programme between Foras na Gaeilge and Bòrd na Gàidhlig, promoting the use of Irish Gaelic and Scottish Gaelic in Ireland and Scotland, and between the two countries.
Address: Foras na Gaeilge, West Gate House, 2–6 Queen Street, Belfast BT1 6ED
Phone: (028) 9089 0983
Email: mscott@forasnagaeilge.ie
Website: www.colmcille.net

Comharchumann Ráth Chairn
This cooperative is based in the Ráth Chairn *Gaeltacht* in County Meath and its website contains the latest local news and information about Irish language courses and cultural holidays in the area.
Address: Comarchumann Ráth Chairn, Ráth Chairn, Baile Átha Buí, Contae na Mí
Phone: (046) 943 2068
Fax: (046) 943 2381
Email: rathcairn@eircom.net
Website: www.rathchairn.com

Concos (Comhchoiste na gColáistí Samhraidh)
Comhchoiste na gColáistí Samhraidh (Concos) is a federation of dozens of Irish Summer Colleges, both inside and outside the main *Gaeltachtaí*. Summer course information for each *coláiste* (Irish college) is provided by Concos.
Address: Tír an Fhia, Leitir Móir, Contae na Gaillimhe
Phone: (091) 577 050
Email: eolas@concos.ie
Website: www.concos.ie

Conradh na Gaeilge
Conradh na Gaeilge (The Gaelic League), established on 31 July 1893, is the democratic forum for the Irish-speaking community and promotes the language throughout the whole of Ireland and around the world. The organisation runs Irish language classes and its headquarters in Dublin house a bookshop and social club.
Address: 6 Harcourt Street, Dublin 2
Phone: (01) 475 7401
Fax: (01) 475 7844
Email: eolas@cnag.ie
Website: www.cnag.ie

Cruinneog
Technology services company which produced the GaelSpell Irish language spelling checker and the Anois grammar checker.
Email: eolas@cruinneog.com
Website: www.cruinneog.com

Cultúrlann McAdam Ó Fiaich
This west Belfast based cultural centre contains space for artistic and theatrical expression, a café, a tourist information office, a community radio and the north's largest dedicated Irish language and media book and gift shop.
Address: 216 Falls Road, Belfast, BT12 6AH
Phone: (028) 9096 4180
Email: eolas@culturlann.ie
Website: www.culturlann.ie

Daltaí na Gaeilge
Daltaí na Gaeilge, a non-profit Irish language organisation based on the east coast of America, is dedicated to promoting and teaching the language. Daltaí runs immersion programmes throughout the year in New York State, New Jersey and Pennsylvania. These programmes offer classes which are suitable for every level of ability, from total beginners to native speakers, and attract learners of all ages.
The organisation's website contains a comprehensive list of language courses and events held in North America, forums,

a grammar section, a list of proverbs and much more.
Address: Liam Guidry, 1504 NW 3rd Avenue,
Fort Lauderdale, FL
Email: daltai1@daltai.com
Website: www.daltai.com

Department of Culture, Heritage and the Gaeltacht
This government department has responsibility for the Irish language and the *Gaeltacht*.
Address: Na Forbacha, Contae na Gaillimhe
Phone: (091) 592 555 / LoCall 1890 201 401
Website: www.chg.gov.ie

Feachtas
This organisation, established in 1980, caters for young people between the ages of eight and 18 and has branches throughout Ireland. It runs weekly youth clubs, summer camps, adventure courses, table quizzes and other events.
Address: 518 Main Street, Tallaght, Dublin 24
Phone: (01) 466 2487
Email: eolas@feachtas.ie
Website: www.feachtas.ie

Fiontar agus Scoil na Gaeilge
This university department offers undergraduate and postgraduate courses through Irish, with a focus on business and technology. It has also been centrally involved in the development of tearma.ie, the National Terminology Database for Irish, and of logainm.ie, the Placenames Database of Ireland.
Address: DCU All Hallows Campus, Drumcondra, Dublin 9
Phone: (01) 700 5614
Email: ursula.mhiccarthaigh@dcu.ie
Website: https://www.dcu.ie/fiontar_scoilnagaeilge

Fios Feasa
This Kerry-based technology company produces educational CD-ROMs for children and adults, including the popular karaoke series *Amhrán is Fiche*.
Address: An Ghráig, Baile an Fheirtéaraigh, Contae Chiarraí
Phone: (066) 915 2465
Fax: (066) 915 2492
Email: post@fiosfeasa.com
Website: www.fiosfeasa.com

An Foclóir Beag
Online Irish–Irish dictionary.
Website: www.teanglann.ie/en/fb

focloir.ie
Focloir.ie is Foras na Gaeilge's New English-Irish Dictionary, launched in 2013. The dictionary is available free of charge, and has been adapted to work both on desktop computers and on mobile devices. As well as translations for the English content, the dictionary also contains grammatical information and sound files.
Address: 66 Amiens St, Mountjoy, Dublin 1
Phone: (01) 639 8400
Email: aiseolas@focloir.ie
Website: www.focloir.ie

Foras na Gaeilge
This cross-border body, established in December 1999, is responsible for the promotion of the Irish language throughout the whole island of Ireland.
Address: 66 Amiens St, Mountjoy, Dublin 1
Phone: (01) 639 8400
Email: suiomh@forasnagaeilge.ie
Website: www.gaeilge.ie

Gaeilge ar an Ghréasán
This portal site contains information about Irish language classes worldwide, organisations promoting the language, third level courses, online resources, blogs, Irish language grammar, place names, and much more besides.
Website: www.smo.uhi.ac.uk/gaeilge/gaeilge.html

Gaeilge-A and Gaeilge-B
Gaeilge-A is a bulletin board aimed at fluent speakers of Irish. Members are not allowed to write messages in English.
Gaeilge-B is a forum for those who are learning Irish. Messages in both Irish and English are allowed.
Website: www.smo.uhi.ac.uk/liosta

Gael Linn
Gael Linn was founded in 1953 and aims to foster and promote Irish and its heritage throughout Ireland as a living language and as an expression of identity. The organisation runs language classes for adults, as well as summer colleges for teenagers in Donegal, west Cork and north Mayo. It produces a range of support materials for teachers and learners, including publications for post-primary schools, posters, CD-ROMs and teaching kits for primary schools.
Address: 35 Dame Street, Dublin 2
Phone: (01) 675 1200 / (1890) 675 675
Email: eolas@gael-linn.ie
Website: www.gael-linn.ie

Gaelchultúr Teoranta
This Dublin-based company (and publishers of this book) was set up in 2004 with the aim of providing educational services to learners of Irish and fluent speakers of the language. It runs language classes for adults in its headquarters in Dublin city centre and in various other locations around Ireland, including Letterkenny, Carlow, Galway and Cork. Gaelchultúr owns the online shop siopa.ie and the e-learning website ranganna.com.
Address: 11 Clare Street, Dublin 2
Phone: (01) 484 5220
Email: eolas@gaelchultur.com
Website: www.gaelchultur.com

GaelSpell
Irish language spelling checker developed by technology

services company Cruinneog.
Email: eolas@cruinneog.com
Website: www.cruinneog.com/GaelSpell.html

Gaillimh le Gaeilge
Gaillimh le Gaeilge works in association with Galway City Council, Galway Chamber and other groups to develop the city's unique Irish image and promote it as a bilingual area.
Address: Kirwan House, Flood Street, Galway
Phone: (091) 568 876
Email: eolas@gleg.ie
Website: www.gleg.ie

Glór na nGael
Glór na nGael (The Voice of the Gael) is an annual competition, first held in 1962. The main prize is given each year to the community which has done the most to promote the Irish language.
Address: Ráth Chairn, Baile Átha Buí, Contae na Mí
Phone: (046) 943 0974
Email: eolas@glornangael.ie
Website: www.glornangael.ie

Google as Gaeilge
To access the Irish language version of the search engine, go to www.google.ie and click on "Gaeilge".
Website: www.google.ie

Google Translate
On this site, you can translate from Irish into various languages and from those languages into Irish.
Website: http://translate.google.com/#

An Gúm
This organisation is part of Foras na Gaeilge and mainly deals with lexicography, publishing textbooks and school resources, as well as reading material for young people.
Address: 66 Amiens St, Mountjoy, Dublin 1
Phone: (01) 639 8400
Email: suiomh@forasnagaeilge.ie
Website: www.gaeilge.ie

IMRAM
Annual Irish language literature festival, held in Dublin. The festival's programme fuses poetry, prose and music, and events are held in various venues around the city. IMRAM has also featured film, drama, puppetry, debates, lectures, and writing workshops for both adults and children.
Phone: (01) 894 4922 / (087) 291 2797
Email: liamog62@mac.com
Website: www.imram.ie

Leabhar Breac
Conamara-based publisher of fiction and non-fiction books for adults, graphic novels, and books for children and teenagers.
Address: Indreabhán, Conamara, Contae na Gaillimhe
Phone: (091) 593 592
Email: eolas@breacan.ie
Website: www.leabharbreac.com

Litriocht.com
West Cork-based Litriocht.com aims to make all books published in Irish or on the Irish language available for sale on its website. There is a comprehensive selection on offer, including dictionaries, grammar books, novels, poetry, children's books, DVDs, and CDs for children and adults. A bilingual description of each book can be viewed on the site.
Address: Aonad 2A, Béal Átha 'n Ghaorthaidh,
Maigh Chromtha, Co. Chorcaí
Phone: (026) 47 330
Email: info@litriocht.com
Website: www.litriocht.com

Logainm.ie
The Placenames Database of Ireland, developed by Fiontar (Dublin City University) and The Placenames Branch (Department of Arts, Heritage and the Gaeltacht).
Website: www.logainm.ie

Ógras
Irish language organisation which runs events for young people between the ages of eight and 19 years.
Address: 6 Harcourt Street, Dublin 2
Phone: (01) 475 1487
Email: eolas@ogras.ie
Website: www.ogras.ie

Oideas Gael
This company has been running Irish language and cultural courses in the south-west Donegal Gaeltacht of Gleann Cholm Cille since 1984. It offers language classes at all levels of competency, as well as a wide range of bilingual cultural activity courses. Programmes include: hillwalking; environment and culture; marine painting; bodhrán; flute and whistle; Irish harp; archaeology; Donegal dances; digital photography; and tapestry weaving.
Address: Gleann Cholm Cille, Contae Dhún na nGall
Phone: (074) 973 0248
Fax: (074) 973 0348
Email: oifig@oideas-gael.com
Website: www.oideas-gael.com

Oidhreacht Chorca Dhuibhne
Oidhreacht Chorca Dhuibhne, based in Baile an Fheirtéaraigh in the Kerry *Gaeltacht*, is a cultural and heritage project established in 1980. The organisation runs Irish language classes for adults and seeks to promote the culture of the area through traditional arts projects.
Address: Baile an Fheirtéaraigh, Trá Lí, Contae Chiarraí
Phone: (066) 915 6100
Email: eolas@cfcd.ie
Website: www.oidhreacht.ie

Oireachtas na Gaeilge

Annual Irish language festival, held in later October or early November in a different part of the country each year. A wide range of competitions, aimed at both adults and children, are held during the festival, including *sean-nós* singing and dancing, music performance and storytelling. Oireachtas na Gaeilge's literary prizes are announced in the autumn each year and prizes of up to €3,000 are awarded to the winners.

Address: Oifig an Oireachtais, Conradh na Gaeilge, 6 Harcourt Street, Dublin 2
Phone: (01) 475 3857
Fax: (01) 475 8767
Email: eolas@antoireachtas.ie
Website: www.antoireachtas.ie

Peig.ie

This website is an information hub for the Irish language and contains links to the latest news and information about events, Irish language job vacancies and much more.

Address: Conradh na Gaeilge, 6 Harcourt Street, Dublin 2
Phone: (01) 475 7401
Email: peig@cnag.ie
Website: www.peig.ie

Portráidí na Scríbhneoirí Gaeilge

Portraits of Irish-Language Writers is a living collection of portraits that celebrate the Irish-language writer, based on the pioneering work of Máire Uí Mhaicín. Further additions are made to the site on an ongoing basis.

Email: portraidi@comhar.ie
Website: https://portraidi.ie/en/

Raidió Fáilte 107.1fm

Community Irish language radio station broadcasting from west Belfast.

Address: 30 Sráid Dhubhaise, Belfast, BT 12 4AL
Phone: (028) 90 310 013
Email: oifig@raidiofailte.com
Website: www.raidiofailte.com

Raidió na Life 106.4

This Dublin-based Irish language community radio station has been broadcasting since 1993. The station is on air 24 hours a day and also streams live on the web.

Address: 66 Amiens St, Mountjoy, Dublin 1
Phone: (01) 661 6333
Texts: (086) 600 1064
Email: beo@raidionalife.ie
Website: www.raidionalife.ie

Raidió Rí-Rá

Raidió Rí-Rá is a radio station for young people playing all the latest music from the charts and broadcasting completely through the medium of Irish. You can listen to Raidió Rí-Rá all year round online at www.rrr.ie and on the Rí-Rá app for the iPhone.

Address: 6 Harcourt Street, Dublin 2
Phone: (01) 475 7401
Email: eolas@rrr.ie
Website: www.rrr.ie

ranganna.com

Gaelchultúr's e-learning website contains a wide range of courses aimed at adult learners of Irish. There are general language courses at various levels, as well as specialised courses aimed at teachers and others who work through Irish.

Address: 11 Clare Street, Dublin 2
Phone: (01) 484 5220
Email: eolas@gaelchultur.com
Website: www.ranganna.com

RTÉ Raidió na Gaeltachta

RTÉ Raidió na Gaeltachta was first established to provide a comprehensive radio service for the people of the *Gaeltacht* regions and for Irish speakers nationwide, and began broadcasting at 3.00 p.m. on 2 April 1972. The station is now available online and attracts listeners from all corners of the globe.

Address: Casla, Conamara, Contae na Gaillimhe
Phone: (091) 506 677
Fax: (091) 506 666
Email: rnag@rte.ie
Website: www.rte.ie/rnag

Seachtain na Gaeilge

Seachtain na Gaeilge (Irish Language Week) is a non-profit organisation which promotes the use of Irish language and culture, both at home and abroad, during a two-week festival held in March each year. It was established by Conradh na Gaeilge in 1902. A wide range of organisations, local councils, schools, libraries, and music, sporting and cultural bodies all register their events with Seachtain na Gaeilge.

Address: 6 Harcourt Street, Dublin 2
Phone: (01) 475 7401
Email: eolas@snag.ie
Website: www.snag.ie

An Siopa Gaeilge

Oideas Gael's Siopa Gaeilge sells a range of products of special interest to the adult Irish language learner and to teachers (at adult, as well as primary and secondary level). It carries a wide selection of materials for children and a variety of traditional music resources, bilingual greeting cards and books on Irish history, culture and music.

Address: Oideas Gael, Gleann Cholm Cille, Contae Dhún na nGall
Phone: (074) 973 0500 / (074) 973 0248
Fax: (074) 973 0348
Email: eolas@siopagaeilge.ie
Website: www.siopagaeilge.ie

An Siopa Leabhar
Conradh na Gaeilge's bookshop, which also sells CDs, posters and other items of interest to speakers of Irish and those learning the language.
Address: 6 Harcourt Street, Dublin 2
Phone: (01) 478 3814
Email: ansiopaleabhar@eircom.net
Website: www.cnag.ie/siopa

siopa.ie
Gaelchultúr's books for learners of Irish can be purchased in the company's online shop. Books by other Irish language publishers, as well as games, greeting cards and other items aimed at Irish speakers, are also sold on siopa.ie.
Address: 11 Clare Street, Dublin 2
Phone: (01) 484 5220
Email: eolas@siopa.ie
Website: www.siopa.ie

teanglann.ie
Teanglann.ie is an online dictionary and language library, which is being developed by Foras na Gaeilge in parallel with the New English-Irish Dictionary project. The aim of the website is to provide users of the language with free, easy-to-use access to dictionaries and to grammatical and pronunciation information relating to words in the Irish language. The site enables the user to search for dictionary entries, grammatical information and sound files for any individual word.
Address: 66 Amiens St, Mountjoy, Dublin 1
Phone: (01) 639 8400
Email: aiseolas2@forasnagaeilge.ie
Website: www.teanglann.ie

tearma.ie
The National Terminology Database for the Irish language, developed by Fiontar, Dublin City University, in collaboration with An Coiste Téarmaíochta (The Terminology Committee), Foras na Gaeilge.
Email: tearmai@forasnagaeilge.ie / tearma@dcu.ie
Website: www.tearma.ie

Teastas Eorpach na Gaeilge
Teg is an examination system for adult learners of Irish that is linked to the Common European Framework of Reference for Languages (Council of Europe, 2001). Examinations test the four skills: speaking, listening comprehension, reading comprehension and writing. Examinations are available at six levels, from Absolute Beginners (A1) to Advanced 2 (C2). There are examination centres in various parts of Ireland, including Maynooth, Belfast, Letterkenny and Cork, as well as overseas, in New York, Paris, London and Prague.
Address: Lárionad na Gaeilge, Maynooth University,
County Kildare
Phone: (01) 708 3737
Fax: (01) 708 6499
Email: teanga@nuim.ie
Website: www.teg.ie

TG4
TG4 is a public service broadcaster for Irish language speakers. The channel, which is based in the Conamara *Gaeltacht*, has been on air since 31 October, 1996. The station's programmes can be viewed live on the TG4 Player and there is also an archive containing a wide range of content.
Address: Baile na hAbhann, Contae na Gaillimhe
Phone: (091) 505 050
Fax: (091) 505 021
Email: eolas@tg4.ie
Website: www.tg4.ie

Tuairisc.ie
Online Irish language newspaper, updated on a daily basis. Tuairisc.ie provides a news service in Irish for the Irish speaking community in Ireland and abroad. Their objective is 'to serve the interests of that community through the generation, collection and publication of high-quality news, information, analysis and entertainment'.
Address: Bearna, Contae na Gaillimhe
Phone: (091) 867 458
Email: nuacht@tuairisc.ie / eolas@tuairisc.ie
Website: www.tuairisc.ie

Údarás na Gaeltachta
Údarás na Gaeltachta, the Gaeltacht Authority, is the regional government agency with responsibility for the economic, social and language/cultural development of the *Gaeltacht* areas of Ireland. An tÚdarás pursues its core language preservation and development objectives through job and wealth creation and a wide range of community, arts, language and cultural initiatives.
Address: An Ardoifig, Na Forbacha, Contae na Gaillimhe
Phone: (091) 503 100
Fax: (091) 503 101
Email: eolas@udaras.ie
Website: www.udaras.ie

Topics index / *Innéacs topaicí*

Grammar index / *Innéacs gramadaí*